Introduction to the City

Anthony J. Filipovitch
Mankato State University

KENDALL/HUNT PUBLISHING COMPANY
2460 Kerper Boulevard P.O. Box 539 Dubuque, Iowa 52004-0539

Photos by H. Roger Smith used by permission.
Cover: Photo by John LaFond.
        Stained glass window entitled ''Exploding City'' by H. Roger Smith

Copyright © 1989 by Kendall/Hunt Publishing Company

ISBN 0–8403–5500–9

Printed in the United States of America
10 9 8 7 6 5 4

Contents

Preface

The city is central to our lives. Three quarters of American live in or near cities. The foci of finance are in our large cities. The head offices of most of our major industries are located in cities. The major libraries, most of our symphony orchestras and dance theaters, the world-class museums are all in cities. In fact, the very word "civilized" means "citified."

Yet the overwhelming majority of Americans think of cities in negative terms: "pollution," "crime," "crowding," "dirty." For them, cities are places to be avoided, even to be feared.

There is no denying that there are problems in cities. Many of these problems (e.g., assault and murder, poverty, inadequate housing, political corruption) are share with rural America. Other problems seem to be unique to cities (e.g., traffic jams, crowd control). They are all problems that demand solution. Despite these problems, 80% of students will find themselves living at one time or another in a large city. The city is where they will work, play, and mature.

- A central goal of this book is to help students get a feeling of what it is like to live in a city as well as what people are doing to make cities livable, even enjoyable.

- A second goal is to convey an understanding of some of the factors which contribute to both the excitement and revulsion that many people feel toward cities.

- Third, students should learn to understand, identify, and ultimately incorporate into action an appreciation for the way their actions contribute to making cities what they are.

- Finally, students should learn to see the city urbanely, and appreciate the interdisciplinary nature of cities.

The text is framed not around theoretical and abstract concepts, but rather around tangible and usually visual elements of urban life which are either attractive or repugnant, beautiful or ugly. But simple recognition of these issues is not enough. It is even more critical to have some comprehension of creative problem solving—to have some idea of what to do about these issues. Students should come away with more than an understanding of the dimensions of urban problems (and an appreciation for what may be good or exciting about the city). They should

also develop insights into what they can do, as individuals or as part of a collective body, to turn the liabilities of the urban place into assets for the future.

This text is written from the perspective of urban studies, which is a generalist field. It strives for breadth of scope, occasionally to the detriment of detail. At any given level of analysis, the special disciplines will show more detail. Students are encouraged to contribute the insights that their special discipline might offer to the subject at hand. What is unique about urban studies is its attempt to identify the relationships between the events and phenomena which occur in cities: Our purpose is to understand what is a city. While the special disciplines may provide greater accuracy at a more detailed level of analysis, the positions we present are accurate at the level of generalization which we are intending (or at least, that is our intention). Urban studies tries to see the *pattern,* to understand the process of the city.

The text focuses on those factors which contribute to the formation and further development of human settlements, and the interaction of the residents of those settlements with each other and their urban environment. These factors can be put into four groups:

- The Meaning of "City," which includes the history, literature, and philosophy of cities.

- The Design of Cities, which includes the natural, economic, social, and aesthetic context of cities.

- The Operation of Cities, which includes governing, managing, and planning cities.

- The Future of Cities, both the likely and the possible.

A thorough understanding of cities cannot be achieved by grasping any single characteristic, nor even by grasping the simple effects of the four characteristics separately. Cities are properly understood only through the interaction of meaning, context, praxis, and possibilities. Accordingly, the text includes an appendix of a dozen field projects which provide the opportunity to **experience** what is being discussed.

This is a text for a first course on the City. The text should be supplemented by lectures and discussions in class. In many cases, the text will be a useful *preparation* for a class session. Since this is an introduction to the city, the intention is not to provide the groundwork for a career in city service, nor even to provide a comprehensive survey of urban theory. The primary purpose of the text is to provide students with an appreciation for the richness and diversity of city living. Detailed study of urban professionalism and the solution of urban problems is reserved for other courses.

Finally, I wish to acknowledge the contribution of so many people to this project. I am from the first generation of students to receive a doctorate in urban studies. My mentors taught me from the perspective of their special disciplines, holding out the promise that I might be able to synthesize what each of them offered. I do not know if they would be satisfied with the synthesis I offer here; I hope they are at least a little challenged by it.

Most of those who helped me think through the ideas in this book must remain nameless, but a few deserve special mention. Nancy Chapman and Chuck Bolton at Portland State University taught me to think about the lives of people in cities; Roger Jennings and Dave Cressler taught me to watch those people as they go about the city. Jim Weiss and Dick Lycan taught me to see how the patterns of life are translated into the arrangements of space. John Hanson taught me to think about how people use economic resources in the city, and even got me to suspend my disbelief in the economist's assumption that people act rationally. Nohad Toulan, a man of great patience, taught me not only planning but also how bureaucracies work; he continued to teach me long after I had graduated from his program, Earl Reeves at the University of Tulsa continued my training in organizational behavior. My colleagues at Mankato State—Bob Barrett, Roger Smith, and David Rafter—have all had a hand in this. Much of the material in the text came from Smith's lectures; much of the editing is owed to Rafter's insightful comments; the time and the support to continue with this project is Barrett's doing. It is a truism that a teacher learns from his students, but in more than the usual way I a m indebted to George Birt, on of my students at Tulsa, who taught me the importance of the land on which a city is built. And there are others who might be surprised to find themselves listed here: Lorraine Nadelman, at the University of Michigan, who first taught me just to look and describe what I saw; and John Sallis, a philosopher at Duquesne University, who taught me that understanding was not just knowing the facts but also the context which gives them their meaning.

I am particularly indebted to Tony and Valerie Kurtzweil Filipovitch, my parents. One of peasant stock, the other a farmer's daughter, neither graduated from college. But both loved learning and shared it with their children. They taught me to respect common wisdom and they tried to teach me common sense.

These, and many others, have unselfishly shared what they know with me. I have taken it and done things to it which they no doubt had not intended. The errors which remain are my doing.

Anthony J. Filipovitch
Mankato State University

Part I

The Meaning of *City*

1

The City Through Time

Stadtluft macht frei!
(*"City air makes one free!"*)
Medieval German saying

Athenian Acropolis (H. Roger Smith)

This chapter is concerned with the historical city, the city for which some record remains. Frequently, this record is written, although in some cases the record is nothing more than the remains of the old walls, buried in the earth. But no matter what form the record takes, it still has to be interpreted. Apparently the people of the past were not **that** different from us; what differences there are, are subtle ones. But it is those subtle differences which can lead one to completely misinterpret the meaning of the historical record. What follows is our best understanding of the role which the city played over time in the lives of its people; there is a great deal we do not understand, and probably much that we misunderstand. In a brief introduction such as this, it is not possible to remain faithful to the individuality of each city in a cultural period. Almost every generalization can be contradicted by evidence from one or another city of any period, although the general pattern would hold across most of the cities of that period.

Early Cities

In the earliest cities, streets were defined by the edges of the houses. The "street" was whatever was left over between the houses (Fraser, 1968; see also Sjoberg, 1960). The form of the city itself was determined by a wall built around the city. This form of city-building can be seen, for example, in the Babylonian cities like Ur and Tepe Gawra, and was the standard form for thousands of years (Lampl, 1968).

The Egyptians imposed some order on this hodgepodge by laying out straight, dedicated streets for the major roadways, often laying them out in a rectilinear (straight lines crossing at right angles) pattern, as in Kahun and El Amarna. This new development was found, not in the capital cities, but in the work-camps that were built to house the people who worked on the pyramids (Macaulay, 1975). In other words, it was seen as a practical device for making things work more efficiently. The residential street continued, however, to be defined by the neighboring buildings.

Around the world from Egypt somewhat later in time, innovations in city-building were also being developed independently in the New World. The Anasazi (the Old Ones of the American southwest) built cliff-dwellings, which were high-rise apartments with sophisticated heating and cooling characteristics (Lekson, *et alii,* 1988). The Toltecs in Mexico built Teotihuacan. It was a planned city with straight arterial streets (and the usual jumble of residential streets) and several high-rise buildings. The Toltec culture was a high culture with sophisticated government, agricultural, and commercial systems and skilled crafts (the stonemasonry in Teotihuacan is remarkably fine). In more recent times, similar city-building occurred throughout the Americas in the Incan and Aztec cultures (Hardoy, 1968). In the central United

States, the Mississippians built similar cities of wood and dirt rather than stone. Little of their cities remains today.

The Greek City

Greek cities were characterized by "the human." They scaled their buildings to the proportions of an idealized human body. Their structures may be imposing, but they are never overwhelming (Haselberger, 1985).

The Greeks also built their cities near agricultural land, but not on it. Greek cities were designed to minimize the use of arable land, since the agricultural goods were needed to feed the local population.

There were several standard features in the design of Greek cities. They were generally built on hills and designed so the rain would scour out the streets of the city. The size of the city was limited to the carrying capacity of the surrounding land—water and food supply, transportation, etc. In the case of Athens, this was 40,000 citizens (landholding free males) or a total of 100,000–150,000 people (including women, children, slaves, and freemen). More commonly, cities grew to 10,000 citizens.

The focus of the city was the Acropolis, the sacred precinct, which housed the major temples to the gods. The business of the city was carried out in the *agora,* the

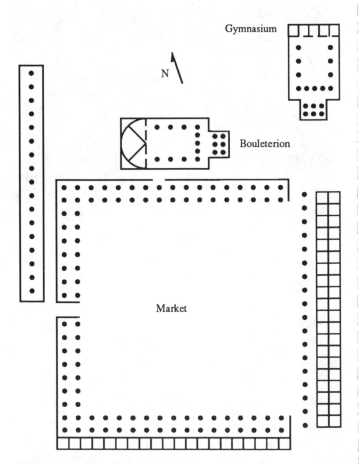

Figure 1.1. Agora of Miletus, 2nd Century B.C.

marketplace, which was the center of public life (Ward-Perkins, 1974). Here people came to exchange information, participate in the government, and just socialize. In contemporary terms, the equivalent of the *agora* is the downtown. The sacred and secular districts of the city were linked by the theater. The plays were originally intended to instruct the citizens in the values and the religion of the city: They taught through example. Production of the plays was a religious duty borne by the wealthy. The Greeks also provided public space for exercise and the practice of sports. In part, this came from their conviction that a sound mind requires a sound body. In part, it was to train their army, which was composed of all the citizens.

Greek society was responsible for several innovations in building and design:

The Greeks opened up the wall and let nature flow into the their structures. They did this with "post-and-lintel" construction, a beam (lintel) supported by a row of columns (posts). This provides a sense of closure, defining an "inside" and "outside" while allowing openings in the "wall."

Parthenon—Athens (H. Roger Smith)

The Greeks also devoted much of their energy to the design of the columns that hold the lintel. They carved the columns so they were slightly smaller at the top and bottom, slightly fatter in the middle. This tricks the eye when one looks up at the columns from their base, so they appear perfectly straight. They also developed three standard styles ("orders") which they used for decorating the tops of columns ("capitals"). The three orders of Greek capitals are the Doric (a flat top with a "pillow block" supporting it), which denotes strength and virtue; the Ionic (scrolled top), denoting wisdom; and the Corinthian (the most decorative, with leaves carved into the capital), denoting beauty.

A third innovation lay in the techniques used by the Greeks to decorate their public buildings. They decorated the top of their buildings with colored tile and bas-relief sculpture made from terracotta (baked clay). This was called a "frieze." Short pillars or supports were sometimes carved into a human form and used as decoration. These "caryatids," while large, were not monumental forms like those used by the Egyptians; the human scale still ruled. The Greeks also used statues (bas-relief sculpture on the friezes or free-standing marble or alabaster statues) as part of the design of their public buildings.

A fourth innovation was their use of open space. Early Greek temples were made of solid walls with internal columns (much like the Egyptian temples earlier). Unlike the Egyptians, the Greeks used wooden rafters and roof members (wood was not as scarce), so the walls could enclose a greater volume of space with the lighter roofs. In time, the columns were placed outside the solid walls. Eventually, the columns supported the entire structure and solid walls were used only as a screen on two sides of the building. The structures has become a roof enclosing a large open space.

The Greeks also developed the sidewalk. The *agora* was enclosed by a walkway. This walkway, called the *stoa,* was covered by an extension of the roof of the neighboring buildings. The *stoa* provided a public space (like our contemporary sidewalks), but one that was protected from rain and the harsh sun.

The last of the Greek innovations was the use of complete street plan (Ward-Perkins, 1974). While earlier cites show some use of straight streets set at right angles to each other (for example, Kahun in Egypt), most early cities let the street be defined by the casual placement of houses (for example, Ur in Babylon). The Greeks are credited with being the first to lay out a plan for all the streets of a city, a plan based on a grid of straight streets set at right angles to each other. Hippodamus, who laid out the street plan for Miletus and Olynthos, is generally given credit for first using this scheme.

The Roman City

While the Greeks were humanists (concerned with the place of man in the world), the Romans, their successors, were Imperial (domineering, colossal, militaristic). Roman cities were very carefully laid out. Every inch of property within the city was very carefully described in legal terms

| Doric | Ionic | Corinthian |

Figure 1.2. Orders of Greek Capitals

and recorded at the Court. The plan for colonial cities was drawn up in Rome, and was imposed on the landscape regardless of the natural landform. If necessary, the Romans were not adverse to modifying the landforms to fit the preordained plan.

The Romans were best known for their engineering feats; in matters of design, they were copycats. They copied from almost every culture they conquered. Their art and even their religion were originally copied from the Etruscans and the Greeks, and later incorporated elements from Egypt, Persia, and even Judea.

Roman city design (except for Rome herself) was based on the military encampment (Vitruvius, 1931; Macaulay, 1974). The Romans maintained their empire first by force but then by trade, as can be seen in the form of the cities they built. The colonial cities were built on the site of the barracks of the conquering army. The old parade ground became the new *forum* (the Roman version of the Greek *agora*). The cities were all walled (including Rome). The walls were for defense, in the days when the city was a barracks; in times of peace and commerce, the

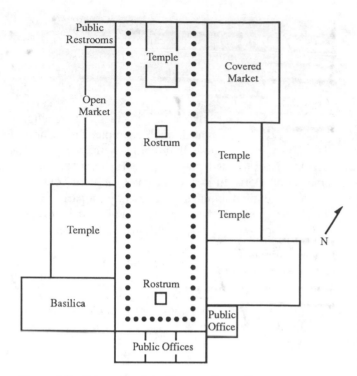

Figure 1.3. Schematic of the Forum at Pompeii

Roman *Via*—street (H. Roger Smith)

walls served to identify the city and its limits (Weber, 1958). The streets were laid out in a strict gridiron pattern, with one major north-south street (the *cardo*) and one major east-west street (the *decumanus*). These streets crossed at the *forum*. Because the major streets were laid out according to the compass, Roman cities were forced to grow along those lines rather than along the lines defined by the lay of the land (Grimal, 1983).

As in the Greek cities, public life in Roman cities focused on the market (the *forum* in Rome, the *agora* in Athens). The buildings around the forum had shops on the main floor and offices on the second floor. The size of buildings and their location throughout the city were controlled by building codes written into the law. In the *forum* was a raised platform surrounded by open space (the *rostrum*) from which news bulletins, public meeting

notices, and laws could be announced. It was sort of a newspaper/towncrier combined. Unlike the Greeks, the Romans placed their temples in the *forum;* there was no separation of the sacred and the secular. The Roman temples were also more enclosed than Greek temples, and were designed to be approached from only the front. Not only was the *forum* the focus of religious and economic life, it was also the seat of government. The Roman civic buildings (the *curia,* where the local legislature and the law courts would meet, and the *basilica,* the local governor's office) were also placed on the *forum*.

Although the focus of public life was the *forum* (downtown), larger Roman cities were divided into neighborhoods and each neighborhood had its own fountain and central marketplace. Upper-class residences (called *villas*) were built around a central open space (the *atrium*), just as they were in Greece. In addition to villas and smaller single-family dwellings, Roman cities contained apartment buildings; in larger cities they could be as high as 8 stories. Like many large contemporary cities, the emphasis was on density: In Imperial Rome, there were 46,602 tenement blocks and only 1,797 private housing blocks (Watts & Watts, 1986).

The major innovation of Roman city-building was to solve the technical problems of large-scale cities. The availability of water always limited the size of cities. Water was needed for drinking and for carrying away the city's waste products. As cities grew, the need for water would outstrip the local supply and the city's wastes would inevitably pollute the local water sources. The Romans built the first complete system of waterworks.

Roman aqueduct at Nimes—France (H. Roger Smith)

The system usually began with water from a mountain stream. Using tunnels and *aqueducts* (bridges which carried water pipes across valleys), mountain water was piped into the cities (Hodge, 1985; Hauck, 1989). Using the water pressure from the mountains, the Romans delivered water to a central waterworks (the *castellum*). From there, it was piped under pressure beneath the streets and into the houses (up as far as 4 stories) through a system of pipes. Many of the water pipes were lead, although some were of wood or ceramic; as long as the water did not stand in the pipes, there was little danger of lead poisoning and, in time, the inner surface of pipes was coated with calcium deposits from the water. By the way, lead water service pipes running from the street to the house are commonly found in many sections of American cities today. Since the Romans could deliver water under pressure, they were able to build fountains which released a stream of water into the air. Public fountains were located on the corner of every block, so households did not have to haul water from a common well or nearby stream. All the water coming into the city had to be removed. The Romans channeled waste water back down to underground sewers, and the streets themselves were cleared by a system of storm sewers which carried the water out of the city and into a nearby stream.

In architecture, the Romans are primarily known for the development of the arch. The did not invent the arch—it was already used in First Dynasty Egypt, around 3000 BC (van Beek, 1987). The Romans advanced the simple arch by inventing the keystone, a wedge-shaped stone in the center of the arch. The Roman arch could bear more weight than the lintel because it translates the downward pressure of the roof into lateral force which can be transferred from the center of the arch to the sides where it can be carried by the walls. The arch permits slenderer columns and larger structures. Rotating the arch through 360 degrees produces the dome—an arched roof.

The Romans also built the first superdome, although they called it the *ampitheatre*. They took the Greek theater out of its natural setting and built free-standing structures. A Roman theater was typically built in the shape of a horseshoe (which held the seating area) closed off at the end by a stage and its backdrop. The ampitheatre has cables stretched from the tops of the walls and large canvasses (''Roman shades'') could be pulled across the cables to shade the stage and the seating areas from the sun.

The Romans also built the first hot-tubs, called *thermae* (usually translated as ''baths''). They used their waterworks to provide the public baths, which in many ways were like contemporary health clubs. One would move from pools of cold water (the *frigidarium*) to lukewarm water (the *tepidarium*) to hot water (the *callidarium*). The *thermae* also included a swimming pool, a steam room, a massage room, a barber shop, athletic courts for running and wrestling, and meeting rooms. In many ways, it was like a contemporary health club. A typical visit to the baths would take the better part of a day.

The Romans also invented reinforced and hydraulic concrete (McCann, 1988), inventions that were subsequently lost until they were reinvented in the 1800s.

The Medieval City

The Medieval city was characterized by a social system called **"feudalism."** All land and everyone on it was owned by the lord of the manor. People on the land (called serfs) owed allegiance to their lord, and he had a right to anything that they had. In turn, the lord was bound to his serfs and retainers by a duty to defend them and to provide for their needs.

The Medieval city was also characterized by **fear.** This was a period immediately following the fall of Rome—the end of civilization as people knew it. Barbarians sacked cities and roamed the countryside. Vikings raided the coast at will. People believed in witches and ogres. Strangers were feared.

This was also a time of **disease** (which reinforced the fear). Cities had only rudimentary sanitation, the structures were vermin-ridden, fire would sweep through entire towns, and poverty was common. The solution to the epidemics of plague and other disease was to burn the town to the ground—purify it by fire.

When the Roman Empire fell, Western Europe also felt the **loss of technology.** The knowledge and skills which built and maintained the waterworks and the ports was lost. This in turn led to a loss of the surplus that was firing the economy, and people's lives during this period shifted from trying to expand their markets to trying to stay alive. The focus of high culture shifted away from Western Europe as the remains of the Roman Empire held out in the Byzantine world (Eastern Europe and Asia Minor) and a new, vigorous culture was developed in the Islamic world.

During the Medieval period, the old patterns of city design returned (Saalman, 1968). There was no formal planning, no legal land description (since the land was all held by the lord or the bishop, there was no need for it); cities just grew like Topsy. Cities sprang up wherever people put down their baggage.

Thatched housing (H. Roger Smith)

Castle at Carcassone—France (H. Roger Smith)

Since the purpose of the feudal system was protection, the castle (fortress) dominated the city (Macaulay, 1977). The castle was a warehouse for storing supplies for defending against a siege, an armory for housing the lord's standing army, and the lord's residence. The castle was surrounded by a high, thick wall built for defense, and the wall usually had one (or at most two) entrance. The entrance was a very elaborate gate, designed to impress and defend. Inside the castle wall was a hodge-podge of houses and streets in no particular order. This had a defensive advantage; if an enemy breached the wall, he still might get lost in the maze of streets. Many of the serfs lived inside the castle wall and journeyed out every day to farm the land. As a city grew, more and more undefended structures would be built outside the castle walls and their residents would flee inside during times of attack.

Unlike the Greek and Roman cities, Medieval cities placed the market outside the town. Markets were places where people would meet to exchange goods, and many of these people were wandering traders. Some of them could, therefore, be spies sent to reconnoiter the town for attack. As a result, no strangers were allowed inside the castle gate without special permission from the lord of the castle.

The castle was made of stone and hung with rugs (tapestries) to cut down on drafts. Castles were for the rich; most people lived in "half-timbered" houses. Wood was used as the structural element, but the spaces between the posts and beams were filled with **wattle** (reeds,

caning) and **daub** (plaster, mud). Roofs were of **thatch** (straw). To make the most of limited space, the second floor of the houses was cantilevered out over the street. As with the Romans, the first floor was generally shops, living space was on the second floor, and animals (pigs, cows, occasionally a horse) were kept in the rear. Unlike the Romans, there was no public sanitation and the houses were built much closer together. In the winter, animals were kept in the living quarters—it kept them warmer, and their body heat contributed to warming the house. Windows were small and unglazed; the houses were gloomy, smokey, and drafty. The streets followed the cowpaths and the normal flow of drainage across the ground. In other words, the streets served as open sewers (a situation that did not change until the 1800s). The streets drained into the moat, a very large ditch which ran just outside the walls of the city. In effect, the moat was an open septic tank.

The Medieval city was primarily a pedestrian city. There were very few wheeled vehicles inside the city gates, and even few beasts of burden. To get anywhere, one went on foot. This limited the practical size of any city to about 2 miles in diameter (the distance one can walk in half an hour). Shops and residences were jumbled together in the medieval city, and since most of the people were illiterate they needed some method other than words to identify the shop they wanted to find. They used signs that represented the type of establishment and/or the name of the establishment. The signs were an early form of corporate logo—the message was conveyed by pictures rather than words.

The Gothic City

The late Medieval period is often called the Gothic. It was a period of relative stability. As the western world began to recover from the fall of the Roman Empire, affairs of state became more organized and predictable.

Feudal lords formed coalitions, fledgling states began to develop. Trade between the cities began to flourish. As these new kings and nobles needed money to finance their intrigues, they turned to the merchants in the cities to finance their operations. The city merchants, in turn, held out for their independence. During this period, more and more cities won their independence, electing their own *burgemeister, maires,* and mayors. This was also a period when the Guilds (craft unions) came to power. As the feudal lords found themselves spending more and more time at the seat of government and leaving their fiefdoms to managers, the cities came to be dominated more and more by the merchants and craftsmen—the *bourgeoisie,* the middle class (Pirenne, 1952).

In design, the Gothic city is marked by shift from the castle to the cathedral. This shift coincides with the rising power of the merchants and craftspeople. The cities no longer needed to focus so heavily on defense (the nation-state provided that), so the castle could be de-emphasized. Besides, the local nobility were always at the national capital. The citizen ("city dwellers") turned to the cathedral for several reasons: The Church served as a force that could counter the power of the nobility, and did so on occasion. The common people also had more contact with the church and religion during the earlier, harder times than they had with the new nation-state, which was the domain of the nobility. In fact, the Guilds (the organizations of working people) started as church organizations and every Guild had its patron saint (Mumford, 1961).

Around the 11–12th centuries, order was reintroduced into Western cities. With increased security and less need for defense, major streets were cut directly from the gates to the cathedral (which was built in the center of the city). The marketplace was moved to the square in front of the cathedral, where all the major roads met. This made it easier for traders who were strangers to the town to find their way to market: The Church steeple could be seen from several miles away, and the road one was travelling led right to its foot.

The focus of Gothic design was the Cathedral (Macaulay, 1973). Its groundplan was always laid out in the shape of a cross (**"cruciform"**). The sacred precinct (the **"apse"**) was always to the east, so the rising sun would shine on the altar. Between the apse and the body of the church was the **"choir,"** which was reserved for the monks and other clerics (who, incidentally, also served as a choir for the sung parts of the ritual). The north and south branches, or arms of the cross, were called the **"transepts"** and often contained shrines or secondary altars. The body of the church, the public space, was on the west side and was called the **"nave."** This form of church-building is very common even today.

The first European universities were also developed during this period. The first places of learning were the monasteries, where the monks preserved traditional learn-

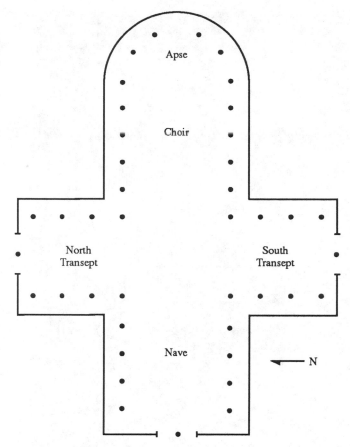

Figure 1.4. Plan of a Gothic Cathedral

ing through the medieval period. But as the nobles grew in power and became a force which sometimes found itself pitted against the Church, they had a need for learned people of their own who were not loyal to the Church—clerks, rather than clerics. The merchants, and later the craftspeople, also found reading and writing to be useful skills in recording and maintaining their business affairs. The universities arose to fill these needs, and to provide lawyers and doctors (other roles which used to be filled by monks).

Ordinary life, however, was not changed very much in the Gothic period. The peasants (and much of the new middle class) still lived in daub-and-wattle cottages. Sanitary conditions continued to be very poor. There was less starvation, but the problem of poverty was not solved. And the worst epidemics of the plague occurred during this period.

There were two major innovations of the Gothic period. The first was a new form of arch. The arch was "broken," made higher and coming to a peak. This permitted both taller structures and wider spaces under the arch. By combining arches, using a main arch with a bracing arch at the side (called a **"flying buttress"**), the main pillars inside could be more slender, providing an even greater impression of height and openness (Mark & Clark, 1984). Where

Gothic Cathedral (H. Roger Smith)

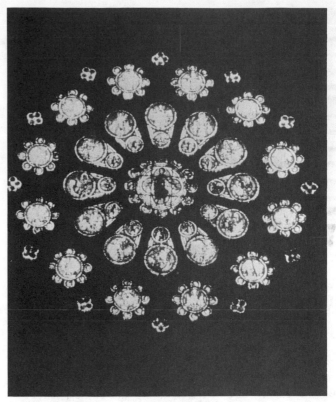

Rose Window at Chartres—France (H. Roger Smith)

the choir and the transepts meet in a Gothic cathedral—where rows of arches cross each other at right angles—was called a **"groined arch."**

The Gothic period also developed to a fine art the piercing of stone walls. They placed windows near the roofline (**"clerestory** windows"), and windows in the walls above the pillars (**"triforium** windows"). They developed a large, round window in the apse (**"rose** window," so named because it was circular and the pattern of stone supports suggest the petals of a rose). In effect, they turned the walls of their cathedrals into lace, a lacework of stone.

The Renaissance City

The word "renaissance" means "rebirth." The Renaissance was marked by the rediscovery of classical culture: Greek and Roman literature, classical sciences and engineering, and classical design. The arts, previously used only in the service of the Church, came to serve the monarchs. The great artists of the time (da Vinci, Michelangelo, etc.) were commissioned to work on buildings, both the design and the decoration.

The Renaissance was also a period of new technology. The Duke of Venice sent Marco Polo to Cathay (China), where Polo found all sorts of unfamiliar inventions. The three most important of his finds were gunpowder, which Western men used for slaughtering each other (the Chinese only used it for fireworks); coal, which freed technology from dependence on charcoal and was particularly useful for smelting iron; and the compass, which permitted more sophisticated mapping and led to an explosion of exploration.

The extensive growth of exploration during the Renaissance brought with it a surplus of physical goods, including new inventions, gold and silver, and exposure to the products of other cultures. It was from another culture, the Arabs, that the Western world recovered the writing of much of the classical Greek and Roman civilizations. Exploration brought a return of surplus, expanding the Western world's stock of capital, goods, and ideas.

The most typical element of Renaissance design was the tearing down of the walls. In the Renaissance, with the development of the cannon, the last ditch of defense was no longer the castle, but the plaza (Argan, 1969). City walls were no longer a defense, since the cannon could breach them or fire over them with ease. But from an open plaza, cannons could be mounted to enfilade all incoming streets.

Castles were transformed into palaces, suited no longer for defense but for pomp and display. As the state grew in

Chateau at Chenoceaux—France (H. Roger Smith)

Two major innovations of the Renaissance shaped the development not only of cities but also of society. The first was the **cannon.** The development of gunpowder as a weapon changed the design of cities. Designers began to lay out cities according to geometric forms to facilitate clear lines of fire from the plaza in the center of town. The second major innovation was the **printing press,** invented by Johannes von Gutenberg. The growth of literacy led to increased demand for written material, but handwritten manuscripts were costly and time-consuming to produce. Gutenberg developed a way to mass-produce written material. Books were still expensive in the Renaissance, but not nearly as rare as they were in the Middle Ages.

The Baroque City

The Baroque was an extension of the Renaissance, characterized by an intense, decorative treatment of detail. There was also heavy use of color.

The hallmark of a Baroque city is the use of wide avenues and *rond points* (traffic circles). This style came from the French, who laid out hunting forests with wide paths for mounted hunters and circular clearings (the *rond points*) where the hunting party could regroup. This radial system in the forest was translated into diagonal and radial streets in the cities. These wide avenues in the cities provided a parade ground for reviewing the troops as well as providing a fine field of fire for defensive cannon.

In the Baroque period, the cathedral was replaced as the central point in the city by the plaza, its fountain, and the radial streets spreading out from there. Not since the Romans had European cities seen so many fountains. The old aqueducts were being repaired and water lines replaced, although Baroque planners still did not pay much attention to the sewer system. The common people continued to live in half-timbered houses with thatched roofs, working at farming or one of the trades (cottage industries were beginning to develop). The cities were filthy and the streets were dirty. The larger cities had some paved streets and some public lavatories, but public sanitation was almost nonexistent (Clark, 1975).

The Baroque also marks the beginning of city planning as a profession. Cities had been planned prior to this, but by artists or engineers who happened to work on one or another city. In the Baroque period, people began to devote their major energies to designing and constructing buildings and cities. The first city planners were most often hired to design the placement of monuments in the plazas and the arrangement of buildings around the plaza.

power, they devoted more money and effort to the construction of public buildings. These buildings were to demonstrate the power and authority of the state. it was time of great wealth for the upper class, and the palaces and public buildings were heavily embellished. Attention was given to the landscaping of buildings. And, with the Roman revival, the dome became fashionable again. During the Renaissance architects even went beyond the Romans and succeeded in placing the dome on a square foundation (the Romans always supported their domes with a cylinder).

St. Peter's Basilica—Vatican City (H. Roger Smith)

The joining of the imperial to the classical is one of the major differences between the Renaissance and its Greek roots. The human scale and the humanism of the Greeks was replaced by the colossal, outdoing even the Romans. The residence of the chief of state of the Papal States (the Pope), St. Peter's Basilica in Rome, was designed to look like a three-story building. It is, in fact, about ten times larger and is completely out of human scale.

The Industrial City

The development of science in the Renaissance led to new technologies, technologies which permitted craftspeople to harness other sources of energy than muscle power, technologies which permitted them to work

11

extensively in materials which could only be worked by machine.

These new technologies changed both the nature of craft and the nature of selling. The craftsperson was replaced by the laborer and the engineer as the mechanical systems became too complicated to be maintained by a single person. The efficiencies which the machine permitted led to a demand for huge quantities of raw or unfinished material, and produced huge quantities of finished products. The producers no longer mined the ore, smelted it, shaped it, and sold it all at one place. Some places specialized in extracting raw materials, others assembled it, others worked it, still others sold it, and through it all others were transporting the various elements from one place to another (Mumford, 1961).

The first phase of the Industrial revolution really began in the Renaissance, and it resulted in a widespread mercantile system. This created a large middle class of entrepreneurs. Once the craftspeople found that there was an almost unlimited market for their goods (if they could produce them cheaply enough), they had the incentive to find ways to produce more, and do it more cheaply. The steam engine provided the energy, and machines were designed which could do the tasks more quickly than people. Unskilled labor was needed to tend the machines. This drew poor people from the countryside (where they were overcrowded and starving) to the cities (where they were still crowded, but at least there was *some* work). Competition among the unskilled laborers kept their wages low—barely above starvation. Thus the feudal system of a rich lord and poor peasants was replaced by a system with a middle class of skilled professionals and a lower class of unskilled laborers. Since the lower-class had some means of income, it also created a new, even lower class of the destitute (Chudacoff, 1975).

In the Americas, this was the period when the frontiers were being pushed back to gain access to the natural resources which were there. At first, the resources were agricultural land and furs. In time, mineral resources drove the expansion.

There were many distinct styles of design during the Industrial period. Early in this period, the American colonists built their houses of wood and shingle rather than stone, masonry, or half-timbering. The buildings maintained but modified the elements of European classical design. For example, they used squared wooden pillars rather than rounded stone ones, but included carved capitals and frieze-work. On the frontier, log cabins with cedar-shake roofs were the norm.

As the colonies and the young nation expanded, towns were platted in advance of their construction, usually from a city far removed from the new townsite. To make things easier, the plats were usually drawn in a gridiron pattern, no matter how the topography fell. The Ordinance of 1785 established a rectangular surveying system for all new land in the United States (basically all the land west of the Appalachians). Because of this Act, most cities on the Plains developed in a north/south gridiron plan with major roads every mile.

The Industrial Period is outstanding for the innovations which it introduced. The first was **movable power.** Farmers were freed from the horse as steam and then gasoline tractors were developed. Mechanical engines were also harnessed to boats, trains, and carriages (cars). **Stationary power** was also transformed. The Industrial Revolution began with water power (the old medieval water wheel), but quickly passed to steam engines driven by coal, to electrical power generated by steam, to internal combustion engines driven by petroleum, and now to electrical power generated by steam from nuclear fission.

There were also innovations in **housing design.** With industrialization and the shift from cottage industry to large factories, the middle class came to dominate city life. This is reflected in their housing. The middle class built decorative houses (using machine-made parts) that once were the domain only of the aristocracy. Wood and stone parts could be mass-produced rather than custom built by artisans.

Cast-iron facade—New York City (H. Roger Smith)

New **construction materials** were also brought into common use. The Crystal Palace, built in London in 1851, use mass-produced glass to completely sheathe a building (Kihlstedt, 1984). Prior to this, glass was handmade and too expensive to use on such a scale, and the technology of iron and steel was too new to provide thin columns that could be made strong enough to support the weight of the glass. By the mid-1800s reinforced concrete and Portland cement had been developed. This permitted the fabrication of entire buildings which could be slip-formed in concrete (concrete poured into forms which could be removed and re-used once the concrete had set). Mass production of cast iron permitted the construction of iron skeletons which could carry a large building on a light foundation.

Since the walls did not bear the weight of the building, they could be hung from the iron framework ("curtain-wall" construction). The walls usually incorporated large areas of glass, and many of the architectural decorations were cast in iron to appear as if they were carved from stone or wood. In recent times, aluminum and stainless steel have also been used to decorate the facades of buildings.

Finally, The Industrial Period saw rapid changes in **movement** (Miller, 1973). Vertical movement was increased by the elevator. The invention of the elevator depended on the use of steel and electricity. The invention of the skyscraper, in turn, depended on the invention of the elevator. Horizontal movement was also increased by the invention of the electric trolley (which ran on railroad tracks set into the street and drew power from overhead electric lines), then electric buses (which ran on rubber wheels and did not need special roadways), then gasoline buses (which did not need overhead power lines), and then away from mass transit to inexpensive private automobiles.

The Modern, Post-Industrial City

Inexpensive private **transportation** broke the bonds of distance that used to hold cities together. Suburbs—begun in the streetcar city of the nineteenth century—became the focus of city growth. The core city lost its dominance.

Automation (the natural progression of industrialization) meant that fewer and fewer workers were needed to produce industrial goods. Put in other words, the productivity of individual workers was dramatically increased. This shifted the bulk of employment from manufacturing to services, like sales, education, accounting, etc.

Parallel to the transformation of transportation, **communication** also underwent a revolution. To the telegraph were added the telephone, radio, television, and computer. The entire globe was now linked aurally and visually, and with only a little delay it was also linked physically.

These three events transformed American society from a federation of relatively independent farm communities and a few trade centers into an interdependent national society. The effort to coordinate this transformation led to a parallel increase in government.

City design in the post-industrial period has predominantly followed a functionalist aesthetic. Contemporary architecture leaves bare its structure, following slogans like "less is more" and "form follows function." The dominant form has been the skyscraper, usually sheathed in glass and steel. The functionalist philosophy has also produced such structures as geodesic domes (much admired, but so far little copied) and Habitat, an apartment complex built for the Montreal World's Fair. Recently functionalism has given way to Post-modernism, which uses the facade of buildings for decoration (a chippendale-like pediment was placed at the top of the

Johnson Wax building and the Portland Office Building is trimmed with bunting).

The Shape of American Cities

The contemporary American city has been shaped most profoundly by transportation. **Accessibility** (i.e., transportation) has been the key to ordering or defining our cities. **Morphology** (i.e., geography) has been an expression of the access routes. The morphology of a city, its shape and the organization of its parts, is a function of the access provided by transportation, a function of time, and a function of the relative advantage which parcels of land derive from the transportation system.

Concentric Ring Model

For most of history, cities have been largely pedestrian cities where both goods and people generally moved at an average speed of 3 miles per hour. A normal walking speed is about 3 mph and a loaded dray wagon could be pulled by a team at about the same speed over a long distance.

This mode of transportation tended to create a city which could best be described as a series of concentric rings focused on a central business district (CBD, or downtown) located at the core (Burgess, 1925). In the industrial era, each ring generally had a distinctive character in its population and land uses, and as the city grew each ring expanded along its outer edge. The users or residents came together in each ring because of a common economic or socio-economic need which could be satisfied there:

1. Central Business District
2. Light Manufacturing Whls. & Whs.
3. Low Income
4. Mid Income
5. Upper Income

Figure 1.5. Concentric Ring Model

Central Business District: The hub of a concentric city was the retail/commercial district. Other institutions such as government, education, religion, entertainment, banking, and personal services frequently shared this location. Although the cost of land was high, the advantages of easy accessibility and centrality were more important.

Warehouse District: The second ring often had a strong symbiotic relationship with the CBD, since it was the source of many goods provided by the downtown. Here one would find wholesale houses, warehouses for bulk materials, light industry, moving and storage firms. It was also the location for the teamster barns that provided drayage both to the market and to the consumer. In the early industrial city, most of the manufacturing was small scale, often designed to service the local market. Businesses such as blacksmithing, harness-making, wagon- and buggy-building, lumber and brickyards, small foundries, grain milling, breweries, meat cutting, cigar making, tanneries, shirtwaist manufacturing, and creameries were typical. Most of these businesses employed fairly large labor forces and were often dirty or produced noxious odors or undesirable by-products.

Low-Income District: The third ring of the city housed low-income households, often the people who worked in the factories, mills, sweatshops, stables, foundries, and warehouses in the second ring. Their quality of life was far from gracious. Living conditions were crowded, poorly served with water, sewerage, rubbish removal, or paved streets. The low-income district buffered the wealthier classes from the dirt, dust, smells, smoke and other undesirable byproducts of the warehouse district. Often residents of this third ring were relatively recent immigrants who had come to the city to find jobs. But their homes were close to work, so they could walk there conveniently.

Middle-Class District: The fourth ring was associated with the middle class. They had an adequate income to provide a single-family home on a city lot convenient to city services such as sewer, water, gas, and paved streets.

Commuter Zone: The fifth zone was not a ring, but a loosely defined area of the city associated with the wealthy and the upper class. Large houses on large lots with pleasant pastoral or urban vistas were the norm. Often the homes were in a desirable section of the city, located along a river or on a lake, or perhaps on a hill or bluff overlooking the city yet relatively inaccessible to the rest of it.

Sector Model

By the 1880s the pattern of city growth was transformed. The railroad tied the nation together and the electric streetcar was becoming common in most of the progressive cities. Until the 1920s these two innovations, railroads and streetcars, transformed the shape of the city. The pattern of mobility shifted from the pedestrian to high-speed linear systems which moved goods and people within the city at the awesome rate of 15 mph.

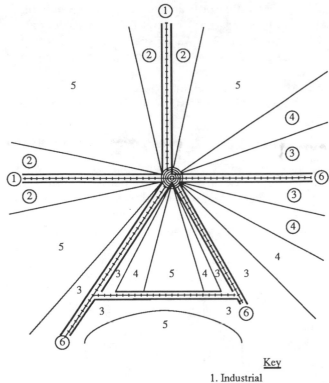

Key
1. Industrial
2. Low Income
3. Apartments - Mid Income
4. Duplex - Mid Income
5. Single Family Resident
6. Commercial (Strip)

Figure 1.6. Sector Model

The previous concentric rings remained, but superimposed on it was a new system of people-and-goods transport. The city rapidly expanded outward from the old core along either side of the new rail lines. This resulted in a characteristic land-use pattern of pie-shaped wedges fanning out from the older core of the city (Hoyt, 1939).

The city continued to focus on the CBD, with the streetcars converging downtown. But streetcar-riding people could now live as much as 5 times further from the city core and still get downtown in the same amount of time as when they walked. As the city sprawled outward along the transportation lines, land developers and speculators found that it was now possible to develop land in the formerly remote surroundings of the city which had been inaccessible in preceding years.

Along with the mobility provided by the streetcar came a rising demand for housing and business locations. Shops and stores were built along the sides of the streets which had streetcar lines, providing the neighborhood shopping and business needs of the commuter. Grocery stores, meat and fish markets, bakeries, taverns and pool halls, doctor/dentist and professional offices, hardware stores, and small variety stores all found a place there. The traffic and exposure the streetcar provided gave them an advantage in these locations which were less expensive than the CBD but convenient to the local neighborhood and the commuters who rode past their doors each day.

The value of land on or near the streetcar line also encouraged the growth of 3- to 5- story apartment buildings offering relatively low rent in good-quality living environments attractive to the middle-class renter. Within a block or two of the streetcar line there would be an area of duplexes and townhouses. The value of the land under these duplexes was somewhat less than that for apartments, but the demand for such housing was considerable. Further away where the price of land was relatively low there would be district of single-family homes. As the numbers in the middle class continued to swell, so did the market for detached single-family homes.

The railroad transformed the location of industry and manufacturing. As businesses grew and expanded, their demand for land and space outstripped the capacity of the CBD and Warehouse districts, which were already tightly congested and often had access problems. The railroad opened new areas beyond the old ring-city for industrial development, just as the trolley had for residential and commercial uses. These new areas had land to grow on and the railroad opened national markets at relatively cheap rates. Factories and mills moved out of the old core not only for more room to expand and access to larger markets, but also for rail access to raw materials for manufacturing and coal to drive steam turbines to power the factories.

Many industries built company towns near their new railroad-oriented factories and provided cheap, relatively good housing for their employees. These workers' housing districts grew up along and beside the mills and factories that lined the railroads leading into the city. Once again, these provided a living area for the "blue collar" workers who tended the mills, fired the boilers and fed the machines of industry while buffering the "better class" residential neighborhoods from the dirt and noise of the railroads and factories.

As the demand for streetcar service grew and the population of the city expanded, the streetcar lines were extended and "crosstown" lines were added. Thus a person could board a streetcar, ride to a major intersection, transfer to another line going off in a different direction, and gain access to sectors of the city previously unserved by public transportation.

It was along these streetcar lines that new businesses emerged to take advantage of the commuter market. For example, Lake St. in Minneapolis became a major automobile sales district in the teens to the thirties. The auto was the "wave of the future" and all the commuters were exposed to the new and used cars displayed along the street in car lots and showrooms.

At the transfer points where two streetcar lines crossed, large secondary business districts emerged to take advantage of the potential customers who were waiting to transfer to another line. Banks, department stores, supermarkets, and haberdashers opened their doors and competed with downtown at these locations.

The streetcar even influenced where such basic urban services as funeral homes and cemeteries were located. Not everyone could afford a lavish funeral with a hearse and vault. So the streetcar was often engaged to take the deceased to a final resting place in a cemetery conveniently located on a trolley line which had special equipment to transport the bereaved and bereft.

Multiple Nuclei Model

By 1920 the automobile was becoming the norm and a growing proportion of the population owned a car or had access to one. Cities found their streets congested with cars which were often in violent conflict with the streetcar. But the car was independent of tracks and wires, schedules and bus stops.

By the 1940s it was apparent that transportation shifts had, once again, reshaped the morphology of American cities (Harris & Ullman, 1945). In the 1950s and 1960s streetcar tracks were paved over and expressways ran from the city across the countryside opening up areas far removed from the old urban core. With the expressway came new opportunities for developers and speculators. The planned shopping center, designed for the convenience of the automobile, emerged at the interchanges of the belt-line highways. With the shopping center came planned residential developments with thousands of acres of tract housing. This swelled the populations of once-small unincorporated hamlets and villages, previously considered remote and isolated from the city but now playing a major role in the growing metropolis. Formerly inner-focused (or "centripetal") cities had suddenly lost their single focus in the central business district. They had exploded outward with a great surge of **centrifugal** force.

This resulted in a metropolis which focused on many diverse communities—a "multiple nuclei" city (Harris & Ullman, 1945). The suburban communities blossomed into full-scale cities themselves while remaining tied to the primary metropolitan center. The old core city had expanded, encouraging the growth of suburban middle-class communities.

The 1920s saw middle class flight to the suburbs. By the 1950s the flight was becoming a stampede. The old urban core was abandoned to the low-income, minority, poorly educated people, many of whom were leaving the farms or migrating north from still more-impoverished southern States. The Depression Years of the 1930s and the War Years of the 1940s made the plight of the old urban core even more apparent. The post-War baby boom and the plight of the city caused an even greater number of former city dwellers to seek a haven of peace and tranquility in the suburbs, the build the "American Dream" manifesting itself in a split-level rambler with a Weber grill on the patio.

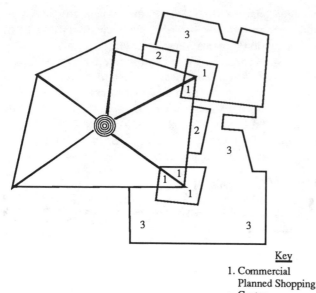

Key
1. Commercial
   Planned Shopping
   Center
2. Industrial Park
3. Suburban Residential
   Single Family

Figure 1.7. Multiple Nuclei Model

Much of the centrifugal flight to the suburbs was a realistic manifestation of the "urban problem"—deterioration, blight, worn-out public services, congestion, crime and the social problems of the poor and minorities. These of course led to higher taxes, more controls on land by cities, redlining by banks which refused to lend money in certain neighborhoods, deteriorating education systems, and a whole host of other problems. But most importantly, it was no longer fashionable to live "in town."

Business and commerce fled to the suburbs from downtown to take advantage of the "new, environmentally controlled, planned shopping center." They were also attempting to get away from the congestion and parking problems of the downtown where the inefficient physical plants had not been modernized in 40 years. There was a general decline in downtown shopping because of a declining market and general image problems.

The middle class abandoned their old-fashioned "inner city" houses and in turn converted them into multiple units for the rental market. Industry likewise found the suburbs attractive. Land was cheap, taxes were low, the railroads no longer served their needs as the truck became the primary means of moving raw materials and finished products. Thus a location in a new industrial park convenient to the expressway and the middle-class, well-educated suburban labor pool generated the forces for relocation. The result was a further enhancement of the multiple-nucleated centrifugal city of the 20th century.

"Back" to the Cities

During the 1960s the primary concern of many urban planners was urban sprawl. CIties had now grown so large

that many predicted that by 1999 the nation would be one large city. But in the process of growth in the 20th century, "leapfrog" development of land occurred. Many large tracts and parcels of land within the "built up" area of the city were skipped over and remained vacant for speculation rather than being developed. Much of the land was served by public services and thus had an advantage over speculative land on the urban periphery which did not already have the amenities of public services. Approximately one-third of the total land area of most of our major metropolitan areas is underdeveloped and considered developable.

This ready, available resource of land convenient to urban services, often previously platted and registered as a subdivision, has assumed a new importance as a result of the advantages they possess. New land development is now taking place not (as before) on the periphery of the city but within the already built-up areas of the city. Much of this new development is coming in as condominiums rather than as single family residential units. This trend is a result of the economics of the '70s and '80s which has escalated the cost of building an average home to nearly $92,000 (1986 national average). The effect of these costs is exemplified by the fact that in 1983 homeownership in the United States declined for the first time since the early 1950s.

With interest rates on home mortgages near 12–14% and downpayments of 10–30%, the cost of housing in the traditional single-family home had risen beyond the means of over 60% of the potential homebuyers in the '80s. These trends further enhance the market for condominiums and (for some) mobile homes.

Coupled with the changing trends in housing America's urban population, there has been a significant change in the demographics of the American city. Since the end of the "Baby Boom" years, there has been a general increase in the number of "empty-nester" suburban families. These are people who own a home but whose family has moved away, leaving a house which is too big for the needs of the parents. Often their income is relatively high, their mobility is high and their remaining debt is low. Add in the time, effort, and money required for maintenance and operation of the house and the result is a perception that a new life style is needed, one different from the traditional suburban family of the '60s and '70s.

These "empty nesters" are finding that the convenience of condominium life is better suited to their new lifestyle. The condominium often provides services which are not part of a suburban home or traditional apartment living, such as security services, enclosed secure parking, recreation and exercise facilities, convenience to transportation, shopping, entertainment, recreation and cultural activities. The attractive qualities of condominium life—particularly in the inner city—have been a significant force in attracting people back to the cities.

Another group attracted "back" to the cities are young people recently out of school, employed (but often at entry- or near-entry level salaries), sometimes married but with no children. Some are attracted to the condominiums, but for many the inner city "distressed" properties are more important. These are properties built 60 to 100 years ago as single-family homes, often in the Victorian traditions of the old-city lifestyle. The structures have usually been adapted to rental uses and divided into smaller apartments. In many cases the are seriously blighted by the combined effects of neglect, overuse, abuse and a general deterioration both of the building's systems and its neighborhood context. Some have been declared unfit for human occupancy or are abandoned and delinquent on their taxes. The cost of improvements far exceeds the sale price of the property, but the cost of improvements can be reduced if owner-labor is substituted for contract-labor (this is called "sweat-equity"). Young people frequently have more energy than money; for them, sweat equity provides an attractive means for obtaining what will eventually be valuable housing at a low entry cost and modest materials costs spread over time.

The Housing Act of 1949 made it possible for cities to condemn properties in neighborhoods which are seriously blighted and resell them at a discount. Many large cities have initiated a program of Urban Homesteading which permits the city to acquire "distressed" properties and resell them by lottery for as little as $1.00. In many cities an outright grant of $5,000 comes with the property, provided the new owner agrees to live on the property for three years, bring the property to the standards in the building code, and restore the exterior trim decoration and landscaping to a minimum level.

Many communities have found that the Urban Homestead programs (and the newer "Urban Shopstead" programs) have revitalized their neighborhoods in a relatively short time, increased tax revenues, restored the local quality of life, and improve the quality of urban services. At the same time, they also experienced a decline in juvenile delinquency and a reduction of vandalism and crime.

The "Back to the Cities" movement is not without its problems. One of the most serious problems is directly related to the housing shortage which is created by an economy which cannot afford to build new low-income housing on the one hand and on the other hand by the **displacement** of low-income residents who formerly occupied the restored housing. This displacement of low-income and minority renters by middle-class owner-occupants is called **"gentrification."** Frequently four or more lower-income households are displaced by one gentrifying household.

The provision of safe, sanitary and wholesome living environments for low-income rental households has been seriously retarded by rising building costs. The limited income of poor households and the high rents required to pay to cost of new construction have created a steadily declining supply of low- and moderate-income housing. In 1978 there was a surplus of 370,000 low-rent housing units; by 1985 there was a deficit of 3,700,000 (Berg, 1989). Incentive programs from the federal government have provided rent subsidies to developers for new low-income housing, and these subsidies have generated some new construction (although condominium construction allows a developer to recover an investment much more quickly). But even these subsidized low-income units are endangered. The subsidy was conditioned on a 15- to 25-year guarantee of low rental rates, after which time the units could be converted to market-rate (i.e., middle-class) rentals. More than 300,000 of the 15-year timeclocks are expiring in the 1990s.

Many former tenement or apartment structures in revitalized and distressed neighborhoods have been purchased, rehabilitated and made more aesthetically appealing, and sold as condominiums rather than apartments, thus continuing the gentrification cycle. In some cities, the "air rights" (unused development potential of a property) of a condominium (but not an apartment building) can be sold, thus reducing the time it takes for a developer to cash out the original investment. This has put pressure not only on apartment buildings in distressed areas but also on apartments for the elderly and the middle class. The profit incentive from condominiums has led to such a significant decline in rental property in many cities that legislation has been enacted to limit condominium conversion and protect tenants from arbitrary displacement for quick profit gain.

Questions for Discussion

1. How important is the division of labor, a hallmark of the Industrial Period? List ten economic activities—whether they be the manufacture of some product or the provision of some service. How might each have been produced by the Romans or the Medieval British? How many distinct steps are there today in the production of each activity?

2. America is mostly a nation of immigrants. For as far back as you can trace your family tree, what were your forbearers' experiences of "city" in each of the generations? In what ways did cities help and support your family? In what ways did cities hinder and frustrate them?

3. Many of the core cities today still bear the wounds of white middle-class flight in the multiple-nucleated city. What opportunities/advantages/resources do these core cities possess which could be turned to the advantage of the people left behind?

Terms to Remember

Ur	nave	El Amarana	clerestory
Kahun	gothic arch	Teotihuacan	rose window
Anasazi	groined arch	Acropolis	plaza
Greek city size	triforium	post-and-lintel	cannon
agora	renaissance	orders of Greek capitals	rond points
capital	palace	caryatid	planning profession
frieze	printing press	Hippodamus	social class
stoa	radial streets	design of Roman cities	Ordinance of 1785
gridiron street plan	division of labor	cardo	stationary power
forum	colonial-style house	rostrum	curtain-wall construction
decumanus	movable power	basilica	electric trolley
curia	slip-cast concrete	atrium	functionalism
villa	elevator	aqueduct	post-modernism
tenement	bus	sewers	morphology
castellum	3 forces in post-industrial	keystone	CBD
Roman arch	city	ampitheatre	low-income district
dome	accessibility	feudalism	commuter zone
thermae	concentric ring model	castle	impact of streetcar
4 characteristics of	warehouse district	half-timbered houses	multiple nuclei model
medieval cities	middle-class district	moat	centrifugal city
market	sector model	bourgeoisie	"empty nesters"
daub-and-wattle	impact of railroad	Guild	urban homesteading
size of medieval cities	centripetal city	cruciform	gentrification
cathedral	"back" to the cities	transepts	displacement
apse	sweat equity	universities	
choir	Tepe Gawra	flying buttress	

References

Argan, Giulio C. (1969) The Renaissance City. NY: George Braziller.

Berg, Steve. (1989) There's a growing crisis in low-income housing as costs rise, supply falls, StarTribune, May 3, 1A and 11A.

Burgess, Ernest W. (1925) The growth of the city: An introduction to a research project, in The City, ed. by Park, Burgess & McKenzie. Chicago: University of Chicago Press.

Chudacoff, Howard P. (1975) The Evolution of American Urban Society. Englewood Cliffs: Prentice Hall.

Clark, Peter, ed. (1976) The Early Modern Town. NY: Longman.

Fraser, Douglas. (1968) Village Planning in the Primitive World. NY: George Braziller.

Grimal, Pierre. (1983) Roman Cities, tr. and ed., G. M. Woloch. Madison, WI: University of Wisconsin Press.

Hardoy, Jorge. (1968) Urban Planning in Pre-Columbian America. NY: George Braziller.

Harris, C. D. and E. L. Ullman. (1945) The nature of cities, Annals of the American Academy of Political and Social Sciences, 142, 7–17.

Haselberger, Lothar. (1985) The Construction Plans for the Temple of Apollo at Didyma, Scientific American, 253 (6), 126–132.

Hauck, George F. W. (1989) The Roman aqueduct of Nimes, Scientific American, 260 (3), 98–104.

Hodge, A. Trevor. (1985) Siphons in Roman aqueducts, Scientific American, 252 (6), 114–119.

Hoyt, Homer. (1939) The Structure and Growth of Residential Neighborhoods in American Cities. Washington, DC: USGPO.

Kihlstedt, Folke T. (1984) The Crystal Palace, Scientific American, 251 (4), 132–143.

Lampl, Paul. (1968) Cities and Planning in the Ancient Near East. NY: George Braziller.

Lekson, Stephen H., Thomas C. Windes, John R. Stein and W. James Judge. (1988) The Chaco Canyon community, Scientific American, 259 (1), 100–109.

Macaulay, David. (1973) Cathedral: The Story of Its Construction. Boston: Houghton Mifflin.

Macaulay, David. (1974) City: A Story of Roman Planning and Construction. Boston: Houghton Mifflin.

Macaulay, David. (1975) Pyramid. Boston: Houghton Mifflin.

Macaulay, David. (1977) Castle. Boston: Houghton Mifflin.

Mark, Robert and William W. Clark. (1984) Gothic structural experimentation, Scientific American, 251 (5), 176–185.

McCann, Anna M. (1988) The Roman port of Cosa, Scientific American, 258 (3), 102–122.

Miller, Zane L. (1973) The Urbanization of Modern America: A Brief History. NY: Harcourt Brace Jovanovich.

Mumford, Lewis. (1961) The City in History. NY: Harcourt, Brace & World.

Pirenne, Henri. (1952) Medieval Cities: Their Origins and the Revival of Trade. Princeton, NJ: Princeton University Press.

Saalman, Howard. (1968) Medieval Cities. NY: George Braziller.

Sjoberg, Gideon. (1960) The Preindustrial City: Past and Present. NY: Free Press.

van Beek, Gus W. (1987) Arches and vaults in the ancient Near East, Scientific American, *257* (1), 96–103.

Vitruvius. (1931) De Architectura, tr. Frank Granger. Cambridge: Harvard University Press

Ward-Perkins, J. B. (1974) Cities of Ancient Greece and Italy: Planning in Classical Antiquity. NY: George Braziller.

Watts, Donald J. and Carol M. Watts. (1986) A Roman apartment complex, Scientific American, *255* (6), 132–139.

Weber, Max. (1958) The City, tr. and ed. Martindale & Neuwirth. NY: Free Press.

2

The City of the Mind

The city is built
To music, therefore never built at all,
And therefore built for ever.

Alfred, Lord Tennyson
Idylls of the King

City at night—Dayton, OH (by author)

The city is more than a physical artifact, more than a collection of buildings and streets. Paul Chombart de Lauwe has called it "culture etched in the ground" (Chombart de Lauwe, 1960). The city both expresses and symbolizes the aspirations which people have for themselves. With only a little practice one can read the city, like a text or a canvas (Clay, 1973), as an object which is layered with meaning built from human experience. These layers of meaning are exposed in two areas in particular, in the arts and in values and customs. In this chapter, we will examine these two areas and come to the question of just what it is we are trying to accomplish by building cities.

The Arts and the City

Following his appointment as Artistic Director of the Guthrie Theater in Minneapolis, MN, Garland Wright articulated his "principles of leadership" for the premier repertory theater in the country. He wrote, in part,

> To the extent we believe and demonstrate that art offers hope and grace to the quality of life, we will have made a difference to our endangered culture and will reaffirm our belief that there is, indeed, a human soul. (Wright, 1988)

Are statements like Wright's little more than self-serving delusions, or is it possible that the arts make a difference in the quality of urban life and in the lives of urban people?

The Arts and Understanding

Yi-Fu Tuan, a geographer, argues that the arts are tools for understanding the environment (Tuan, 1976). The arts both **reflect the times** in which they were created and in which they are being experienced, and they in turn **create and direct the culture** of which they are part. Hadrian's gate, the triumphal arch built in Rome to celebrate the defeat of the Gauls, became in time an inspiration to future empires (and the model for Napoleon's *Arc de Triom-*

Arc de Triomphe—Paris (H. Roger Smith)

phe). Greek civilization created and became a creature of the *agora;* Gothic society focused on the cathedral. As Churchill said of the House of Commons, "We shape our buildings, and afterwards they shape us."

A work of art may reflect the time in which it was created at four different levels, according to Tuan. Not all artworks operate at all of the levels. It might even be argued that the aesthetic quality of a work is determined at least in part by how far down the levels it can take us.

At the surface level, a work of art presents **factual data** from its time. The novels of Charles Dickens describe—document, if you will—the daily life of the urban poor in Industrial England, as de Sevigne's letters document 17th century Paris, Seneca's letters do so for Augustan Rome, and Saul Bellow's novels for contemporary American cities. From *Les Tres Riches Heures de Jean Duc de Barry* we can see many of the details of daily life in Medieval France, just as Edward Hopper's paintings preserve part of the middle Twentieth Century. Some art, of course, purposely distorts the factual: Despite Dali's painting, most pocketwatches do not melt nor or many criminal justice systems as frustrating as Kafka's *Trial.* But Dali could not have produced his painting in a culture that did not use pocketwatches, nor could Kafka have written his novel for a people who had no experience of bureaucracy.

At a deeper level, a work of art presents a **conceptual frame.** From among an indefinite number of details, the artists selects a few which capture her/his point of view. Dickens could have written about middle-class London, as Jane Austen did. Hopper could have painted vibrant, dynamic streetscapes as Hocking would a few years later. In each case, the artist's viewpoint tells us something about people and cities of their time. Dickens (along with others) is concerned that so many poor people are pouring into London, where they will live in squalor. Hopper (along with others of his time) is concerned that cities are anonymous and isolating places. Each artist's choice of viewpoint is deeply personal; at the same time, it is usual-

Hadrian's Gate—Rome (H. Roger Smith)

ly shared by others of that time. If it were not, the artist would find no public and (being human) would have a difficult time pursuing her/his art.

Yet there is a deeper level. Many may have had similar perceptions and thoughts, but part of the artist's craft is to **articulate** that **experience.** As Alexander Pope put it in *An Essay on Criticism,*

True Wit is Nature to advantage dressed
What oft was thought, but ne'er so well expressed. . . .

The conceptual frame of a work may be shared, but the clarity with which it is expressed is what makes it a work of art. Many have said that a building should blend into natural environment; but when one comes to Frank Lloyd Wright's house at Fallingwater in Pennsylvania, there is an instant of recognition that *this* is how it can be done. Many have thought that the city exacts a high price for success; in reading Theodore Dreiser's *Sister Carrie,* the suspicion is crystallized into the experience of its truth. Curiously, where art is most true—when an experience is articulated most clearly—it is the most artificial. Probably no person is forced into a pattern of behaving as inexorably as Dreiser has contrived for Carrie. For all of its effortless suspension between water and hillside, the house at Fallingwater required very sophisticated design, engineering, and construction, and still requires continual maintenance. The truths which artists seek are hidden ones; the "facts" around them must be altered if the truths are to be made plain.

At its deepest level, art grapples with the **mythic.** At its deepest and best, art expresses not only the experience of one time and place, but the basic riddles with which all humankind grapple. The wanderings of Odysseus, the *hubris* of Oedipus, the courage of Beowulf, the ambivalence of Hamlet, the self-indulgence of Lear all speak to universal human dilemmas. Much that is artistic does not reach to this depth. It is usually only through the passage of time that succeeding generations come to realize how deeply a particular work has tapped a universal truth. At the mythic level, the city has been perceived as both the holy city Jerusalem and the whore Babylon.

The City as Symbol

There is a long and respected tradition of using "city" to symbolized the source and keeping-place of "civilization." Lewis Mumford (1961) wrote,

From its origin onward, indeed, the city may be described as a structure specially equipped to store and transmit the goods of civilization, sufficiently condensed to afford the maximum amount of facilities in a minimum space, but also capable of structural enlargement to enable it to find a place for the changing needs and the more complex forms of a growing society and its cumulative social heritage.

In one of humankind's oldest written works, the *Epic of Gilgamesh,* the wisdom of the king is expressed by the city and its walls. The walls were so impressive that "the seven sages laid the foundations." In the Hebrew *Bible,* the city Jerusalem was the "holy city," the sacred place, the focus of worship. In these ancient societies the city was the physical presence of all that was civilized and sacred—it was a **"heavenly city."** A similar tradition can also be found in the Greeks. When Plato, in *The Republic,* inquired into the nature of a just life, he proceeded by examining the nature of a city in which justice might occur. The Christians transferred this to Paradise when they referred to life after death as "the Heavenly Jerusalem."

Such an image of the city as representing the good, the true, and the beautiful has been carried forward into contemporary writing. In *The Wizard of Oz,* the city of Oz reflected (and, as it turned out, magnified) the magnificence of the great wizard, Oz. Shangri-La, the mythical city in the Tibetan mountains, was supposed to be an earthly paradise. And, in a contemporary rediscovery of a medieval story, Camelot represents the city ruled by justice and renowned for its beauty.

There is another sense in which the city is a source of civilization. This is the city as focus of culture and refinement—the **"sophisticated city."** It can be found in the Greek fable (later retold in the medieval versions of Aesop's fables) of the city mouse and the country mouse. The story depends on the ready acceptance of the character of city-dwellers as smooth, polished, and knowledgeable. This convention continued in the Latin playwrights. Both Plautus and Terence drew on the stereotypes of the country rustic and the urbane city dweller. In fact, Quintillian in the *Institutio Oratoriae* defines "urbanity," the characteristic behavior of city-dwellers, as "wit and humor in speaking" (Ramage, 1973). This convention of a country rustic and a suave city-dweller continues in the plays of Shakespeare, for example in the juxtaposition of Bottom and Lysander in *A Midsummer Night's Dream* and Audrey and Rosalind in *As You Like It.* Henry James, the American-born English writer, follows this convention in his novels, although he is less concerned with rustic uncouthness than he is interested in urbane civility as, for instance, in *The Ambassadors.*

There is a third sense of the city as a source of civilization. Not the heavenly city, nor even the sophisticated city, the city is a place where things happen—the **"lively city."** This sense of city was also present in ancient writings like the *Iliad* and the *Aeneid,* but it was so much assumed that it never found full voice. It wasn't until the Industrial Period that we find writers praising the *energy* of their city. Carl Sandburg addresses the city in his poem, "Chicago," as "Hog butcher for the world" and "City of the big shoulders." James Joyce made Dublin a familiar town for millions of readers who have never been there. John Dos Passos did the same for New York City. In all three cases, no effort was made to hide the blemishes; there is much in their cities that is gritty and ugly. But it is forgiven, because it is in the City that these writers feel most alive.

In other words, there is a strong tradition in our literature tying the city to what is good about humanity: It is not for nothing that the root meaning of "civilization" is "city-fied."

But there is another tradition, on which identifies the city as the source of evil and corruption. In this tradition, to be a hero (good, noble, true) and to be in the city is to be a "self-divided man" (Gelfant, 1954).

This tradition extols the simplicity of rural life; the **earthly city** is an imperfect model of nature. Horace, in the *Odes,* praises the simple virtues of rustic life in republican Rome, as did Vergil in the *Georgics.* They found an openness (and open-handedness) and simple honesty in a life close to the soil. This theme was picked up again in the eighteenth century by the Pastoral Poets in England and France who rediscovered these same themes.

Across the ocean a century later, Henry David Thoreau retreated to Walden pond because in nature he could escape from the alienation and distortion of values which he found in cities. For him the city was not only imperfect, it was an **artificial city.** A product of human craft, the city is in one sense an "artifice"; but by placing itself and the human affairs it embodies between the individual and nature and between individuals, the city also creates an artificial way of living (Marx, 1964). Theodore Dreiser, in *Sister Carrie* and *The Financier,* portrays the city as an evil place which seduces the innocent with allurements of fame and fortune. Carrie came from the farm to the big city; she was unknown and innocent when she arrived. By the end of the novel, she was famous but fallen. Upton Sinclair, in *The Jungle,* exposed the profiteering of city businesses. Sinclair Lewis, in *Main Street,* exposed the pettiness of city people and F. Scott Fitzgerald, in the *The Great Gatsby,* portrays the rapid climb to success of city folk, and their equally precipitous decline.

Cities are also seen as the "whore Babylon"—the **corrupt city.** These are cities in the tradition of Sodom and Gomorrah, dens of iniquity which are fit only to be destroyed. St. Augustine, in *The City of God,* identifies the earthly city with sin, evil, and corruption (the better to contrast present life with life in the Heavenly city). There is some basis for such a characterization: In the Middle Ages cities were, in fact, a source of illness and death as they spread cholera, typhus, and the plague. In the *Decameron,* Boccaccio has his storytellers fleeing the city to escape Bubonic plague. Cities have not necessarily been much healthier in recent times. The London of Dickens' novels is dirty, filthy, and decaying—a place for people to be miserable. Jacob Riis, in *How the Other Half Lives,* and Lincoln Steffens, in *The Shame of Our Cities,* exposed the misery in American cities at the turn of the century.

How can such contradictory symbols arise? Is one "right" and the other "false"? Not necessarily. While a *thing* cannot both "be" and "not be" at the same time, our *image* of a thing can easily carry contradictions within it, like the optical illusion which is perceived sometimes as a vase and sometimes as two people looking at each other. This realization is one of the roots of the psychoanalytic interpretation of human experience (Freud, 1900; Jung, 1960). We carry within us a basic **ambivalence** about the city.

Figure 2.1. Optical Illusion: Vase or people?

A person's perception of the city is filtered through experience. Raymond Williams (1973) recalled people saying, "Things were better in my father's day. . . ." So he went to the literature of their fathers' day, and found authors saying, "Things were better in my father's day. . . ." He traced an unbroken line of this yearning for the better times of a recent past—a line which extends through English literature all the way to *The Vision of Piers Plowman* (and, says Williams, one that probably goes all the way back to Adam and Eve, were there a written literature by which to trace it). Searching times past is risky business. It is likely that cities are *both* corrupt and civilized, a veritable *Tale of Two Cities.* It is also likely that we perceive the present corruption and remember the past civility, as in Thorton Wilder's *Our Town.* It should be no surprise that people are capable of carrying such conflicting perceptions together. Unlike the musical, *Camelot,* in Mallory's *Moret d'Arthur* the city of the Round Table always maintained an uneasy truce with the internal forces which caused its eventual destruction. Consistency of principle seems to be more common in the abstract than in human behavior.

The city has also played a traditional role in art forms other than the written word. Peter Breughel, the Elder, painted scenes of town life in the Gothic period. His cities were crammed with things to do, people to see, and mischief to get into. He was an early observer of the city as a place "where the action is," but he was an exception. Most artists of the Medieval and Renaissance periods use the city as a backdrop against which action occurs, as in "October" from *Les Tres Riches Heures de Jean Duc de Berry*. Here the artist portrays peasants working in the field against a backdrop of the castle of Paris; all the action is in the foreground.

Cities remained as decorative objects for painting until the Industrial Period when Romantic artists discovered the common folk all around them. Just as Dickens described the city as filthy and decaying, Daumier drew city people as impoverished and grotesque. He highlighted the plight of the lower class and the shallowness of the upper classes. On the other hand, the Impressionists (such as Pisarro or Renoir) focused on middle-class city life, and drew street scenes full of activity—activity suggested not only by the actions of the characters portrayed, but also by the play of light and color on the scenes. In this century, the premier painter of cities is probably Edward Hopper. His pictures display everyday street scenes in the city, frequently lit by the flat, bright light of a streetlamp. The people tend to be isolated, each sitting or standing apart from the others, few facing the viewer. Hopper's city is the anonymous city of strangers. Less literal, perhaps, but equally reflecting the city is the work of Alexander Calder, especially his "stabiles." These sculptures, anchored in the ground yet constantly moving, constantly releasing energy, can be seen as abstractions of urban life itself. So, among modern visual artists we find the tension of city as good/city as evil just as it is found in the language arts.

City in the Electronic Media

The ambivalence between the city as evil and the city as desirable is also found in the way the city appears in contemporary media. The news media, especially the medium of television news, focus on problems. Cities make the news by having problems like riots, crime, bankruptcy, graft, welfare fraud. When good things happen, they tend to be attributed to individual people or maybe a small neighborhood community, but rarely to a city as a whole. The net effect is that cities seem to have nothing but problems.

The popular media, again especially television, also draw on these cultural stereotypes in presenting their stories. The stereotypes of the city as dangerous is a common convention. When you think of TV series which have featured a city, *Streets of San Francisco, Dallas, Hawaii Five-O,* or *The Naked City* come to mind. All of these are crime stories (if you will grant that the melodramatic an-

tics on *Dallas* are larcenous). When you think of TV series which feature the country, *Little House on the Prairie* or *The Waltons* come to mind, stories which, while they have their dramatic tensions, stress the basic goodness of people. The picture is not always so black-and-white, of course. *The Cosby Show, The Mary Tyler Moore Show* and *Welcome Back, Kotter* portrayed city neighborhoods sympathetically and *The Dukes of Hazzard* and *Mayberry, R.F.D.* play on the stereotype of the country bumpkin.

The curious thing about the relationship between the city and the electronic media is that the media have transformed the United States into an urban nation. In terms of culture and values, there is little distinction any more between urban and rural locations. Isolated, rural farmers wake up to clock radios, set to a channel which reports the commodity market closings from the day before. After a hearty breakfast in front of a television set tuned to a national morning news program, the farmer climbs into the air-conditioned cab of her/his tractor, tunes in the radio or TV to a channel from a nearby city, and goes about the chores. In the afternoon, driving into town to pick up some supplies and repair parts, the farmer catches up on the progress in the days' commodity markets and maybe stops off at the broker to invest in (or maybe to sell) some commodity futures. In the evening, national network news brings the farmer up-to-date on the market closings and the antics of leaders around the world.

How Cities Transform Art

Not only does art support "the City" by capturing and expressing our feelings about such places, but the city also supports the arts. For one thing, a city serves as an **art gallery**. In many cities, the commissioning and display of public art is a regular part of the budget. Portland, OR, requires that 1% of the construction budget of major buildings be devoted to public art. Some cities are identified by their statues, like "The Spirit of Detroit" or Chicago's Picasso statue. Cincinnati and Los Angeles both commission fine arts competitions for downtown billboards. Atlanta has become a home for the National Black Arts Festival. There is also a growing body of research demonstrating the economic impact of the arts on cities (Jordan, 1988; Metropolitan Council Regional Arts Council, 1985).

Wall murals are a form of public art commonly found in cities around the world. They are part of a tradition which goes back to Egyptian, Greek, and Roman wall art. Wall murals can span the range from graffiti to picture histories to decorative painting. Frequently wall murals express the identity of a neighborhood or a people, like the People's Wall in Berkeley, CA, or Diego Rivera's murals in the Detroit Institute of Arts. The rural town of Good Thunder, MN, has even painted its grain elevator to portray the history of the town.

Mural: People's Wall—Berkeley, CA (by author)

Mural: grain elevator—Good Thunder, MN (by author)

Contemporary cities have taken the role played previously by wealthy **patrons of the arts.** They provide museums to collect art objects and display them for their citizens. In the past, this was done by private citizens and usually was not made available to the general public. Many cities also provide grants to encourage and support young artist in their work. Some cities (like San Francisco) even support local and neighborhood art centers to train new artists.

Finally, the city has transformed **how we view art** by changing the way in which we move around the art object (Wines, 1973). Because of the automobile, most public art is **oversized** and lacks detail. It has to be, if it is to make an impact on a person who will be viewing it from a rapidly moving vehicle. Since the artwork will probably be seen only from the front window of a car as it speeds by, the artist thinks in terms of **limited angles of sight** (like the Roman public buildings, which were designed to be approached from only one side). And, since the object will be framed by the rectangle of the front window of the car, a certain **format** or shape for the design tends to be dictated.

The Conscience of the City

Values

The city has had an important impact on human values. Throughout recorded history, city folk have had to find a way to deal with strangers in their midst. In smaller communities, strangers are few and readily recognized as such. In cities, there are too many strangers and they are too regular a part of life to be ignored. Cities are often so large that even the local residents are strangers to many of the other local residents (Lofland, 1973).

This living in a world of strangers has had two effects on city-dwellers' values: First, time has become **"deprivatized."** Time in the city is no longer the duration of one's own activity, but it is instead a measure, external to oneself, within which and against which one pursues an activity. If the independent activity of thousands of individuals is to be coordinated, they must regulate themselves by some common rhythm. A farmer in the field can eat when s/he is hungry; five hundred assembly-line workers must eat on a schedule to keep the line running. The clock (and, worse, the pocket- and wrist-watch) is an urban invention.

Second, city folk live their lives among **anonymous others.** In our society we are so used to it that we barely notice it, but city folk learn to live by and for "the record." Many of city folks' actions are determined by and directed, not to another person, but to some generalized other, an anonymous, faceless "them." Memos, newspapers of record, formal courtesies are all examples of this. Bureaucracy (a city invention) is based on the anonymity of others.

Even though cities have changed the values of people who live in them, it does not necessarily follow that these shifts are bad. They are adaptations to the pressures brought by a certain type of environment. If such adaptations permit city folk to maintain higher, more cherished values while also enjoying the benefits of city life, perhaps the adaptations are useful.

Ethics: The Secular City

In *The Secular City,* Harvey Cox argues that ethical behavior in a city is different from ethical behavior in small towns (Cox, 1966). In big cities, one often treats other people (the strangers) **impersonally,** sometimes even mechanically. But, Cox argues, given the number of people in a city, it would be impossible to maintain a personal relationship with each. "You don't have a personal relationship with the parking lot attendant," he argues. As long as you and the other agree to it, each of you treat the other as a piece of the city's machinery. This is necessary to simplify life to a bearable level of complexity.

There is a second ethical implication to living in a city of strangers. City people have to be more **tolerant** of diversity in ethical positions. Strangers also have strange values. If one wants the benefits of commerce with strangers (whether those benefits be economic, artistic, or cultural), one will also have to allow them into the community, differences and all. The mercantile revival of the Gothic era required that cities return the marketplace (and the strangers) to the center of town. The economic and cultural revival of the late Medieval and Renaissance could not have occurred had the market remained outside the walls. The stranger can represent an opportunity as well as a threat.

These two claims of ethical relativism imply an acceptance of "situation ethics" (Fletcher, 1966). Proper behavior depends on the circumstances in which it occurs. Perhaps it is permissible to ignore a drunk on the street in the big city, while in a small town one would have a duty to intervene. Perhaps in the big city it is no cause for proselytizing if a neighbor stays home on Sunday morning and reads the paper—or prostrates himself three times a day and prays to Allah, or goes to temple on Saturday. If situation ethics is to work, if moral relativism is not to degenerate into moral absence, the diverse moral communities must each be strong enough to be comfortable in their beliefs yet willing to allow others to express their own beliefs. Faced with the impersonalism and tolerance of the city, too many abandon their own beliefs and replace them with nothing else. The result is not tolerance, but normlessness ("anomie," in the language of sociology).

Aside form structural differences in ethics, cities also generate and support **diversity** and differences in lifestyle. The city and the town represent different values. The city stands for mixture (of a finer or coarser grain, but a mixture in any event) of classes and races, of opportunities and advantages. The town stands for homogeneity. The city is a very concentrated, densely-built environment. The town is more dispersed. The city depends on specialized labor from its residents, while the town draws on its residents to perform a great variety of roles.

Suburbs stand somewhere between the city and the town. Suburbs share many of the physical characteristics of towns (dispersion, homogeneity, multiple roles). But, as Gans (1961) points out, city and suburban people are primarily different only in age and economic status; many share similar intentions and goals. The popular image of the suburb is that it is an area for childrearing and socializing. Suburbs are thought of as areas of low-density, single-family housing units with plenty of open space. According to Sylvia Fava (1956), the suburban way of life stresses neighboring and other social contacts. However, in a survey of suburbs across the United States, William Dobriner (1958) found that the only things suburbs had in common are that they are outside the core municipality, their residents commute to work, and the residents are more likely to know each other. He did not find that all suburbs were homogeneous, nor that they were all bedroom communities (i.e., cities with very little local employment),

nor did he find a single suburban life-style. In fact, he found that the outer edges of the core municipality were indistinguishable from the first tier of suburbs.

Meier (1962) has also shown that the life-style of cities is closely ties to the communication patterns of cities. An urban culture is one in which interaction occurs between anonymous actors, and which has evolved primarily to facilitate communication among them. Thus, the attraction of city life becomes stronger as time spent in public and professional activity increases. Conversely, the attractiveness of cities decreases as time spent reflectively on matters of personal concern increases.

In other words, the city has influenced our understanding of what is right and wrong. It has also freshened our understanding of what is "acceptable" (as opposed to right or wrong) by providing a greater range of social environments in which to live.

A Philosophy for Urban Living

Most people want not merely to live, but to live "the **good life**." The problem, of course, lies in what is meant by a "good" life. The question is a philosophical one. A. K. Bierman, a philosopher, has developed the argument that philosophy is only possible in the city (Bierman, 1973). Philosophy requires a place small enough for high discourse to have effect, but large enough to engage the full scope of a person's interests. Only the city is such a place. The neighborhood community is too small to provide all of the various activities which are part of the cycle of living, and the modern State is too large to be engaged on a personal level. Following the structure of Plato's argument in *The Republic,* Bierman turns the question, "What is the good life?" into a question of how the city can support the good life—"What is a good city?"

Bierman argues that the good life and the good city are inextricably intertwined. The good life no longer depends on meeting physical needs; we have enough food and other physical goods, even if they are currently poorly distributed. The good life depends on meeting social needs, which he refers to as creating a "morally whole civic community." A morally whole community has the characteristic of **"concinnity,"** a recognition that the parts are fitted together well.

The key issue of concinnity is creating the circumstances in which the **Many** (who are needed if a city is to be a city) can **become One.** How can a morally whole community be created in a world of strangers?

Bierman rejects the social-contract theories which assume a rugged individualism in which persons are independent entities. Rather, he argues, **personhood** lies in relationships. Just as pieces of paper became this book by being placed *in relation* to each other, he argues, human bodies become persons when they are placed in relation to other human bodies. A wild child, raised by wolves from infancy, would be human, but not a person; only when the feral child comes into human society is there a person. It is the relation of people to each other in society that creates persons. It is logically impossible to define a person's interests in terms of self-interest alone, according to this theory. Withdrawn, anonymous, alienated society go together, create each other (see also Bellah, *et alii,* 1985, for a similar argument).

Creating the morally whole person implies creating the morally whole society—the good city. To do this, to achieve concinnity, requires **"understanding,"** which is the ability to take to Other's point of view. Understanding is created through **justice** and **tolerance.** Each person must grant the other what s/he values or in which s/he has a special interest. At the same time, the variety of personal points of view must be modified sufficiently that they converge toward a common social point of view. This common social point of view by its nature cannot be contained in any single individual point of view. Tolerance is the feeling aspect of understanding. Justice is its cognitive aspect.

According to Bierman, art is an essential tool in the creation of the community. It is particularly suited to conveying to an audience a point of view which is different from one's own. Of all the arts, drama is best suited to this function, for not only does it bring individuals to confront the "otherness" of its characters, but the audience comes to this realization in a group rather than alone. The experience of otherness is shared.

What Bierman is calling for is a rediscovery of "the public," a new appreciation for what we have in common. It is in the sharing of what we have in common that the need for and appreciation of the city occurs, and it is through the arts that this sharing is realized.

Summary

In this chapter, we have looked at the city as a human construct. We have seen the city as a symbol for what is good and for what has gone wrong in the lives of people. We have seen how the city transforms the arts, making them distinctly its own. The values which are embodied in the arts are also transformed by living in cities, particularly because of the diversity and the anonymity which characterize city life. Finally, we have seen that the arts themselves become the tool for overcoming the isolation to which cities are prey. The chapter began with the statement that the arts both reflect their times and create their times. For the city, this is certainly the case.

Questions for Discussion

1. What are we trying to accomplish by building cities? What role do the values which a city embodies play in what *you* are trying to do with your life? How do you think your values articulate with "mainstream" American values?

2. As a symbol, the city can be seen as the locus of good or of evil. Select three or four works of art in which the city plays a role, and evaluate is meaning at the other three levels.
3. What has American society lost in the process of becoming urbanized? Which of the original founding values have been lost? Transformed?
4. The arts can be used to "create the community," according to Bierman. What activities would you design into a community arts festival which would advance this goal in your city? Would the activities be different for other cities?

Terms to Remember

dual role of the arts	heavenly city
"city" as symbol	lively city
sophisticated city	corrupt city
earthly city	ambivalence of "city"
artificial city	city as art gallery
city and the news	transforming the way we
city as billboard	view art
"deprivatization" of time	anonymous others
impersonal ethics	ethics of tolerance
value of diversity	city/suburb/rural values
value of public activity	the "good life"
One from Many	"personhood"
concinnity	understanding
tolerance	justice
4 levels of meaning in art	

References

Bellah, Robert N., *et alii.* (1985) Habits of the Heart: Individualism and Commitment in American Life. Berkeley, CA: University of California press.

Bierman, A. K. (1973) The Philosophy of Urban Existence: Prologomena. Athens, OH: Ohio University Press.

Chombart de Lauwe, Paul. (1960) Famille et Habitation. Paris: Editions du Centre National de la Recherche Scientifique.

Clay, Grady. (1973) Close-Up: How to Read the American City. NY: Praeger.

Cox, Harvey. (1966) The Secular City: Secularization and Urbanization in Theological Perspective, Rev. Ed. NY: Macmillan.

Dobriner, William M. (1958) The Suburban Community. NY: Putnam.

Fava, Sylvia F. (1956) Suburbanism as a way of life. American Sociological Review *21,* 34–37.

Fletcher, Joseph. (1966) Situation Ethics: The New Morality. Philadelphia: Westminster Press.

Freud, Sigmund. (1900) *Die Traumdeutung* (The Interpretation of Dreams). Leipzig: Franz Deuticke.

Gans, Herbert J. (1961) Planning and social life: Friendship and neighborhood relations in suburban communities. Journal of the American Institute of Planners *27*, 134–140.

Gelfant, Blanche H. (1954) The American City Novel. Norman, OK: University of Oklahoma Press

Jordan, Fred. (1988) Arts districts can paint downtowns the color of money, Governing, *1* (10), 40–45.

Jung, Carl G. (1960) The Collected Works, Read, Fordham & Adler, eds. NY: Pantheon.

Lofland, Lyn H. (1973) A World of Strangers. NY: Basic Books.

Marx, Leo. (1964) The Machine in the Garden: Technology and the Pastoral Ideal America. London: Oxford University Press.

Meier, R. A. (1962) A Communication Theory of Urban Growth. Cambridge, MA: MIT Press.

Metropolitan Council Regional Arts Council. (1985) The Arts: A Regional Industry. (Publication Number 658-86-006) St. Paul, MN: Metropolitan Council.

Mumford, Lewis. (1961) The City in History. NY: Harcourt, Brace & World.

Ramage, Edwin S. Urbanitas: Ancient Sophistication and Refinement. Norman, OK: University of Oklahoma Press.

Tuan, Yi-Fu. (1976) Literature, experience, and environmental knowing in Environmental Knowing, Moore & Golledge, eds. Stroudsburg, PA: Dowden, Hutchinson & Ross.

Williams, Raymond. (1973) The Country and the City. NY: Oxford University Press.

Wines, James. (1973) Notes from a passing car: The problem of art in a mobile environment, Architectural Forum *139* (2), 66–75.

Wright, Garland. (1988) Principles of leadership, The Guthrie Theater Program Magazine, Summer 1988.

Part II

Making the City

3

Design with Nature

. . . (I)t is obvious that designs for houses ought . . . to conform to the nature of the country and to diversities of climate. In the north, houses should be entirely roofed over and sheltered as much as possible, not in the open, though having a warm exposure. But on the other hand, where the force of the sun is great in the southern countries that suffer from heat, houses must be built more in the open and with a northern or northeastern exposure. Thus we may amend by art what nature, if left to herself, would mar.

Vitruvius
On Architecture

St. Anthony Falls—Minneapolis, MN (by author)

In this chapter, we consider the natural foundation on which cities are built. The focus ranges from water and the land, to climate, to other forms of life with which humans share space. The chapter will also look at ways of designing cities (and elements within cities) to make best use of the natural environment, and programs designed to conserve natural resources.

The Land

The city is the ultimate expression of humankind's ability to transform the environment. In the city, almost everything you see around you was built there or placed there by someone for some purpose. These decisions to locate or build something were primarily made by a large number of individuals, each acting basically in his/her own interest and with no knowledge of the future actions of other individuals. It is really quite remarkable that cities work at all under these conditions, since the environmental interactions which must be balanced through these individual actions are quite complex.

The urban environment is a complicated **feedback system** with a combination of environmental inputs, transformations, and outputs. The city takes in air, water, people, materials, fuel and other energy, and food. In the city, these are transformed through work, storage, and internal flows of goods, services, and energy. And from this the city produces ideas, information, education, technology, and services; the city also releases noise, waste, dirty air (compared to how it came into the system), and dirty water (again, relatively speaking). Air, waste, and water feed back, in turn, into the inputs which go into the city, and in the city all of these inputs, transformations, and outputs are balanced by literally thousands of individual, daily decisions (Detwyler & Marcus, 1972).

Flooding

One of the major environmental considerations in building and maintaining a city is the control of water. Many cities were built on waterways for easy transportation. Those same waterways can also destroy a city through flooding.

River valleys, when they are young, take a typical **V-shaped profile.** The banks of the river are steep, the river runs a fairly straight course down the slope, and the river is actively cutting down and into its banks.

An older river valley typically has a **U-shaped profile.** The banks are much wider apart and slope gently to the river bed; in fact, sometimes it is hard to recognize them. The river cuts back and forth across the floodplain created between the banks, and river moves slowly and tends to cut sideways rather than down into its bed.

This sideways cutting which transforms young river valleys into old ones is called **"lateral cutting."** The water in the river moves faster on the outside of a bend and slower on the inside. The faster water cuts into its

V-shaped river valley—Montana (by author)

U-shaped river valley—rural Minnesota (by author)

bank, and the slower water deposits its load of silt (the soil carved from the previous banks) on the inside of the curve. Over time the river sweeps back and forth, carving ever-widening banks, and laying down a fertile, stable layer of soil (silt) in the bottom of the valley. This stretch of land deposited by the river in the valley bottom is called a **"floodplain."** (Van Dusen, Dozier, & Marsh, 1978).

The first settlers usually settled on this fertile soil, and the first towns were usually located there to provide easy access to the river-road. As cities grew, the floodplain location created problems. It is not always immediately apparent where the floodplain is. For most of the year, the river stays within its banks and does not rise to the plain. Even during spring rains, the river will not necessarily rise to fill the entire floodplain. In fact, floodplains are defined by the probability that an area will flood: The 100-year floodplain is that portion of the valley bottom which has a

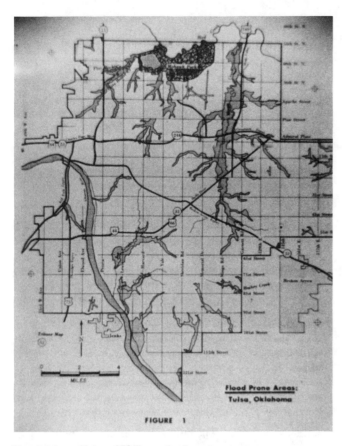

Floodplains—Tulsa, OK (by author)

1-in-100 chance (a "1% probability") of flooding in any given year.

The issue of flooding is further complicated by the fact that the forces which create a floodplain are not static. The size of a floodplain depends on the amount of water that a river has to handle at flood stage. The amount of **stormwater runoff** that flows into the river, in turn, depends on the type of soil, the time of year, and the type of groundcover.

Groundcover: A forest can absorb 80–100% of the rainfall which reaches it. As the raindrops strike the leaves of the trees, they are broken into smaller droplets and fall more gently on the soil, which is covered with the litter of dead leaves. An evergreen forest will absorb almost all of the rain falling on it, as the needles turn raindrops into a mist.

A cultivated field might absorb only 40–50%. Much of the soil under cultivation is kept bare, to facilitate the circulation of air between the rows of crops and to keep down the growth of weeds. Raindrops striking the bare soil will compact it and draw the clay particles together so they become sun-baked into hardpan. When the next rain comes, the water runs across the ground over the soil rather than being absorbed.

A suburban, residential environment can absorb 50–60% of rainfall. Much of the soil is covered with imperme-

able surfaces—roofs, driveways, sidewalks, and streets—and absorbs no water. But some of the land is devoted to lawn; the blades of grass break the raindrops, and the thatch on the surface of the lawn absorbs the droplets, and little of the rain falling there runs off.

In a built-up central city, no more than 10% of a rainfall is absorbed. Most of it runs off the roofs and sidewalks and streets, into storm sewers, and from there into the creeks and rivers (Marsh, 1978). In other words, as an area is built up it shunts more and more of the rainwater into the river, thus increasing the chances of flood.

Time of Year: Whether or not a river will flood also depends on the time of year. Typically, the soil is water-logged in the spring. During the summer, there is less rain, the plants draw moisture out of the soil through transpiration, and the air draws moisture out of the soil through evaporation. Summer soil can absorb more rainfall, other things being equal (Bellovich, 1976).

Soil: A third factor in the volume of stormwater runoff is the type of soil. Clay soil absorbs very little water, and in fact can become impermeable. Sandy and gravelly soils absorb more water than clay when dry, and continue to absorb more water over time (Strahler & Strahler, 1973).

A common solution to flooding problems is **channelization:** Straighten the stream and line the riverbed with concrete. The channel will remove water from the floodplain more quickly, and the liner will keep the stream from cutting into its banks or its bottom. The problem with channelization is that the straightening increases the speed

Channelization—Riverwalk, Flint, MI (by author)

with which water goes through the stream, which increases the force with which water hits its banks at the end of the channel. Channels have a tendency to erode rapidly where they end (Creath & Birt, 1976).

A better solution to flooding is **impoundment:** Construct holding ponds which will capture part of the rainwater runoff and release it slowly into the watercourse. Properly designed holding ponds can provide a runoff rate no different from the rate prior to development in the area. The problem with impoundments is that they can require a large amount of land and eventually pressures for development will come to bear on the space, too.

The ideal solution (but one rarely taken) is to **stay out** of the floodplain altogether: Build on the ridges and the high ground (McHarg, 1969). The problem can be resolved by being avoided in the first place.

Soil and Subsurface Structures

Besides water, the second major environmental force in the city is the ground itself—soil and subsurface geology. The ground under a city is not uniform. It is composed of layers, or **strata,** of rock. These strata are usually tipped slightly, so the different strata come to the surface (outcrop) in different parts of the city. This will have an effect on the soils (which are composed of eroded particles from the exposed rock) and on the runoff characteristics of those parts of the city.

The different rocks which constitute the strata have different characteristics. Limestone is hard, but it can be

Rock strata—St. Paul, MN (by author)

worn away by water. Shale is strong under compression (loads which push straight down), but it is weak under lateral force and it is very slippery when wet. Granite is very strong and is impervious to water. Sandstone acts like a sponge, soaking up water; it is also easily eroded.

Soils also have different characteristics. Sand is loose and porous. Loam (soil which is rich in organic matter)

holds water and takes a shape. Clay swells when it is wet and becomes waterproof (Marsh, 1978).

These simple elements can create some very difficult problems in cities (Gray, 1972):

A common problem is **"differential settling."** Sometimes a builder will have to carve out part of a hillside to provide a flat foundation for a building. Often the material cut from the hill will be used to fill in part of the foundation site ("cut-and-fill"). Normally this creates no problems. But if the soil is loose and the fill is not compacted enough, the fill material can compress under the load of the building, shift, and cause the foundation to crack. A similar problem will occur if the fill is clay, since wet clay fill will shrink as it dries out and dry clay fill will swell when it gets wet. Also, if the cut into the hill crosses the boundary between two strata, the water-carrying characteristics of the strata can cause groundwater to eat away at the fill, again cracking the foundation.

Erosion is another common problem. Roads are usually engineered to run straight and have only a moderate incline. When the landforms do not comply with these specifications, the hill is frequently cut away. But the typical profile of the hill (a gentle curve to the top) represents the balance between the various forces of wind, rain, freezing, drying, and vegetation which are acting upon the hill. A roadcut upsets that equilibrium, and nature will attempt to restore it. The hill will attempt to even out the steep inclines created at the site of the cut. Erosion is particularly troublesome because it increases the risk of mudslides. A large burden of soil can fail to hold its shape and come sliding down the hill. This is particularly troubling to people who build on the crest of a hill or bluff and find that they suddenly have an unobstructed (if unwelcome) view of the bottom of the hill.

The use of **groundwater** (the rainwater which was absorbed into the soil—and from there into the rock—rather than running off into the waterway) also carries its own problems. If a city, or residences within a city, draws water from a well, it is drawing on the groundwater. Usually wells are not drawing on moisture in the soil, but instead are driven down into a stratum of moisture-bearing rock. This rock is recharged by water which filters into it wherever the stratum is exposed to the surface. This area is called the **"aquifer recharge area."** If the aquifer recharge is small, building over it may seriously lessen the ability of the aquifer to recharge itself. No matter how large the recharge area, if pollutants which are not biodegradable are introduced into the aquifer, its usefulness can be destroyed (for all practical purposes, permanently). For this reason the location of waste disposal sites, particularly hazardous and nuclear waste disposal sites, is so important. Finally, if the aquifer is structurally weak (for example, a large bed of sandstone) and too much water is drawn out of it, the whole structure can collapse into a sinkhole.

Earthquakes

A final problem to consider is the threat of earthquakes. Because of geologic processes, there are huge cracks in the structure of the strata. These cracks are called **"faults."** As the crust of the earth moves, it tends to adjust itself along these cracks. On the surface, these adjustments are experienced as **earthquakes.** In some areas, there are many faults and they are "active," movement occurs along them regularly. Such places are not ideal locations for building a city. If a city must be built near an active fault, there are designs which can be used to minimize the damage should an earthquake occur (at least, up to a point—given a large enough earthquake, no amount of clever design will help). Tall buildings and overhanging cornices and decorations should be avoided. Special reinforcement should be built into the structures, and some can even be built to absorb some of the stress (Tokyo had a hotel built on springs).

The Climate

Cities have a different climate than the surrounding countryside (Bryson & Ross, 1972). There are four primary differences:

Heat

The city is a **heat island.** It absorbs heat during the day and releases it during the night. The concrete of the city is, in effect, a stone; stone heats up slowly (absorbs heat), but it then keeps its heat longer (releases it slowly). Cities also have a heavy concentration of dark surfaces (blacktopped streets, dark shingled roofs) which absorb heat. As a result, temperature readings in the city are usually higher (as much as 10° to 15° higher) than the surrounding countryside.

Wind

Cities also present a rough surface to the wind. As a result the city overall is less windy than the countryside or open water. On the other hand, the aerodynamic roughness of the city also creates more turbulence and local eddies; there are places in the city which are **windier** than anywhere else around. Very tall buildings capture the wind and funnel it down to the base of the building. New York City has had to require that any new skyscrapers have a wind analysis performed, since the **"wind tunnel"** effect has gotten so bad in Manhattan.

Dust

The third element of city climate is dust. In a light wind (less than 8 mph), one can see (literally) a **"dust dome"** around any large city. This phenomenon is the result of several forces acting together. Since the city is warmer than the surrounding countryside, air in the city rises over the center of town (the hottest area) and falls back down on the outskirts as the air cools. The cooler air is pulled back along the streets in the center of the city, eventually rising in the center as the air is heated. This is a convection process, just like the one which occurs in a pot of boiling water. As the breezes hit the rougher city surface, they slow down and drop whatever particles were suspended in the air. The cooler air coming into the city carries some dust with it from the countryside. In addition, it picks up dust from the city streets—dust ground finer by the wheels of cars running along the street. The dust is ground finely enough that it rises on the convection of air in the city center and settles back down with the cooled air on the edge of the city, where it get picked up by the air coming back into the city and gets recycled.

On windier days, the dust dome turns into a **"dust plume."** Rather than hanging over the city, dust is carried by the wind downrange, often forty miles or more. When the wind is from the south, Chicago smells like Gary, IN.

Rain

The fourth climatic difference in cities is rain (and clouds). The dust particles lofted into the air in the dust dome over the city provide a nucleus on which condensation (clouds and rain) can form. The cooling of the dust dome wrings moisture from the rising hot air. In effect, cities have their own cloud-seeding operation. Studies have found that cities receive more rain than the surrounding countryside, and that the increase is more marked from Monday to Friday (when there is more activity, and hence more heat and dust).

Plant and Animal Life

Biologists have a phrase for the interrelationships between plant and animal species. They call it **"commensalism,"** partners at the same trough. It is used to describe a relationship between plants, animals, and people in which they share space and resources without necessarily harming each other.

It takes a certain kind of plant to survive in the city (Elias & Irwin, 1976). It must be disease-resistant, since disease spreads so rapidly in cities. It must tolerate air pollution, salt pollution (the salt used to clear winter roads gets plowed and splashed onto the soil), and heavy metal pollution (from industrial smokestacks and auto exhausts). It must withstand drought, since much of the soil is packed from constant auto and pedestrian traffic.

The prototypical city tree is the ailanthus, the "tree of life," an escapee from India which grows like a weed in cities. It can take root in a crack between a concrete alley and the foundation of building. It will survive and grow, cracking the foundation and the concrete in the process. Other (more decorative) urban trees include Norway maples, London plane trees, ginkgo, honey locust, some ash and some oaks. The city is also home to a great variety of wildflowers and plants (Page & Weaver, 1975).

Typical urban animals must tolerate many of the same environmental stresses as plants—air pollution, drought, contaminated soils. They must also survive the destruction of native habitat and with it, the loss of former food supplies (Stearns, 1972). Typical urban animals include roaches, ants, rats and mice, pigeons, squirrels, dogs, cats, sparrows, jays, and robins (Gill & Bonnett, 1973).

The different tolerance which plants and animals have for pollution may even be used as a rough indicator of the spread of pollution around urban areas. Lichen, for instance, do not tolerate air pollution. Their death could indicate a worsening of the pollution problem. Black and gray squirrels do not tolerate each other; black squirrels are less hardy in polluted air, and are replaced by the grays. Again, changes in the population of black squirrels may indicate changes in the air quality of an area.

Designing with Nature

How can this information about the physical basis of cities be used in the design of cities? Put another way, can this information be used to design cities which make fewer demands on the natural environment, including energy demands? The answer to this question must successfully meet four basic **environmental concerns** for any building: The structure must keep the rain out. It must let light in, more during the winter, less during the summer. It must maintain an internal temperature within tolerable limits; it must keep the heat out during the summer and keep it in during the winter. And it must provide air circulation, more during the winter, very little during the summer (Fitch, 1972).

Topography

One resource which can be use in the design of buildings is the **topography,** the lay of the land itself. Cold air pools at the bottom of hills. The air is also cooler at the edge of plateaus, because it speeds up as it starts to fall down the bluff. The tops of hills are usually windy. Mid-slope is the warmest location.

One can use this information to select a more **preferred site** on a hillside, depending on the climate. In cool, temperate climates (Minneapolis, MN, for example), south-southeast mid-slope is the ideal location. It will be sheltered from prevailing northwesterly winter winds, it will capture the sun on the south, and it will take advantage of the mid-slope warmth. In a hot, humid climate (New Orleans, LA, for example), however, the considerations are different and a north or south hilltop is preferable. Because of the humidity, one wishes to take advantage of the properties of wind and would choose the location which gives the greatest exposure to the wind. The bottom of the hill might be cooler, but the pooling of cool air will also cause higher humidity. The choice of the north or south face of the hill depends on the severity of

the winters and the desire for capturing the winter sun and avoiding winter winds (Olgyay, 1963).

Solar Control

One can also design the structure itself to provide greater solar control. **Shading** can be provided for the windows. This can be done through the structure of the building, by designing wide overhangs like those Frank Lloyd Wright built into his designs. Or one can attach fins and awnings to the structure in order to shade the windows. It is also possible to provide curtain or blinds which

Window overhangs—University of MN (by author)

block much of the sun (if the curtains are insulated, they will also block some of the heat). In all three cases, it is necessary to design the shading so it blocks summer sun (which is high in the sky) but admits winter sun (which is lower in the sky). With overhangs or awnings, this is done by designing them to be deep enough to shade the window in the summer, but shallow enough that it does not shade the window in the winter. With curtains, one simply adjusts them as the season demands. They should be closed during the day and opened at night during the summer; reverse the process in the winter (Eccli, 1976). Another technique uses deciduous trees (trees which lose their leaves in the autumn). Planted on the south side of a structure, these trees will (in time) shade an entire wall in the summer but let winter light through.

Shape is also a factor in the solar control of a building. In cool climates and in hot, arid climates, minimal roof area is preferred. The greatest heat loss and heat gain in a building is through the roof. The smaller the roof area, the less heat lost to the cold in the winter and the less heat beating into the cooler interior in the summer. In hot, humid areas the need to control humidity is greater, so one would seek a sprawling structure which would capture more wind (Olgyay, 1963). The "ranch-style" house, popular in the 1960s, is perfect for south Texas, but ill-suited to northern Montana. These same principles apply to town forms as to building forms. A dense, compact city is more efficient in cold climates; an airy, sprawling one is better for humid climates.

The use of **materials** may also help with solar control. Thick walls with few openings, especially walls made of a dense material like stone or concrete, absorb heat during the day and release it at night. This principle was used in the Hopi pueblos and in Middle Eastern architecture (from Babylonian times to contemporary Saudi Arabia). It works as well in hot climates, where the interior of the dwelling stays shaded and cool during the day, as it does in cold climates, where the stone absorbs heat during the day and moderates the cold which the heating system has to work against during the night. This is also the principle behind earth-sheltered housing (to which we will return later). Such design is not appropriate for humid climates, however. Moisture in the air will condense on the cool stone walls and cause dampness problems similar to those found in some basements during the summer.

Heat absorbing materials—Hopi pueblos (by author)

Air Motion

Air motion is another consideration in designing with the climate, although the design is a little trickier. Prevailing winds may shift with the seasons. This can be turned to an advantage if one is aware of it and designs for it.

The most common technique for controlling air motion is the **windbreak.** You may be familiar with the windbreaks which farmers plant beside their fields to cut down on soil erosion. A similar effect can be obtained in the city, although the forces involved are more complicated. In cities, the buildings themselves often act as windbreaks.

The **profile** of the windbreak affects the pattern downwind. Structures set in parallel will reduce the flow of wind—the same principle racecar drivers use in slipstreaming. If the structures are staggered, they will channel the flow around each other. Which pattern is preferable depends on the climate and the season. A winter wind should be obstructed, but a summer breeze might be usefully channeled around the buildings. If the winter wind and summer breeze tend to come form different quadrants, it is possible to place the structures so they shield each other in the winter and channel the summer breezes. If the structures of the windbreak are angular (i.e., if the buildings are square-cornered), setting them at an angle to the wind will reduce the turbulence (gusting) as the wind flows around them.

Airflow patterns may also, of course, be modified by **landscaping.** The same principles apply, with a few new wrinkles. One does not want to plant trees or large shrubs too close to a window, because it will hinder maximum ventilation. In fact, shrubs close to the windows can make humidity problems worse since the shrubs will be transpiring (releasing water vapor) through their leaves. Landscaping may also be used to create beneficial airflows for structures which are not ideally sited. Planting at an angle to the prevailing wind can direct the air to and through the windows of a house, trapping breezes which might otherwise have been missed.

The use of **windows** will also affect the airflow. The optimal arrangement is to have a small inlet and a large outlet for the air. This will cause the incoming air to speed up (and thus cool down) as it comes in the window (Olgyay, 1963). This arrangement can be created with more than one window, as long as the total area of the open window on leeward side is greater than that on the windward. Airflow may also be directed by "offsets" (partitions); the interior walls and doors of a house may be used to control and direct the flow of air. Partitions parallel to the direction of flow can be used to split the stream of air. Doors to the far side of a flow pattern will redirect it, creating dead spots in the corner. The lower the inlet, the greater the cooling effect. The ideal arrangement would be floor inlets; more commonly the lower sash is opened on the inlet side and upper sash is opened on the outlet side.

Airflow is important in the winter as well as in the summer, although for different reasons. In the winter the goal is to minimize airflow since the outside air is so much cooler than the desired temperature. The major problem in the winter is the "chimney effect." Hot air rises, and will leave by any high opening; in the process, it will draw cool air from any crack in the house. It is for this reason that it is important to seal windows in the winter and to close the flue damper when a fireplace in not in use.

Temperature Control

There are also a variety of methods which deal directly with the control of heat in a structure. The easiest way to control heat (whether to conserve it or to avoid it) is to **prevent heat transfers. Thermal curtains** (window curtains which have insulating properties) or shutters are on method for controlling the transfer of heat across the glass in a window. **Air-lock foyers** (entryways which have two airtight doors, and enough space between them that a person on entering closes the first before opening the second) serve a similar purpose for doors. Insulation (of which there is a wide variety) serves the same purpose for walls. If temperatures will vary widely from the inside of the wall to the outside, a vapor barrier should be installed on the warm side to prevent water vapor condensing in the insulation, thus destroying its insulating properties and probably rotting the wall itself.

In cool climates, one may also wish to create heat transfers. The simplest way to do this is to design a **heatsink** as part of the house. Sun from a south window can be used to heat a concrete floor, masonry walls, or columns of water. These heatsinks will continue to release their warmth back into the room after the sun has set. Two corner windows (southeast and southwest) can be used to create a southern exposure if the structure is not oriented to the compass.

Another option is to build a **solar collector** onto a south wall which has no windows, and vent the heatsink into the house. A variation on this design is to build a greenhouse ("sunspace") on the south side, attaching it to the wall or adding it as a balcony or placing it above a garage. A heatsink, incorporated into the sunspace, can be vented the house.

Passive solar collector—Minneapolis, MN (by author)

Although it is more difficult, costly, and less efficient than a totally **passive solar design** (one which has no moving parts), one may also build **active solar heaters.** These may involve hot air, water, or chemical solutions; they may use convection or forced flow; some incorporate heat exchangers (Eccli, 1976; Olkowski, *et alii,* 1979).

There are several designs which incorporate these ideas for designing with nature. Two, in particular, deserve spe-

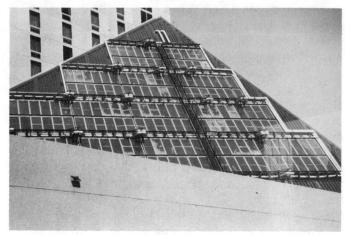

Active solar collector—St. Paul, MN (by author)

cial note. In the Middle East, there is a traditional form of architecture used in hot, arid regions called a **"wind tower."** These are tall structures placed some distance from the residence. They are oriented to capture the prevailing wind in large scoops which funnel the air down the tower and underground to the house. The cooling air condenses water from the ground and enters the house as a cool, moist breeze. It was an early, effective form of air conditioning. In addition, the domed roofs of the houses created a chimney effect which pulled the cooled air through the entire house. It was a very effective, entirely passive cooling system.

The second design is a contemporary twist on the old sod house; it is **earth-sheltered design.** Earth is not a particularly good insulator; what makes earth-sheltered designs effective is the great mass of the earth which surrounds the structure. As a result, the heating and cooling system works against a fairly constant, unchanging external temperature. This, combined with the absolute necessity for a structure with no leaks or cracks, results in a relatively efficient environment for heating.

Earth-sheltered design—Minneapolis, MN (by author)

Programs for Conserving Energy

From the energy crisis of the 1970s, several programs developed which could improve a city's ability to conserve energy. Most involve alternate energy sources (wind, sun, water), although **"district heating"** is one program which cities can undertake that would save energy using conventional methods. In district heating, a single source of heat is established, frequently using waste steam from some other source (such as a power plant). The steam is distributed throughout the city (or a neighborhood) in underground pipes. It is distributed inside the buildings to radiators which heat the rooms. This idea has been used in Scandinavia for some time; in Iceland, they use steam drawn underground from geysers. Many cities have developed downtown district heating plants (Minneapolis and Baltimore, for example); some even supply district heating to neighborhood residences (e.g., St. Paul, MN).

Another program which is being discussed involves **"Solar Access Zoning"** (Erley & Jaffe, 1979; Jaffe & Erley, 1979). Passive and active solar collectors will not work if they are shaded. Presumably, the owner would not allow a structure or a tree on her/his property to shade the collectors. But in cities, houses are often quite close to each other and a neighbor might take action which would deprive an owner of the use of her/his solar collector. Many cities have no ordinance regulating such a situation. Solar access ordinances specify that, once a solar collector is in place, the sunspace for that collector is protected. A neighbor may not infringe on another's solar space if it is in use.

A third program which has shown promise is a system of **"energy audits."** People have been trained to inspect a building, examining it for insulation, airtightness, and usability of alternate energy and passive energy sources. In addition, they are trained to "cost out" any improvements, estimating the time it would take the improvement to pay for itself (assuming current costs of energy and current costs for improvements). The owner is then free to take whatever action s/he considers appropriate.

A fourth program, so far not developed very far beyond the discussion stage, involves various schemes for redesigning the city. One, dubbed the **"compact city"** (Dantzig & Saaty, 1973), is designed to minimize transportation needs. This can be done by building to higher densities (building up instead of out), and by mixed-use zoning (combine residences with employment and services). It can also be done by providing the support system ("infrastructure") needed for people to use alternative transportation modes (mass transit, bicycles, walking, etc.). In either case, minimizing automobile transportation would significantly decrease the energy economy of a city.

A second scheme, dubbed the **"edible city"** (Britz, 1981), would keep current densities but use the open land around the dwellings to raise food. Energy would be saved both from economies in the transportation and warehousing of perishable foods and from the savings from packaging (plastic bags, foam trays, etc.) and disposal which accompany the retail sale of perishable foods. The Farallones Institute in San Francisco has created a demonstration project in which a single-family house was converted to be almost self-sufficient in energy and food production (Olkowski, *et alii*, 1979).

Summary: Hard vs. Soft Energy Path

In this chapter, we have seen how humankind shapes and is shaped by the land, the climate, and the plants and animals with which we share space. Although there are occasions when the relationship between people and the land becomes seriously imbalanced (floods, earthquakes, landslides, poisoned water), most of the time people establish a rough equilibrium with nature.

The issue is *how* that equilibrium is established. Flooding can be alleviated by channeling, or by building away from the floodplain. Building temperature can be maintained by furnaces and air conditioners, or by insulation and solar control. Buildings can be constructed where desired and the landforms modified to accommodate it (the way the Romans did), or they can ben placed where the natural forces will most readily accommodate them.

Amory Lovins (1977) calls these the "hard" and "soft" energy paths. The "hard" path uses human engineering and mechanical devices to harness and augment the forces of nature. The "soft" path gathers what is readily available. The soft path gathers solar energy through south-facing windows and stores it in a stone floor; the hard path pumps liquid through solar collectors and stores it in a heatsink. The hard path will harvest more of the available energy—but at a greater cost, both in the initial investment and in operating and maintenance expenses. The soft path makes fewer demands on the earth's resources, but demands more from those who use it.

While these two approaches are not contradictory, they do often conflict. The resource demands of the hard path and the ability to circumvent natural constraints which it offers can also upset the fragile balance with nature on which the soft path depends. The really important—and really difficult—environmental problems are the technical ones; human have generally found ways to engineer satisfactory fixes (at least, for the short run). The really significant problems come from differences in values.

Questions for Discussion

1. What can differences in river valleys tell you about the land? What can they tell you about good locations for building?
2. Impoundment ponds are spaces which are designed to capture the stormwater runoff from a develop-

ment and release the water slowly in to the watercourse. What creative solutions might you employ to integrate stormwater impoundment into planned-unit development? (Hints: What might you do with the space when it isn't raining? What spaces which already have other uses might be redesigned to also hold stormwater?)

3. What are the relative merits of the various solutions to flooding? Under what conditions would you recommend each one?
4. Examine a topographic map (a map which shows changes in the elevation of the land) for an undeveloped area near your city. Where would you locate a new residential development? What modifications might you have to make so the area would be fit for development?
5. Examine a topographic map for a developed area in your city. What environmental problems do people in that neighborhood have to cope with? What could be done to ameliorate them, given that the land is already developed?
6. How can structures be designed to minimize heat transfers? to create heat create transfers?
7. What programs might be developed in your region to improve its ability to conserve energy and resources?

Terms to Remember

urban environment	V-shaped river valley
feedback system	lateral cutting
U-shaped river valley	factors in stormwater
100-year floodplain	runoff
channelization	impoundment
ideal solution to flooding	strata
differential settling	erosion
groundwater	aquifer recharge area
faults	earthquakes
heat island	wind tunnel
dust dome	dust plume
rain	commensalism
characteristics of urban	4 elements of buildings
plants	preferred site
topography	building shape
shading	windbreak
building materials	landscaping windbreaks
windbreak profile	preventing heat transfers
use of windows	air-lock foyer
thermal curtain	solar collector
heatsink	active solar heater
passive solar design	earth-sheltered design
wind tower	solar access zoning
district heating	compact city
energy audit	hard vs. soft path
edible city	

References

Bellovich, Steven J. (1976) An introduction to the extent and nature of the flood problem in Tulsa, OK, in Proceedings of the Floodplain Management Symposium, A. J. Filipovitch, ed. Tulsa, OK: University of Tulsa.

Britz, Richard (1981) The Edible City: Resource Manual. Los Altos, CA: William Kaufmann, Inc.

Bryson, Reid A. and John E. Ross (1972) The climate of the city, in Urbanization and Environment: The Physical Geography of the City, Detwyler & Marcus, eds. Belmont, CA: Duxbury Press.

Creath, William B. and George Birt. (1976) Steam flow, erosion, and floodplain development, in Proceedings of the Floodplain Management Symposium, A. J. Filipovitch, ed Tulsa, OK: University of Tulsa.

Dantzig, George B. and Thomas L. Saaty. (1973) Compact City: A Plan for a Liveable Urban Environment. San Francisco: W. H. Freeman & Co.

Detwyler, Thomas R. and Melvin G. Marcus. (1972) Urbanization and environment in perspective, in Urbanization and Environment: The Physical Geography of the City, Detwyler & Marcus, eds. Belmont, CA: Duxbury Press.

Eccli, Eugene. (1976) Low-Cost, Energy-Efficient Shelter for the Owner and Builder. Emmaus, PA: Rodale Press.

Elias, Thomas S. and Howard S. Irwin. (1976) Urban trees, Scientific American 235 (5), 110–118.

Erley, Duncan and Martin Jaffe. (1979) Site Planning for Solar Access. Washington, DC: USGPO.

Fitch, James M. (1972) American Building, Vol 2: The Environmental Forces That Shape It. Boston: Houghton Mifflin.

Gill, Don and Penelope Bonnett. (1973) Nature in the Urban Landscape: A Study of Cit Ecosystems. Baltimore, MD: New York Press.

Gary, Donald H. (1972) Soil and the city, in Urbanization and Environment: The Physical Geography of the City, Detwyler & Marcus eds. Belmont, CA: Duxbury Press.

Jaffe, Martin and Duncan Erley. (1979) Protecting Solar Access for Residential Development. Washington, DC: USGPO.

Lovins, Amory. (1977) Soft Energy Path: Toward a Durable Peace. Cambridge, MA: Ballinger.

Marsh, William M. (1978) Soils and drainage, in Environmental Analysis for Land Use and Site Planning, W. M. Marsh, ed. NY: McGraw Hill.

McHarg, Ian L. (1969) Design with Nature. Garden City, NY: Doubleday.

Olgyay, Victor. (1963) Design with Climate. Princeton, NJ: Princeton University Press.

Olkowski, Helga, Bill Olkowski, Tom Javits and the Farallones institute staff. (1979) The Integral Urban House. San Francisco: Sierra Club Books.

Page, Nancy M. and Richard E. Weaver, Jr. (1975) Wild Plants in the City. NY: Quadrangle Books.

Sterns, Forest. (1972) The city as habitat for wildlife and man, in Urbanization and Environment: The Physical Geography of the City, Detwyler and Marcus, eds. Belmont, CA: Duxbury Press.

Strahler, A. N. and A. H. Strahler. (1973) Environmental Geoscience. Santa Barbara, CA: Hamilton Publishing Co.

Van Dusen, Peter, Jeff Dozier, and William M. Marsh. (1978) Floods and floodplains, in Environmental Analysis for Land Use and Site Planning, W. M. Marsh, ed. NY: McGraw Hill.

Vitruvius. (1914) The Ten Books on Architecture, tr, M. H. Morgan. Cambridge, MA: Harvard University Press.

4

Design for Working

The modern city . . . is primarily a convenience of commerce, and owes its existence to the market place around which it sprang up.

Park, Burgess, & McKenzie
The City

Mobile, AL (H. Roger Smith)

You regularly read in the newspapers these days about one business or another which is proposing to move a major facility to town. In return, the only thing they ask is just a little assistance from the city. The assistance may be special permission to use a parcel of land in an unusual way, or perhaps help in assembling a number of properties and clearing the structures which are already on them, or maybe a low-interest loan or a property tax reduction. The question is whether it is worth it for the city to give special consideration to one or another business. The answer, in no small part, depends on an understanding of the economy of cities and how business and industry affect the quality of city living.

Process of Urban Development: A Fable

There was once a continent with a mountain range, a forest, a swamp, and a lake. The nomadic people who lived there would spend the winter in the warmer regions. As summer came and the weather became hotter, food would dry up. So the tribe would travel to a cooler climate, following the migration of the animals and the growth cycles of the berries. When the weather turned cold, they would wander back to the warmer areas again. This cycle of folks wandering back and forth in search of food went on for a long time.

Then one day two people, call them George and Mabel, were wandering around and they discovered that a black rock which was found in one area kept a sharp edge when it was broken. Up to this time, if they wanted to catch a rabbit they would grab a fallen tree limb and throw it at the rabbit. George and Mabel tied a piece of this broken rock to the end of a stick and discovered that it was easier to kill rabbits by throwing these rock-tipped sticks at them. The throwing stick did not have to be as heavy, so it was easier to carry it on long trips. It was just basically a superior killing device.

This was an *innovative perception*. They looked at this broken rock and realized that it was a better way to kill animals.

George and Mabel carried this nifty throwing stick around with them as they wandered up and down the continent. Watching them kill rabbits, folks would say, "My, that's a neat throwing stick. Where can I get one?"

One day, wandering around by a mountain range, they went off the trail a bit to chase a rabbit. They discovered a whole pile of the special black rock on a spur of one of the mountains.

Mabel looked at it. "Hey, George, black rock!"

George looked at it and said, "Black rock."

"No George, *lots* of black rock—we'll have lots of throwing sticks!"

And George said, "Lots of throwing sticks, big deal. We only use one."

But Mabel said, "No, no! You don't understand. We don't have to look all over for it, it's right here. Lots of it."

Finally George got the idea. George was not too bright. He was always chasing rabbits, but Mabel spent a lot of time nursing the kids. She had time to think, so she was the smart one.

Mabel told George, "We're going to stay here for awhile and make a bunch of throwing sticks."

They had found a *comparative advantage,* a place which gave them an advantage over everyone else, a place with a lot of black rock. They stayed there for awhile, making throwing sticks.

Then a forest family came wandering down the trail, and said, "Hey, nice throwing sticks. Sure wish I could have one."

George said, "You gotta find your own rock."

But Mabel hit him in the ribs and said, "George!" Then she said, "You give us two rabbits and I'll give you a throwing stick."

The other guy said to himself, It's a good deal because that thing kills rabbits fast and if I had one of those I could kill lots of rabbits. So he went out and killed two rabbits and traded them with Mabel for a throwing stick.

Now Mabel got to thinking about it, and she realized that they didn't need to hunt any more. She and George could just sit there on their mountain and make lots of throwing sticks to trade for food. She realized there was a *demand* for their product.

In time, people started going out of their way to get these throwing sticks. George and Mabel were spending all of their time making throwing sticks. They went into *production*. Eventually, they had more business than they could handle. Then Mabel realized that Biff was hanging around a lot. He was bright enough, and she figured they could teach him how to make throwing sticks. They would give him some of the food they got in trade. In other words, the increased production spurred *employment*.

Eventually, George, Mabel and Biff were turning out so many throwing sticks that they had more than they could trade—they developed a *surplus*.

Mabel thought about that for awhile, then she said, "George, we're going to take all these rocks and move them closer to the main trail. Everyone will be going by there, so we can trade more of our throwing sticks for rabbits." Besides, since they would be farther away from where they got their rock, it would be harder for anyone to discover their source and take it away from them. And so they developed a *market*. A market depends on flow of trade; a market works because there are lots of folks going by on whom you can unload your surplus goods.

This was the beginning of the first city. It started with an innovative perception, although innovative perception by itself is pretty useless. But when George and Mabel found the comparative advantage (a location that allowed them to use their innovation) then they had the beginning of something that was really going to work. The superiority of their product created a demand. But the demand is no good unless there is a surplus to trade, so demand also works to create production, employment, and markets.

This same thing that worked in the beginning works today. Why is your town located where it was? What made it happen? What was the innovative perception that led to it? Maybe your town is located on a river. But why *that* place, rather than another location on the river? When you move to a new city, you should look for the comparative advantage that caused that city to be built there in the first place. But, second, you will want to know what comparative advantage remains today. Is the river *still* a comparative advantage? You may need to discover what the comparative advantage is today, because what started the city is not necessarily what keeps it going. If a city loses all of its advantages, the city will die. Duluth, MN, is a large port, but it has lost its comparative advantage. Barge traffic through Minneapolis and St. Paul has replaced much Great Lakes shipping of grain. The Mesabi iron ore industry near Duluth has been mined out. And other port cities on the Great Lakes are growing. The same thing happened in Colorado on the West Slope. A lot of towns were built there in the 1970s to explore oil shale. The oil companies have decided that it is not going to work, so they are pulling out. There are twentieth century ghost towns in western Colorado (although it is strange to think of split-level ramblers in a ghost town).

Just as there is a link between innovative perception and comparative advantage, there is also a relationship between surplus and demand. It is not enough to have a surplus. Consider the case of Pittsburgh, PA. When you melt iron ore and limestone together to make steel, the impurities that are left over are called "slag." Pittsburgh in its heyday would run trains of slag to the edge of town (which is now the middle of town) and dump it in slag heaps. There are some uses for slag—it can be crushed and substituted for gravel as the subbase in roads. But that uses only a small portion of the available surplus. If somebody could make rocketships with slag, or *anything* with slag, Pittsburgh could meet the demand. With such a new market, the town would be completely rejuvenated because it is sitting on such a huge pile of the raw material; so far, no one has found a use for it. You can have a surplus that it useless; you may have to *generate* the demand. George and Mabel may have had to go out and convince people that they really wanted to buy their throwing sticks. The same thing is true with any industry, with any city. A city has to sell its industries.

The process of urban development begins with an innovative perception which is turned to an advantage. If a demand can be found for the innovation, it goes into production which eventually leads to increased employment to create a surplus (Figure 1). The surplus can be used in either of two ways. The surplus can be plowed back to meet demand—George and Mabel could make more throwing sticks. This is a *maintenance mode*. The city keeps itself going. On the other hand, the surplus can be turned to developing new ideas. Instead of using the surplus to produce more throwing sticks, George and Mabel could start experimenting with other things like combining fire and rock to produce bronze (which would make even better throwing sticks). Developing the advantage of other innovations is the *growth mode*.

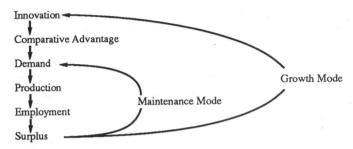

Figure 4.1. The Process of Urban Development

If a city stays in a maintenance mode it risks dying when its product is no longer in demand. Detroit was an innovator in automobiles, but the focus of automobile manufacture has shifted and Detroit's maintenance strategy is threatened. Pittsburgh has gone through the same failure with the steel industry. The Twin Cities of St. Paul and Minneapolis, MN, started out with lumber and grain, but it plowed the surplus back into specialized manufacturing and computers. The region is not as dependent on a single industry, and stands a better chance of surviving shifts in the market.

Industrial Mix

The primary base for any city is industry (or, what amounts to the same thing, employment). The development, production, and marketing of a comparative advantage are essential for the continuing existence of any settlement; without it one has only a campsite. The mix of industries will influence the income of a city's residents and the growth of the city itself.

Types of Industries

Cities are tied to a geographical location; from a city's point of view, industries can be distinguished based on their spatial requirements. In this sense, "industry" does not necessarily mean manufacturing. It is the application of skill to the provision of a good or a service, usually for a profit. In Las Vegas, gambling is an industry; in San Francisco, tourism is an industry; in Washington, D.C., Government is an industry; in Phoenix, retirement services are an industry. "Industry" is how people make a living.

Some industries are resource-oriented. They need to be located near the source of the raw materials which are used to make their product, usually because for the type of work they do it is cheaper to ship the finished product than it is to transport materials. The newsprint industry, for example, consumes large amounts of wood pulp. It would be difficult to locate a pulp mill in the Arizona desert.

Other industries are market-oriented. They need to be located near the consumer. This is particularly true when the finished product does not ship well, such as perishable food, or really cannot be "shipped," like house construction or retail shopping.

Some industries are labor-oriented. They need to be near either a specialized supply of labor, like Silicone Valley in California which has attracted top computer engineers from the nearby universities and from around the country, or need a great amount of labor, like the automobile assembly lines of the 1930s and 1950s in Detroit. In the 1980s, many corporations shifted their operations from the industrial North, where labor was unionized and expensive, to a new industrial strip which ran from San Antonio to Austin, TX. While the price of labor was lower, many of the firms found that they had to undertake expensive employee training programs which they had not needed in the North. Some of the corporations eventually returned their operations to locations which could supply the type of skilled labor they needed.

Finally, some industries may be "footloose." Footloose industries are not tied to any specific location. The resources they need are either ubiquitous or easily transported, their markets are not concentrated, and their labor needs are either simple or so specialized that no single location can routinely meet them. Fast food restaurants are footloose, on the low-tech side; computer software development and even some microchip design and manufacture is footloose on the high-tech side.

Types of Cities

If businesses can be distinguished based on their need for specific factors of production, cities can be distinguished based on their size. Smaller urban areas tend to be dominated by concern for their competitive position in relation to other cities. They frequently have relatively few major employers, and the local economy is heavily dependent on those few. As a result, the city is particularly sensitive to local job formation. If one of the major employers expands, it is likely to bring a significant increase in local jobs (and local housing, shopping, taxes, and other economic activity). If a major employer were to cut back or even leave, the city could be left with high unemployment, housing vacancies, lower tax revenues, and a declining retail market.

Larger urban areas are not as concerned with increasing their rate of growth, but concentrate instead on managing the growth which is naturally occurring. It is not that the loss of a particularly large employer does not hurt, but in a large city there are generally enough major employers that no single firm is dominant and the shock of one firm's departure can be absorbed. The decline of a whole industrial sector (like the automotive industry in Detroit) is another matter, and will be considered later. For the most part, large cities generate their own growth and spawn many feeder businesses and nurture many start-up businesses which are spun off the other business activity. The problem, rather, is to manage this growth and the dislocation it causes, both as it expands into new areas and as it leaves old ones. While the city as a whole may have a healthy employment rate, there might easily be pockets of high unemployment in selected areas.

Industry Mix and City Income

Urban areas can be considered as a more or less distinctive mix of industries (Thompson, 1967). Whether the urban area is large or small (whether it is a congregation of cities in a metropolitan region, or an isolated rural city), the unique mix of industries in the area will have a profound impact on its economic life. Both the distribution and the stability of local income depends on the mixture of businesses in the local economy. There are three key elements in the industrial mix which will affect local income:

Labor: Skilled labor can command a higher wage than unskilled labor. Two regions may have similar employment rates, but the region with a higher proportion of skilled labor will also have higher average incomes (other things being equal). For example, Austin and Fort Worth are roughly the same size and had roughly the same unemployment rates in 1980. In Austin, more than 30% of the residents had graduated from college and the median income was $19,500. In Fort Worth, 17% of the residents had graduated from college and the median income was $18,200.

Productivity: the more the business can automate its activity—the more the effort of an individual employee can be magnified through machinery—the higher the wages a business can afford to pay. Although assembly-line work in the auto industry is not particularly skilled, autoworkers are able to command a high wage because the industry is so highly automated. Through automation, each worker's effort is more productive. One of the problems with the economic recovery in the 1980s was that high-paying manufacturing jobs were lost and replaced with low-paying service jobs (former autoworkers found jobs at MacDonald's). The amount of effort by the worker on the two jobs was the same, but the income was much less. This has had a deep impact on the economy of former manufacturing cities like Detroit, MI.

Market: Businesses which have little market competition for the sale of their products ("oligopolistic" markets) also tend to pay higher wages. There are relatively few firms manufacturing automobiles or computers or drilling for oil; wages in those industries are high. There is more competition among businesses which produce, say, paper or corn. Wages in those industries are lower.

Clearly, then, the ideal business for the growth of a city is one which uses highly skilled labor in an automated process to manufacturer a good which is sold in an oligopolistic market. In a word, the computer industry and, increasingly, hospital health care (which is becoming highly automated, unlike nursing care).

Industry Mix and City Growth

The mix of business activities in an urban area will also effect the growth rate of the area. The rate of growth will depend on three factors:

New Industries: The proportion of new industries in the local economy can have a significant impact on the rate of growth. Not all new industries succeed; most fail. But if a new industry succeeds, the local region stands to capture most of that growth. Mature businesses tend to remain stable. There is less growth, but there is also less failure. When a mature business does expand, it is as likely to relocate as it is to expand at its present location.

Demand for Product: Basic goods and services tend to experience slow, steady growth. "Luxury" goods and services experience rapid increase in demand when times are good, and see a sharp decline in demand when the economy turns down. They are said to show "elasticity of demand" based on income: As income increases, demand for the good increases; as incomes fall, demand falls (but usually not back to the previous levels). Food and clothing are usually "inelastic"—there is only so much you can eat or wear. But dining out and designer clothing are highly elastic. When times are tough, people stay home and wear last years' clothes. When times are flush, they celebrate and buy new wardrobes. Businesses which produce income elastic products ride an economic roller coaster, but with reasonable planning the peaks can carry the business (and the city) well over the valleys.

Market Share: Businesses can grow even in a mature industry which is fairly inelastic, if they can capture a large share of the national (or international) market for their product. Most of the textiles produced in the United States are milled in North Carolina; Josten's, in Owatonna, MN, makes most of the school rings; Carlson Craft, in Mankato, MN, is the largest engraver of wedding invitations in the country.

The size of the urban area will also affect its growth strategy. Larger urban areas tend to plant and harvest growth industries; they have a larger share of rapidly growing industries but their share declines as the industry matures. Because larger urban areas already have a wide range of support services (for the other existing industries), because they tend to be the focus of transportation lines, because they can provide a spectrum of skilled labor—for all these reasons, it is easier for rapidly growing industries to find what they need in big cities. But once the industrial product is standardized and the process is routine, the advantages of the big cities become disadvantages. Skilled labor is more expensive; locations at the center of transportation systems cost more; support services—once they are clearly specified and routinely purchased—can be supplied anywhere. Mature production will often be shifted to smaller towns where prices are lower. For example, 3M (the manufacturers of Scotch tape and Post-It Notes) does most of its research and development just outside St. Paul, MN, but most of its production is scattered among rural cities throughout Minnesota and the country.

The size of the local area will also affect the stability of the local economy. The growth of a single business or even a group of businesses will have the greatest impact in a small city, where each employer is a (relatively) greater share of total employment and income base of the local economy. Larger cities can absorb more growth with less transformation. It is easier for large cities to weather the loss of a business, and it is harder for them to reap the benefit of the growth of a business.

The benefits of local growth are particularly advantageous for lower income workers. If a city grows too rapidly (say, faster than the national average), the local labor market will tighten. This will raise the average income as scarcity drives up the price of labor. This increase in income will particularly benefit the lower wage-earners, since wages for skilled labor already reflect something of a "scarcity premium" even when unskilled labor is not in demand (Thompson, 1967). Unfortunately, this process works equally well in reverse. Hard times hit the lower wage-earners hardest.

Summary: Local economic growth comes from having a greater share of the national market and the economic infrastructure (resources, services, etc.) to support it. This is called *depth*. Detroit, until recently at least, was deeply into automobiles. Not only did the city manufacturer cars, they also built batteries and windows and seats and distributors to put into cars. Not only did they produce these "supporting" products, but they also produced ball-bearings and glass and rubber and seat cushions. Not only did they produce supporting services for support services, but they also produced trucking companies to move the ball-bearings to the distributor manufacturers and glass to the window manufacturers and rubber to the tire manufacturers. When the auto industry had a good year, Detroit had a very good year. Unfortunately, when the auto industry had a bad year, Detroit had serious troubles. Pittsburgh pursued a similar strategy with steel, Seattle with aircraft (Boeing), Tulsa with oil, and Akron with rubber.

A city's ability to survive the shock of a market weakness in any single industry depends on diversity. This is called *breadth*. Minneapolis was built on the lumber and grain milling industries. Lumber is gone, but food processing continues to be a central part of the local economy—along with computers, banking and insurance, education, retailing, and some manufacturing. Similarly, Chicago

49

was built on the railroad and the stockyards, but has since expanded to retailing, finance, air transport, and manufacturing.

The two strategies of depth and breadth compete with each other. Resources that are dedicated to broadening the economic base of a community are not available for deepening the community's share of a particularly desirable industry. Yet the more a community becomes dependent on a single industry group, the more the community's future is hostage to that industry. Ideally, a community would want to have depth in a broad base of economic activities.

Economic Forces

It might be useful to examine in more detail the forces which shape a local economy. Many of these forces have already been introduced, although they were not discussed in any focal way. Although there are many factors which affect the growth and health of a business, there are three key forces which drive urban economic development: Economic base, Agglomerative economies, and Scale economies.

Economic Base

No city can live by everyone "taking in each other's laundry"—an entire economy cannot be built on personal service to the local residents. Cities are not self-contained economic units; if nothing else, they need to ship in ("import," if you will) food. To pay for the food, somebody has to be making something to send back ("export," to follow the metaphor) to the farmer in exchange.

"Basic" industries are those which bring money into the city. They are also called "export" industries, because they sell their products to markets outside the city (Alexander, 1954). The concept of a "basic" industry is an abstraction. In real life few businesses export all of their product, or (the opposite case) sell none of their product outside the city. Even the lowly laundry will, on occasion, sell its services to outsiders who are in town on business or pleasure. This concept of "economic base" is part of the common lore of cities. Detroit is identified with automobiles, Pittsburgh with steel, Seattle with Boeing aircraft, Silicone Valley with computers. Every city must have something that it is selling, or the city will die.

It is possible to measure directly how much of each firm's production goes to outside markets. This approach, while obvious, is also time-consuming and expensive. And the local economic profile is so volatile that by the time all the measurements are tabulated and a report published, the data is already dated. Instead, researchers resort to two conventions for measuring basic economic activity in real cities.

One convention categorizes industries as inherently export-oriented. Mining, heavy manufacturing (like automobile or refrigerator manufacturing), and finance are

considered basic in this system, even though local residents will buy cars and use oil and take out loans (i.e., buy money). Retail trade, services (laundry, restaurants, hospitals), and government are not considered basic in this system, even though the tourism industry (which depends on restaurants and often on retail trade) and some hospitals like the Mayo Clinic in Rochester, MN, sells most of their services to outsiders.

The second convention accounts for the fact that any activity can be basic if it sells in outside markets. In this approach, the national average for production of any good or service is taken as the baseline for local consumption. In other words, assume that everyone, on average, uses about the same amount of each of the goods and services which are produced in the country. In that case, any local economic activity which exceeds the national average must be going to markets outside the local area (Tiebout, 1962). This convention provides a better estimate of the economic base of a community, if the distinctions between type of industries are fine enough to capture variations within categories. For instance, an urban area may be at the national average in manufacturing, but above the national average in, say, furniture manufacture and below the national average in all the other types of manufacturing.

Basic industries apply the money they receive from the sale of their products to pay for services (including labor) and goods which are used in the production process. Some of this money is used to purchase goods and services outside the local economy; the rest is spent locally. This local supply of goods and services is called "non-basic" or "service" industry. Service industries provide for the local consumption of goods and services by a community's residents and businesses.

Not all basic industries are alike. Some basic industries buy most of their raw materials (including labor) from suppliers outside the local community. They "import" their factors of production. This does little good for the local community. Other basic industries buy most of their raw materials (including labor) from the local community. As a result, a greater share of the income of those businesses is passed around the local community. There is a way to measure how many times a dollar paid to an export industry is passed around in the local community before it is used up; it is called the *income multiplier*.

Suppose a community—call it "Civitas"—has a firm which sells steel plows to farmers. For ease of analysis, suppose the plows sell for $1.00, and 25% of the cost of the plow is used to purchase resources (materials, financing, etc.) outside civitas. That leaves $0.75 for local services. Again for ease of analysis, suppose that all of that 75 cents is used to pay for labor. Suppose the worker spends all of that 75 cents buying food, and the food store divides it 40% for outside resources and the rest ($0.45) for local service—in this case, new shelving. Suppose the carpenter spends 33% of that 45 cents to buy lumber outside the community, and the rest ($0.30) on a haircut. The barber uses 50% of the 30 cents to pay the interest on a small business loan, and uses the rest ($0.15) to go to a movie. The movie house uses 30% of the 15 cents to pay for the movie, and the rest ($0.11) to pay the ticket-taker. She, in turn, uses 60% of the 11 cents on a shopping trip to a nearby city, and the rest ($0.05) to buy a pack of gum. The candy store uses 60% of the 5 cents to pay its distributer for Chicago, and the rest ($0.02) goes into the shopkeeper's pocket. The shopkeepers spends the entire 2 cents to feed the parking meter on his next visit to Kansas City. The original $1 passed through seven more hands until finally all of it was spent outside the local community. The original $1 generated an additional $1.83 as it was passed around, for a total impact in the local community of $2.83.

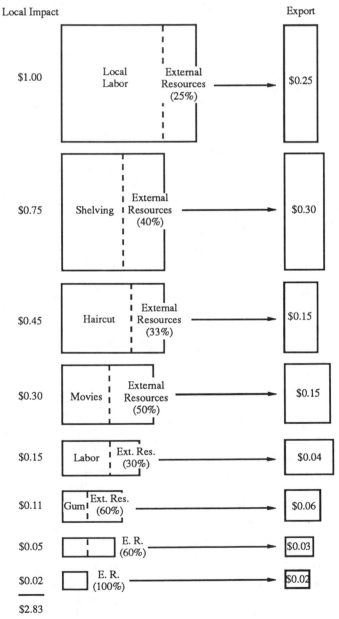

Figure 4.2. Income Multiplier

The calculation of an income multiplier is fairly simple (Isard, 1960). It is the ratio of total community income to basic income. By definition, total income is composed of basic and service income. In the illustration just above, the income multiplier for the plow-manufacturing firm is 2.83, which is respectable for the local economic impact of a firm. The larger the region, the larger the multiplier (since more goods and services will be included as "local" in the calculations). At the global level, all activity is "local."

Agglomerative Economies

In addition to the unique character of the firms an industries which are located in a city, there are also benefits which come from the mass of an industrial sector or related sectors. Economists call these benefits "agglomerative economies," businesses call it "cost sharing" (Vernon, 1960; Chinitz, 1961). In cities, these benefits are the force behind industrial parks and shopping malls.

Why should a department store locate in a shopping mall where it will have to compete with all the specialty stores? Why should the specialty stores want to compete with each other (Have you ever counted the number of shoe stores in a shopping mall?) or, worse, with a department store? Even more, why would *two* department stores want to move into the same mall? Clearly, they must think that they gain more than they lose. One of the most difficult problems—and biggest expenses—of retailers is getting people in the door. Until the customer is in the store you cannot sell her/him anything. In a shopping mall, the stores can share the traffic that each generates and they can even cooperate on advertising campaigns. Even though each is different (unique, they hope), simply by being together they can share common costs.

Industrial plants do not rely on traffic; why do they choose to clump together? In part, they can spread some of the "cost" of neighborhood disruption among themselves. Residential neighborhoods resent the truck traffic, noise, and emissions of industrial plants. Other industrial plants do not. It's a perfect match! Even more, industrial plants need heavy duty roads, high capacity utilities (sewer, water, power), possibly railroad spurs. It would be very expensive for each plant to construct its own roads and utilities; it is fairly inexpensive to share common truck lines and roads. The plants need have nothing else in common—one could manufacture doll clothes, another could manufacture boilers—but there are some common costs in which savings can be realized.

In the 1980s, a specialized industrial park became common, called a "business incubator." Incubators are designed to nurture new industrial firms as they are first getting their feet under themselves. In addition to sharing the cost of highways and utilities, they also provide common sales, secretarial, bookkeeping, personnel, and other support services which larger firms would provide themselves. By sharing these costs, the new businesses retain their flexibility and realize a savings since they need only purchase as little as they need and can pool the overhead costs. The risk with these incubators is that, by making it easy for a firm to start up, they also make it easier for a firm to go away. With less resources tied into the operation, it is easier for marginal activities to "give it a try"—and fail.

Agglomerative economies, then, are the advantages which come to a firm as a result of locating near other firms. The advantages arise because equipment can be shared (by providing enough business to support a rental firm to serve them) and transportation and utility costs can be shared. Information costs can also be shared. If nothing else, being near each other makes the grapevine work more quickly. There is no technical reason for banks, investment houses, and insurance companies to come together in a financial district in the downtown of almost every city—they routinely transmit all their information through computers. The advantage comes from the fact-to-face interaction which common location facilitates.

Scale Economies

A third key element in the local economy is called "economies of scale" by economists, "cost-spreading" and "the experience curve" by businesses. Scale economies are the advantages to a firm which come from providing a greater share of goods or services to the market (Thompson, 1968). Consumers recognize it as "volume discount"—the larger box of cereal costs less, ounce for ounce.

There are several reasons why firms operating at a large scale might produce their products more cheaply. The most obvious one is that "fixed" costs can be spread over more units. Up to a certain size, the firm might need only one accountant, or one secretary, or one building. Those costs remain the same whether the firm produces 25 widgets or 2500. Note that cost spreading does not automatically occur. If the production line can handle a maximum of 2500 widgets, the 2501st widget will force the purchase of a whole new production line and *increase* the cost of additional production. There are other, more subtle advantages to size. A larger firm, with more employees and a greater variety of operations and products, will have resident a wider range of expertise and experiences. It takes time to learn how to do something well; if a firm can draw on that experience already resident, it can save on that time and reach full production more quickly. This is what businesses call "the experience curve." Finally, if a firm is large enough it can dominate the market; less competition might translate to lower prices as distribution and advertising costs can be less.

Location Decisions

Even given that there are advantages to locating in an urban area, there still remains the question of where in an urban area one would chose to locate. Both workers and workplaces go through a similar calculation, although their solutions may be very different.

Residential Location

Suppose you have just accepted a job in a new city. Now you are riding around town looking for a likely spot to live. There are so many good choices; how will you decide?

Economists make the case that the choice of a residential location is basically a trade-off between the attraction of open space and the cost of transportation (Kain, 1962; Lowry, 1968). The American dream is to live out in the country, enjoying the fresh air and surrounded by nature. The wealthy might want 5 bedrooms and 6 baths while the poor might settle for a 2-bedroom cottage, but both prefer to surround it with open space.

The problem for most of us is the journey to work. Transportation costs increase with distance from the workplace. This assumes that most employment is downtown or near downtown and that the commute to work is the greatest share of transportation costs. For simplicity, we will also assume that transportation costs per mile are basically the same for all income classes. It is true that the poorer classes are more likely to rely on public transportation, which may be cheaper (it depends on how much you value time and flexibility). But since public transit outside core city locations is limited, this piece of reality would only strengthen the argument which is about to be made—namely, that lower income people choose central city locations.

While transportation costs increase as one lives further from the center of the city, land costs are cheaper. This is because land closer to workplaces is more highly priced since it carries lower transportation costs. Lower income people, however, have less money to spend on housing. A greater share of their income is taken for food (the first item in anyone's budget) and transportation (the second item, since if you cannot get to work you cannot earn the money to buy anything else). But the food budget is fairly "income inelastic"—with increasing income, a lower ratio of the income is spent on food even though the actual size of the food budget may be larger. Transportation costs per mile are the same for all classes; and while they increase with distance, they do not increase as rapidly as the price of land declines. So the higher income households can exercise their preference for purchasing open land which is further away from the core of the city. And, since the land is cheaper, they can buy more of it than they could afford at close-in locations.

The result of this model is that the affluent live in the suburbs and while the poor live near the core. Transportation is a greater share of a poor household's housing costs, so a greater savings is achieved if that cost can be kept low. The ideal would be to live close enough to work that one could walk, which would drop transportation costs to zero (except for the cost of time). The affluent spend more of their income on land and building, so savings on transportation costs are less important to them.

An implication of this model is that the poor live at the core of the city, on some of the most expensive land in the city. This means the poor must use less space. Although the unit cost of land is higher, by using fewer units the price can be kept low. Landlords in these neighborhoods make their profit from renting many small parcels; it is a high volume business.

Another implication of the model is sprawl at the suburban fringe of the city. As the affluent seek inexpensive open land, they bid the price of agricultural land on the fringe of the city above its value for farming (since the land now has the potential for residential development), but below its market value once it is developed (since, after all, one farm field is much like another and development could go elsewhere). While allowing individual households to realize their preference for open space, sprawl creates problems for delivering services (roads, utilities, city services) to scattered sites. The problem might be solved by regulating the conversion of land on the urban fringe, since by eliminating the risk of the timing of development you would also eliminate the profit due to speculation. The other possibility is to tax the speculative value from the market by taxing any increase in the value of agricultural land which is not converted to urban uses (Clawson, 1962).

This model of residential location decisions is not completely adequate. Not all employment is located at the core. The journey to work is not the major transportation cost of all households (retirees, for example). But the model does seem to explain the dynamics of a process which is occurring; changing the initial assumptions might change the results but leave the model intact.

Industrial Location

The industrial location decisions of business and industry are similar to those of households, but more complex. Businesses must find the location which balances four factors: proximity to market, proximity to raw materials, proximity to labor, and cost of land. Proximity is usually measured by the *cost* of transportation, rather than by mileage (Alonso, 1965; Mills, 1967; Moses & Williamson, 1967).

Businesses differ in their dependence on the various factors of production. For example, resource-oriented businesses will locate at or near their source if at all possible. Frequently, however, a business will need more than one resource. The steel mills in Pittsburgh used ore from Minnesota—but they also needed coal from western Pennsylvania and West Virginia and limestone from western Pennsylvania.

For every business, the problem is to minimize the total costs imposed by each of their needs. Think of the four factors (each of which may have multiple parts) as fixed

anchors and transportation costs as rubber bands stretching from them. When the rubber bands are all tied together, the knot will come to rest at the "best" location (actually, there may be more than one "best" location, in which case the knot could come to rest in any of several location). Now suppose something changes—one of the anchors is moved, or one of the rubber bands becomes thicker (transportation costs increase). The balance of the forces is changed, and the "best" location moves.

In other words, businesses try to locate in places which provide everything they need, and to do it as inexpensively as possible. A business will not remain in a location which cannot supply one of its factors for production. And a business will feel pressure to relocate if the price of supplying the factors changes—not just the price locally, but the price across the entire network.

City/Suburban Competition

Increasingly, the core of the city is losing its comparative advantage for many industries.

Technological changes are sapping the attractiveness of central places. Manufacturing at the turn of the century was labor-oriented, and work was carried (literally) to several floors in the process of manufacture. Downtown land provided easiest access to labor. Now manufacturing has become dependent on cheap land, since the plants need space to spread out their assembly lines. Manufacturing has substituted machinery for labor, and downtown land is too expensive. Other businesses used to need a downtown location so they could move information— paper—easily among each other. The cost of transporting information over any distance was just too expensive. The telephone, computer, and fax machine have changed that; there is little difference between transporting information across that street and around the world.

The economy is also shifting from manufacturing to service. Service businesses tend to be more footloose (especially given the technological advances for moving materials and information). They can make their decisions not on the basic of locational constraints but on the basis of amenities. Part of the attraction of the Sunbelt was cheaper labor; but part of it was also climate.

As businesses are loosed from their downtown moorings, the suburbs beckon them with inexpensive land, less congestion, and attractive residential environs. Suburbs are competing successfully with downtown for many economic activities: Shopping malls have replaced downtown stores, warehouses and factories are located along the beltline freeways, highway strips support a great variety of service businesses from auto repair to medical clinics to light manufacturing. Downtown has not been completely abandoned, but it has been transformed. Banking and finance remain, along with government offices and some corporate headquarters (although production will have shifted to the suburbs). There is still some retail, especially lunch-time restaurants. Frequently the arts, especially the performing arts, will find a home on the fringes of downtown.

This means that the starting assumptions of the location models may have to be re-examined. The professional jobs have remained downtown, but many of the working-class jobs have gone to the suburbs. Excepts for the very poor (who need to walk or ride the bus to the welfare office downtown), lower income households no longer focus around downtown. But when they arrive in the suburbs, looking for housing near work, they find little in their price range. And they find few of the support services they were used to downtown. Downtown, meanwhile, is becoming more attractive to young professionals who cannot yet afford a place in the country. Although transportation costs are not an issue, they are finding that they do not need all that space if they do not have children. Many of their non-work trips are also downtown (to the theater, to the restaurants, etc.) By changing the starting assumptions, the same models can as easily explain working-class suburbs and the return of young professionals to downtown (called "gentrification.")

Value of Growth

Of all of the assumptions underlying this discussion of urban economic activity, the single most important one is growth. Cities compete with each other for business from a conviction that growth is good. This assumption is so central to urban development that it deserves special consideration.

Effects of Growth

If a community grows at less than the national rate of growth, it risks chronic unemployment, assuming that the nation is growing fast enough to provide full employment. Chronic unemployment will have two effects: The city will receive less in taxes, yet it will have to supply more services because of the high unemployment rate. Second, people (especially the young) will move out in search of jobs elsewhere. This will leave the city with an older workforce trained in older skills, which will make it more difficult to attract new industry. A downward spiral of urban decline will follow.

On the other hand, if a community grows at a rate *greater* than the national rate of growth (assuming full employment) there will also be problems. The rapid growth must outrun the city's capacity to provide adequate services (including streets, developable lots, and utilities). This will increase congestion, which will add to transportation costs and lessen the competitive advantage of the city. It will also increase the rate at which existing facilities wear out and will stress the capacity of the natural environment to carry the development. Extended rapid growth is also self-destructive.

In other words, the object is not growth at any cost. The goal is *balanced* growth. Too much growth will destroy the quality the quality of life of a city, while too little growth will make life in the city untenable (Hansen, 1975).

Effects of Size

If the rate of growth is problematic, is there also a limit to the amount of growth? Can a city be too big or too small?

The advantages of size—agglomerative and scale economies—are basically the benefits of choice. The more there is, the more choice one has. A city is too small if it cannot offer a wide enough range of choices (Thompson, 1967). The minimum size of a city appears not to be absolute. Individuals whose interests are less common will need a larger place to find the diversity to satisfy those interests. While one can study piano in almost any city, a budding concert pianist might have to relocate to a large city to find an appropriate teacher.

A city is too large if one can no longer take advantage of the range of choices which are offered. A city is too large when it builds over all of its open space, when traffic can no longer flow in its streets, when its creeks and rivers breed disease. The range of choices it can offer is restricted by the breakdown of its base of physical resources. The upper limit of city size can be extended by substituting technologies. Replacing the private automobile with mass transit (as in New York City) can greatly extend the maximum size of a city. Restricting what households and businesses can put into the river (as in Cleveland's cleanup of the Cuyahoga) can expand the limits of development.

Problems

Traditional economic theory assumes the necessity of growth. It is the fuel that drives the economy. There is no word for "non-growth" other than "stagnation." If an economic organization is not growing, it is dying. There are a few economists who are just beginning to explore what a non-growth, non-stagnant economy—a "steady-state" economy—might look like (Schumacher, 1973; Daly, 1977), but their work to this point has not extended to urban economies. Yet this is a critical problem for cities, since they cannot grow indefinitely. All cities must eventually use up all the land available for new residences and new industries, must reach the carrying capacity of their streets and highways (Finkler, Toner & Popper, 1976).

Traditionally, growth has been offered as the solution to poverty. As the urban economy grows, the unemployed can find work and poverty can be eliminated. The real problem for big cities is not poverty (as damning a problem as that is). Even if poverty were eliminated, a straining resource base would remain. The heaviest strain on the urban economy is not poverty but population growth.

A growing population can be accommodated through horizontal or vertical expansion. Horizontal expansion (which, if uncontrolled, becomes "sprawl") expands transportation demands, put a disproportionate demand on public services, and with increased distances it lessens the communication between population clusters (which, frequently, are class clusters). Vertical expansion (which, if uncontrolled, becomes "crowding") increases interpersonal contacts, but also increases friction—social friction, transportation friction, and wear on the physical structure of the city (Thompson, 1967). There is a third, historical solution to population growth. The Greeks and Romans designed their cities for a maximum population size. When population growth exceeded the carrying capacity of the city, the population was divided and some set out to found a new colony. While this arrangement probably suited the townsfolk, the new colonists might have had second thoughts.

Summary

We began with a question about public encouragement of economic growth. Part of the solution, as we have seen, is technical, drawing on measures like income multipliers and location decisions. But another part of the solution is normative, drawing on decisions like what we want our city to be and how we want to live together. The urban economy is more than economics, more than work. It is how we make a living.

Questions for Discussion

1. Suppose you were a city council member in a rural Midwest city which has a population around 20,000 people. The city has been approached by two businesses, each requesting city assistance to construct a new production facility in town:

   Gung Ho Industries, Inc. will employ 50 people at $5/hour to repackage consumer goods on a contract (job-by-job) basis. They propose to purchase an existing warehouse building and refit it for their purpose. They estimate that they will need $750,000 for their plant; the corporation will bring $250,000 to the project and will borrow the remainder.

   Gunga Din Corp. will employ 10 people at $15/hour to manufacturer components for scientific instruments. This plant will cost $1,250,000, mostly for precision machinery. The company can get $1,000,000 in financing and will bring $250,000 of its own to the project.

   Each firm is asking for loan guarantees and interest write-down from the city (worth about $50,000 in each case). The city can only approve one of the requests. How would you vote?

2. Under what circumstances would you recommend a maintenance strategy for a city's economy? A growth strategy?
3. What is the economic basis of your city? Does the city show depth? Breadth? What recommendations would you make for an economic development strategy for the city?
4. How would you determine the optimum city size for the quality life you seek from a city?
5. What would it take to have an economically healthy city which has no more land for housing or industrial expansion? What would a steady-state urban economy look like?
6. What technological innovations might alleviate the problems of horizontal expansion of cities? Vertical expansion?

Terms to Remember

Urban Development Process	effect of large city size
comparative advantage	innovation
production	demand
surplus	employment
growth mode	maintenance mode
industry	industrial mix
market-oriented industry	resource-based industry
footloose industry	labor-oriented industry
industry mix & income	types of cities
productivity	skilled labor
oligopolistic market	market
new industries	industry mix and growth
elasticity of demand	demand for product
city size and economic growth	market share
depth	growth and lower income
basic industry	breadth
income multiplier	service industry
scale economies	agglomerative economies
cost spreading	cost sharing
journey-to-work	experience curve
industrial location decision	residential location decision
high growth rate	low growth rate
	effect of small city size

References

Alexander, J. W. (1954) The basic-nonbasic concept of urban economic functions, Economic Geography *30*, 246–261.

Alonso, Williams. (1965) Location and Land Use. Cambridge, MA: Harvard University Press.

Chinitz, Benjamin. (1961) Contrasts in agglomeration: New York and Pittsburgh, American Economic Review *51*, 279–289.

Clawson, Marion. (1962) Urban sprawl and speculation in suburban land, Land Economics *38,* 99–111.

Daly, Herman, E. (1977) Steady-State Economics. NY: WH Freeman.

Finkler, Earl, William J. Toner, and Frank J. Popper. (1976) Urban Nongrowth: City Planning for People. NY: Praeger.

Hansen, N. (1975) The Challenge of Urban Growth: The Basic Economics of City Size and Structure. Lexington, MA: Lexington Books.

Isard, Walter (1960) Methods of Regional Analysis. Cambridge, MA: MIT Press.

Kain, John F. (1962) The journey-to-work as a determinant of residential location, Papers and Proceedings of the Regional Science Association *9,* 137–160.

Lowry, Ira S. (1968) Seven models of urban development: A structural comparison, in Urban Development Models. Washington, DC: Highway Research Board.

Mills, Edwin S. (1967) An aggregative model of resource allocation in a metropolitan area, American Economic Review *57,* 211–222.

Moses, Leon and H. F. Williamson, Jr. (1967) The location of economic activity in cities, American Economic Review *57,* 211–222.

Park, Robert E., E. W. Burgess, and R. D. McKenzie. (1925) The City. Chicago: University of Chicago Press.

Schumacher, E. F. (1973) Small is Beautiful: Economics as if People Mattered. NY: Harper & Row.

Thompson, Wilbur R. (1968) Internal and external factors in the development of urban economics, in Issues in Urban Economics, Perloff and Wingo, eds. Baltimore: Johns Hopkins.

Thompson, Wilbur R. (1967) Urban economics, in Taming Megalopolis, C. W. Eldrege, ed. NY: Praeger.

Tiebout, Charles M. (1962) The Community Economic Base Study: Supplementary Paper #16. NY: Committee for Economic Development.

Vernon, R. (1960) External economies, in Metropolis 1985. Cambridge, MA: Harvard University Press.

5

Design for Living

City life: Millions of people being lonesome together.
Henry David Thoreau

Los Angeles, CA (by author)

Personal Space

Sense of Place

Walk into a room for the first time. Almost instantly, you develop a "sense" for that place. A friend, entering that same room with you, might have a radically different opinion of it. All people carry within themselves spatial references to which they ascribe value and meaning—a "sense of place." Suppose the room were a classroom, a windowless space built of painted cinder block with asphalt tile on the floor and acoustic tile on the ceiling. To many, the description fits the basement of their childhood home: a damp, dark, cold place where they were penned up on days that were too inclement for playing outside. Is it any wonder that they become restless when they walk into such a classroom? Or perhaps the color of the walls is the same as the hospital room in which you awoke after emergency appendectomy surgery. For you, walking into such a room might restimulate a physical twinge in the gut even years later.

We all deal with space through the filter of perception. Some of the filters are cultural, and are shared with others from the same culture. The Japanese, for instance, consider a space to be private if it is screened from view. It does not matter that the screen is made from a single layer of rice paper and transmits all sounds easily. Other filters are personal, and are unique to each of us—like the color of the walls in one's first bedroom. The point is that space perceived through different filters—cultural or personal—is different from the same space perceived through different filters. People respond to the city, not as some "objective reality," but as a **perceived** world, a "behavioral environment." To the extent that these behavioral environments are shared, by an entire culture or by some group within it, we talk of such shared perceptions as a "sense of place."

Perceived Space

The perception of space is a function of two process: the sensation of space and the way those sensations are "construed" (or interpreted) to make sense.

All of our knowledge of the physical world comes through our senses, but the various senses do not provide identical information. As Edward Hall (1966) pointed out, some of the senses are "distance receptors" and others are "proximate" receptors. The sense of touch and the sensation of heat and cold are limited to the space immediately around the body. While the distance receptors (sight, hearing and smell) can be used at close-range, they are commonly used to provide information about the world at some distance from us. In fact, each of the senses creates its own unique space: Visual space is bounded by objects which do not transmit light (e.g., walls, but not windows). Acoustic space does not recognize those boundaries: If the door is open, you might hear someone approaching in a hallway long before s/he enters the room in which you are sitting. Conversely, through a plate glass store window you might observe people on the sidewalk outside even though you cannot hear them pass by.

Different cultures stress different sensory receptors. As already mentioned, the Japanese ignore the lack of acoustic privacy in their dwellings. It appears that there are cultural differences in thermal space preferences, too. Northern Europeans seem to prefer to keep some distance between themselves; Southern Europeans seem to prefer to be close enough to sense the heat of the other's body. To the Southern European, the northerner is "cool" and "distant," to the Northern European, the southerner is "pushy" and "invasive."

Sensory space by itself, however, does not carry the full meaning of a space. Besides the physical environment itself, the "social construction" of space is influenced by individual characteristics, the task at hand, and the characteristics of others who are in the space. The physical environment includes all the sensory characteristics, like room size, number of occupants, and the arrangement of furniture. They are the frame on which environmental behavior is hung. Individual characteristics include age, sex, cultural background, previous experiences, and all the other baggage that each of us carries around. These traits make up the personality of the one who is behaving in the environment. The task at hand could involve elements of conflict, cooperation, conversation, or solitary occupation. It is the purpose for which one is behaving in a given environment. The characteristics of others are their personalities, be they traits of leadership, attractiveness, stigma, etc. Humans are fascinated by each other, and cannot help but react to the presence—and even sometimes the absence—of others.

Consider a large room—the classroom described earlier. Imagine that space, with perhaps fifty chairdesks. Suppose five other people are already in the room, reading. Imagine that you are looking for a place to study as you open the door to the room. How do you react? Perhaps you would choose a desk, sit down, and begin to study. Perhaps not—for some people, five people in an open space is too distracting for study; the space would be too crowded. Now imagine the same space, this time without any desks. Instead, there are forty people in the room, and a boom box playing at high volume. Imagine that you are looking for a place to boogie. Is the room crowded now? Hardly; it could probably hold another forty people with no problem. Now imagine the same room, again with the chairdesks, only this time there is only one person in it. Again, you are looking for a place to study. You open the door, look inside, and see your ex- with whom you have had a horrible row the night before. Is the room too crowded? You'd better believe it—there is one person too many in that room.

Lived Space

People live simultaneously in several kinds of space. There is "personal space," the bubble of space that we all carry around with us. There is "territory," the area that a person claims for his or her own. And there is "home range," which is not a coherent territory, but is instead one's familiar world.

Imagine that you are riding an elevator, alone. The Muzak is playing a favorite tune of yours, and you are whistling along, slouched against the back wall of the elevator. The elevator stops, the door opens, and someone else gets in. Now you stop whistling, straighten up, and look straight ahead. You travel on in silence, until the door opens again and two more people get in. Now the elevator is getting crowded, and you move to the side so everyone shares the space equally. You have known your numbers since you were three, but now you watch those numbers from one to ten at the front of the elevator as if they were the most interesting thing in the world. What is happening here? There are social conventions for behavior in different kinds of personal space. Personal space is actually several spaces, each with its own perimeter.

At "public" distances (more than, say, 40 feet), other people are characters on a stage and each of us is a performer. It is difficult to read their facial expressions, or even many gestures. Voices must be loud, movements exaggerated for communication to occur. Communication is usually one-way, with a "speaker" and an "audience." This is the distance from which old-time politicians address a crowd, or from which stage actors ply their craft. It is only from public distances that most buildings can be seen in their entirety, and any decoration applied to the surface of buildings must be large-scale to be appreciated from those distances.

At "social distances," from 5–20 feet, it is possible to carry on a discussion in a normal tone of voice. Facial expressions and subtle bodily gestures can be used to support (or undercut) what is being said. At the near range of this distance, one does not see the whole body, but focuses primarily on the head and upper torso. It is the distance people normally assume when they are introduced—a handshake is extended, then each takes about half a step back and sizes up the other. In the built environment, it is the volume enclosed by a room—whether the room is under a roof or an outdoor patio. The little touches of an interior decorator now come into play, and some of the nuances of texture and fabric come into play.

At "personal distances," from 2–6 feet, it is possible to converse in a subdued voice. It is the distance between friends. Facial expressions and slight gestures often convey more than words, and one focuses on the face of the other. At the near range of this distance, it is possible to feel the body heat of the other, or smell the fragrance of his/her breath. In the built environment, it is a corner of

Type	Distance	Activity	Communication	Visual Field
Public	>40 ft.	Performance	Speech	Total Body/Gross Details
Social	5–20 ft.	Discussion	Normal Voice	Head and Torso
Personal	2–6 ft.	Conversation	Subdued Voice	Face/Small Details
Intimate	<3 ft.	Privacy	Whisper	Proximate Senses

Figure 5.1. Lived Space.

the room. Small details—knickknacks and other artwork, details carved into the furniture—become focal points.

At "intimate distances," no farther than the reach of one's arm, one speaks in whispers. Sight gives way as the primary sensory mode to sound, touch, and smell. It is the space we occupy when alone, or on rare occasions when we invite someone else to be close. Little children are permitted to violate this boundary almost at will, but the rest of us go through elaborate rituals when we must impinge on the intimate space of another. That is why we behave so peculiarly in a crowded elevator.

Territory is home, or home base, or "turf." It is space that each of us takes and defends as one's own. A dog, wandering about in the neighborhood, lifts its leg from time to time and "marks" its territory, defending its claim to the space against any other dogs in the area. People behave similarly. When you moved into the dorm, first you scanned the room to decide which part of it was going to be yours. Then you threw a suitcase on one of the beds to claim it, and put a box of books on one of the desks and hung a poster on one of the walls. After you settled in, you started leaving dirty socks and other clothes around the room, to mark your passage. Homeowners do the same thing. When they first move in, they leave some things in the yard and driveway, to declare their new possession of the premises. In short order, they put a lamp and a chair in the picture window and plant some flowers around the foundation.

Home range is different from territory, but tied to it. Just as a dog will defend its territory but will range some distance outside it, so too are people familiar with a much greater space than what they are prepared to defend as their own. While territory is limited, has boundaries, home range is described in term of destinations and directions (called "nodes" and "paths" by Kevin Lynch (1960)). Like a medieval map, home range describes the spaces one has traversed and there are many blank places where monsters lurk. While personal space and territory can be measured in feet, home range is often measured in time, nearness and accessibility, and friendliness.

City Space

The effect of space—of the city—on the people who live in it is not limited to the personal experience of that space. Recall that the sense of place is determined by cultural as well as personal filters. We turn now to an examination of how cities have affected social perception.

Impact of Urbanization on Society

When you read the papers today, you find all sorts or stories describing how the cities are going to wrack and ruin, giving the impression that ours is the worst of times. Actually, it has often been so (read Charles Dickens if you doubt it). For much of American history, cities have experienced spreading slums and decay, the power and impersonality of giant factories, and ever-widening gulf between the rich and the poor, churning neighborhoods, and competition for space and jobs (Chudacoff, 1975). Nonetheless, cities did provide upward mobility to their residents. Cities also had a profound impact on the family life of their residents.

"Upward mobility" does not mean that, eventually, class differences would disappear (an idea that Chudacoff (1975) labels "The Egalitarian Myth"). Only a small number of people have accumulated large proportions of the wealth, and most of them inherited it. The middle- and lower-classes have improved in an absolute sense, although most of the time they lost ground relative to the wealthy. Despite the occasional rags-to-riches stories, the bulk of mobility occurred in small increments. Nor did upward mobility eliminate poverty, since downward mobility was occurring at the same time, especially among the lower classes.

There are three major types of class mobility: geographical, occupational, and property. "Go west, young man!" is a classic American expression of geographic mobility. Today it is found in the migrations from the Rustbelt to the Sunbelt in search of jobs. It is the ability to take advantage of opportunities which exist elsewhere; sometimes it is the belief that if one only moves someplace else, one's luck will change. Often putting down roots someplace else does provide some improvement; certainly it can nourish the intention to improve one's social standing. In any event, geographical mobility generally occurs by moving into the city, whether it be unemployed autoworkers from Detroit moving to Austin, Texas, or rural high school graduates going off to the city for a first job, or an accountant for one of the Big Ten taking a promotion and moving from a branch office to the head office in New York.

Occupational mobility—the move to a higher-status job—may be individual or generational. Another word for individual mobility is "a promotion." Because of their size, cities support more complex businesses and provide for greater division of labor. As a result, there are more jobs—and more gradations of jobs—in larger cities. Promotions are more frequent, and if a promotion is not forthcoming it is easier to jump to another, similar firm (with, of course, a promotion in with the deal). Even if one spends one's entire career at the same job—furnace repair,

for instance—it is still possible that one's children would find higher-status occupations. Many immigrants of peasant stock came to this country, settled in cities, and worked the rest of their lives as laborers. Their children, better educated than their parents because of the opportunities afforded by the school system, were able to find work in skilled trades and office work. The grandchildren, in their turn, often graduated from college and pursued professional careers.

Property mobility is a peculiarly American from of status-climbing. More than Europeans or other nationalities, Americans have pursued single-family homeownership as the ideal way of living. Perhaps it is a legacy of our frontier days. In any event, because of the size of our cities and the geographical mobility which we enjoy, most city people are not known to each other. In a small town, where everyone grew up together, people meet each other with the background of their history together; in the city, each person is a stranger who is taken on face appearance. Where one lives (a "good" address, or a "bad" one), and the kind of house one lives in, are ways of reinforcing an appearance, and impression we try to make on each other (Cooper, 1972). Consequently, Americans have a tradition of moving to a new residence when they receive a new promotion.

Mobility, urban expansion, industrialization, and economic growth all promoted specialization and fragmentation. Some argue that this, in turn, has led to a "breakdown in community." But it is not clear that "community" ever existed in America—the village was a British convention and never really caught on here. Daniel Boone, the frontiersman, is said to have moved to a new farmsite whenever neighbors moved close enough that he could see the smoke from their chimneys. Specialization and fragmentation have created their own opportunities, and carry with them their own challenges.

Urbanization has affected the family ("households," to be more precise), as well as individuals. In preindustrial cities (and still, to some extent, in rural areas today), work and residence were combined: Shopkeepers lived above their stores; farmers worked the land on which they lived. As a result, children were socialized into work roles and into adult life as part of their home life. The Industrial Revolution, with its division of labor and large-scale production, separated home and work. Children stayed home; parents went away to work. If the family were wealthy enough, the children stayed home with their mother; if not, they stayed with a grandparent or an aunt who lived with them while their mother went off to work. The family was no longer the economic unit: Individuals went off to work and earned their own wages. The family remained a unit of consumption (the fruit of individual labor was still consumed in common), but production occurred among unrelated individuals who were located elsewhere. The world of adults became a foreign world to children.

The mobility—geographic and social—which urbanization fostered also broke the generational ties that used to bind families. Formerly, kin groups settled in a single region and if children, parents, uncles and aunts, and grandparents didn't live under the same roof, they frequently lived within shouting distance. In cities, people move from place to place in search of work or in search of better housing. It quickly becomes cumbersome to juggle the schedules, travel needs, and work opportunities of multiple wage earners. Little by little, the family unit was pared to its essentials: the nuclear family of parents and their children (today, in many cases, it is mother and children). Among the working classes, the need for freedom to move was tempered by the high cost of purchasing housing. Well into the twentieth century, it was customary for working and middle class families to rent "rooms" to lodgers and boarders to augment the family income.

Through all these changes, the role of women in the city was complex and often confusing. With the growth of industrialization, there was also a growing "cult of domesticity" (Chudacoff, 1975) which urged women to tend the hearth and raise the children. This was one solution for the loss of the extended family. But many households could not afford to lose the wages a women could earn, and throughout the nineteenth and early twentieth centuries many factory jobs (especially in textiles and clothing) depended on female labor and many middle-class women were proprietors of small establishments (a pattern which is still prevalent in Latin America today). In other cases, there was no choice: single parents (windowed, divorced, or abandoned) usually had to work. There were some very interesting efforts in the last half of the nineteenth century to apply industrial techniques to household work on a neighborhood scale. For example, in Melusina Peirce's 1868 "cooperative housekeeping" strategy (Hayden, 1984), some would care for children, some would provide the food, and others produce goods for sale (using the proceeds to pay wages to all involved).

Social Structure of the City

Are city people different, really, than country people? The genetic material is the same; are there social and environmental conditions which make a difference? In 1938, the effect of cities on the people who lived there was defined by Louis Wirth in three terms: Large size, density and heterogeneity. (Wirth, 1938). For more than half a century, scholars have been exploring the implications of his simple definition.

Large Size: Cities are, by definition, large aggregates of people. Wirth argues that, simply by virtue of their size, cities cause people to "segment" (compartmentalize) their relationships. City people know less about a smaller proportion of the people they meet. This, in turn, leads to superficiality and anonymity in social contacts. On the one hand, this fits the division of labor and specialization

Large Size—Tidewater, VA (by author)

which industrial society requires; on the other hand, it leads to *anomie* (normlessness), sometimes decried as "breakdown of moral values."

In a 1945 article, James Bossard developed some of the implications of the effects of size. He pointed out that, as the number of people increases arithmetically (i.e., 1, 2, 3, 4 . . .), the number of possible interactions increases geometrically (i.e., 0, 1, 3, 6 . . .) (Bossard, 1945). The point is that one more person is not just "one more." Depending on the complexity of the current social situation, each additional person brings ever greater complexity into the setting.

In 1964, Barker and Gump took this issue a step further by examining the behavior of students in a large and a small high school (Barker & Gump, 1964). They found that size affects a person's access to opportunities. In a small school, there might be 23 Juniors exposed to 48 different settings with each student participating, on average, in 8 or 9 activities. In a larger school, although there was a greater number of settings (189) the increase was not as great as the increase in students (almost 800 Juniors). As a result, students in the large school participated in an average of 3 to 4 activities. The small school is "undermanned"—it has few people to perform the necessary roles; the large school is "overmanned."

In an undermanned setting, Barker and Gump argue, each person must play several roles and is unable to concentrate on any one. The result is a "jack of all trades" mentality. In an overmanned setting, people will specialize in only one or two roles. This results in specialists and experts, rather than generalists. If one has a variety of interests and talents, a small school (and, presumably, a small town) would provide the best environment for pursuing them. If one has a special talent—playing the violin or playing football—then a large school might be preferable.

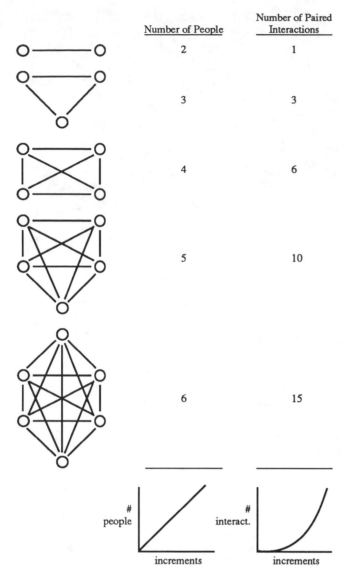

Number of People	Number of Paired Interactions
2	1
3	3
4	6
5	10
6	15

Figure 5.2. The Law of Interaction

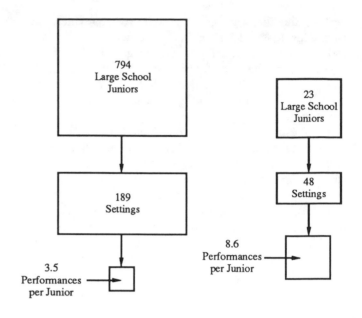

Figure 5.3. Undermanning/Overmanning

not work if they do not reinforce this purpose. The trick, in other words, is to provide enough opportunity to encourage interaction without providing an overload.

Density: The second of Wirth's characteristics which define cities, density is the degree to which people are concentrated in space. Wirth argues that density is necessary for differentiation and specialization to occur. Jane Jacobs (1961) concurs, arguing that it is precisely the high density of Greenwich Village which makes it an exciting and livable place.

In the intervening years, research has clarified the meaning of "density." **Physical density** is the number of

If larger size creates increasingly greater complexity, it is logical to expect that there is some upper limit to the complexity (and therefore the size) that human beings can tolerate. Georg Simmel first explored this idea in 1903 (Simmel, 1971), and Stanley Milgram returned to it in 1970 (Milgram, 1970). If the environment presents more stimulation than an individual can process, they argue, the human organism automatically acts to filter and cut down the incoming stimulation. Simmel (and Wirth) argue that this results in social relationships which are superficial, anonymous, transitory. Milgram reasons that city people are less likely to help each other than town people.

There is a contradiction inherent in the concept of sensory overload, for (as Christopher Alexander, [1967], points out) cities are above all "mechanisms for sustaining human contact." The primary purpose of cities is to provide people with the opportunity to interact. Cities do

Density—New York City (by author)

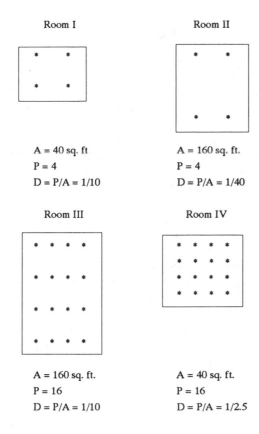

Room I

A = 40 sq. ft
P = 4
D = P/A = 1/10

Room II

A = 160 sq. ft.
P = 4
D = P/A = 1/40

Room III

A = 160 sq. ft.
P = 16
D = P/A = 1/10

Room IV

A = 40 sq. ft.
P = 16
D = P/A = 1/2.5

Figure 5.4. Social Density

people living on a unit of land. In other words, physical density is the population per acre (D=P/A), to use the Census Bureau definition. But there is another type of density, **social density,** which is the number of interactions per unit of space (Loo, 1973). Consider the difference between these two definitions: Suppose you have four rooms, two of 40 square feet and two of 160 square feet. Suppose two of the rooms (one large, one small) have 4 people in them, and two have 16 people in them. Which room is most "crowded"? Clearly, the small one with 16 people in it. Which is least crowded? Again, clearly the large one with 4 people in it. The remaining two rooms are identical, at least in terms of physical density. But would they *feel* the same? For most people, the larger room with more people would feel more crowded than the smaller room with few people. This difference is what is meant by social density.

There is a third term, introduced into the discussion of density, which also needs to be more carefully defined: **Crowding.** There was a time when the Census Bureau defined crowding in terms of the number of people per room. A household which lived with more than one person per room was, by definition, crowded. A family of five needed a five-room house (kitchen, living room, and three bedrooms); a family of seven needed a seven-room house. Current research no longer treats crowding as some objec-

tive function, but as a perception. Crowding is the feeling that there are too many people in one place. When you shoehorn yourself into the bleachers at a football game, you do not feel crowded—part of the reason you went is to shout yourself horse and have the guy behind spill beer down your collar. On the other hand, when you walked into that almost-empty classroom and spotted your ex-, the space definitely had one person too many in it. It was crowded.

There is a large body of research which focuses on this issue of crowding. John Calhoun (1971) argues, based on the behavior of lab rats, that crowding leads to a "behavioral sink," a total social breakdown. Lab rats, held in confined quarters, stopped caring for their young and stopped grooming themselves; some became bullies and others cowered in corners. For Calhoun, the parallel to urban inner cities was inescapable. He also recognized that "crowding" was tied to perception in human beings, hypothesizing that cultural inventions at crucial junctures have permitted humans to achieve greater and greater densities without feeling crowded. Stokols (1972) reasoned that the perception of crowding occurs when the demand for space exceeds the supply. At a football game, 3 square feet may be all you need; when you are studying, it may take a minimum of 20 square feet. Jeanette Desor (1972), on the other hand, tied the perception of crowding to excessive social stimulation—the amount of space is less important than how much is going on in it. Chalsa Loo (1973) takes this a step further and argues that it is the structure of the social stimulation which affects the sense of crowding. The more structured the social density, the less likely one is to feel crowded.

But how do these theories relate to what really happens in cities? In an article dating from the 1930's, J. S. Plant argued, based on his experience as a clinical psychologist, that family living space has a negative effect on the personality development of children who grow up in a crowded environment (Plant, 1960). He argued that personality development needs a closed information system, and overstimulation from crowding results in lack of objectivity, lack of self-sufficiency, and the loss of illusions (children in crowded environments have seen it all). Later research was unable to confirm Plant's theory; it appears he may have confused the effects of poverty, mental illness, and other factors with the effects of crowding.

Festinger, Schachter, and Back (1950) studied the formation of friendships among people who moved into a new development. They found that friendships are formed on the basis of "functional" distance ("propinquity") rather than physical distance ("proximity"). In other words, it is more important to examine people's paths rather than measuring space on a map. People seemed to develop acquaintances based on many recurring opportunities to see each other—first comes recognition, then "nodding acquaintance," then speaking acquaintance, and finally friendship. If people's paths cross, there is more opportunity for them to go through these steps. As predicted, they found that people who lived on the corner knew more people in their neighborhood, while people at the end of a cul-de-sac knew fewer. In apartment buildings with a single mailbox for all the residents, the people who lived near the mailbox knew more of the residents.

Leo Kuper (1953), writing about new towns in England, noted that the placement of doors, windows, and party walls will also affect the pattern of friendships in new housing developments. For instance, if the "back" door is on the side of the house and faces directly into the adjoining neighbor's "back" door, friendship will be discouraged. Apparently it creates a feeling that the neighbor is "too" close. Similarly, in one set of duplexes the master bedrooms were designed in such a way that the only place for the headboard of the bed was against the party wall shared by the master bedroom of the adjoining duplex, and the soundproofing was none too good. While most households living in duplexes developed friendships with their "housemates," people in these duplexes avoided each other. Apparently they already knew more about each other than they cared to admit.

Heterogeneity: "Heterogeneity" means diversity, the presence of different types of people in the same place. Wirth argued that cities, because of their large size, contain a great variety of people. On the one hand, this leads to a perception of the world as unstable and insecure; on the other, it lends itself to sophistication and cosmopolitanism. City dwellers tend to be members of a variety of different types of groups, but because of mobility, turnover in these groups is high.

As it turns out, the issue of urban diversity is more complex than Wirth suggested. While the city may be heterogeneous, areas within the city are often more or less similar in their social characteristics. Generally, people who identify with a particular status level tend to be spatially concentrated in neighborhoods which possess an identification with that status.

Edward Laumann (1973) in his study of Detroit found that people tend to live in neighborhoods with others like themselves. Like seek like, especially if they are alike in ethnic/religious and occupational characteristics. Lynn Lofland (1973) explains this phenomenon as a way of bringing order to what would otherwise be a chaotic environment in the urban "world of strangers". City life, she argues, is made possible by categorizing people in terms of appearance and spatial location so that those who live in a city could know a great deal about each other just by looking. While city people know nothing about individual persons they encounter, they can at least react to each other based on the category to which each appears to belong. In the modern city, where individual appearances are easily shifted, there tends to be more reliance on spatial ordering. Activities—and people—are assigned to specific locales. As a result, skilled urban dwellers use appearances, location, and behavior to make identifications—and to make impressions.

The central issue of urban diversity is one of balance. Homogeneity provides a source of identification for those who are among the "in" group, but it makes coordination with other groups difficult. The more isolated (i.e., the more homogeneous) the group, the harder it is to see another group's side. As some of the major American cities have become minority-dominated, it has fostered the growth of minority leadership: Henry Cisneros of San Antonio, Coleman Young of Detroit, Andrew Young and Julian Bond of Atlanta, the late Harold Washington of Chicago, Tom Bradley of Los Angeles. At the same time, the White flight which abandoned these central cities to minorities has deepened class and racial cleavages in metropolitan areas. Herbert Gans, the sociologist and planner, proposed what he called the "Balanced Community": heterogeneous sectors ("neighborhoods," if you prefer) composed of homogeneous blocks.

Neighborhood and Community

Most people do not directly experience "the city." The city is too complex, too grand to be taken in whole; in its raw form, it is (to take William James out of context) a "blooming, buzzing confusion." For most of us, the city is known through the neighborhoods, our own and others that we visit.

The Concept of Neighborhood

The idea of neighborhood has undergone something of an evolution. At the turn of the century, Ebenezer Howard proposed in effect the city as a neighborhood. In his plan for "garden cities" which would be developed in farmland around industrial London, the towns were to be about 1 mile in diameter, tied to the core city by mass

Heterogeneity—Toronto, ONT (by author)

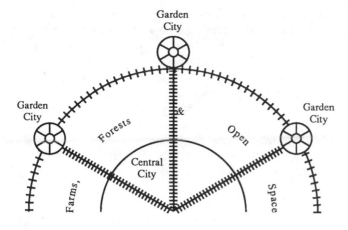

Figure 5.5. Garden Cities

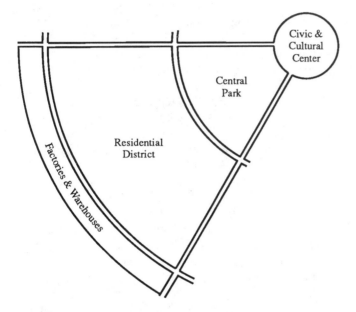

Figure 5.6. Detail, Garden City Ward

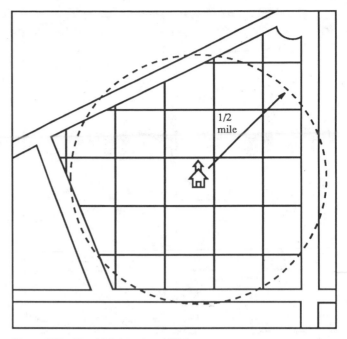

Figure 5.7. The Neighborhood Unit

transit, and would focus on parks, shopping, and schools at the center with industrial establishments on the periphery (Howard, 1965).

Pieces of Howard's idea were taken up in this country by Clarence Perry (1929) in his "neighborhood unit" plan. In his plan, districts (i.e., neighborhoods) would be focused on the elementary school. Accordingly, each neighborhood would be about 1/2 mile in diameter (the maximum walking distance one would expect an elementary school child to go) and 2–4 such neighborhoods could support a high school which would be no more than 1 mile from any residence. The neighborhood was designed around children, auto traffic was discouraged, adult activities like shopping were relegated to the edges of the neighborhood. Perry's plan works, as long as the households generate enough children. As households age

or social norms shift to smaller families, the "neighborhood unit" becomes less and less workable.

More recently, research has focused less on the physical boundaries of neighborhoods and has paid more attention to the social and psychological processes by which people divide cities into neighborhoods. Gerald Suttles (1968) in his work on Chicago has found that people can reliably and consistently identify neighborhoods within parts of the city with which they are familiar. From his research, he concludes that they are working on the basis of the frequency, convenience, and continuity of the contacts between people in the neighborhoods; he calls this "ordered segmentation." Further, he found that people use this compartmentalizing of contacts to maintain boundaries between the neighborhoods. He relates examples in which behavior, condemned when performed by outsiders, is explained away when it occurs inside the neighborhood. In other words, we know more about the people with whom we share space, and so find it easier to understand their actions.

Suttles studied the space with which people were familiar; Terence Lee (1968) studied the patterns in how people became familiar with space in the first place. Lee found that "the neighborhood" is less a physical space than a mental construct. Depending on the context people recognize three types of neighborhood: social acquaintance (the largest, and it may have unknown spaces within it), homogeneous (which probably comes closest to what planners mean by "neighborhood"), and personal. The personal neighborhood is built from the space that a person knows best. Its size depends on how active one is in his/her space; its dimensions depend on the pattern of

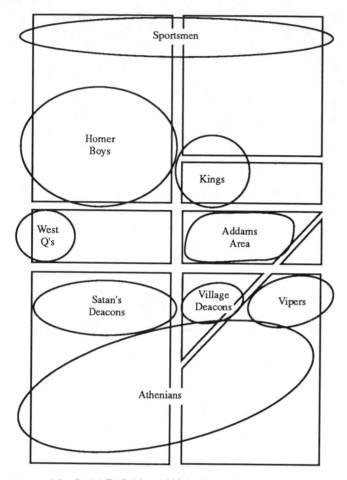

Figure 5.8. Social Definition of Neighborhood

one's activity. Lee found that most people frequent one or two places for shopping, laundry, recreation, etc. Often such a place is on or near the route that one takes to work. Over time, places in this target area and places on the route from home to the target area become better known, places away from the target area are less well known. The result, Lee found, is that the "mental map" of the neighborhood is asymmetrical, pulled in the direction of the target and foreshortened on the back. Further, "the neighborhood" probably has no discrete limits since it is constituted by these individual mental maps and expresses overlapping focusses and interactions. While there is a common core, the boundaries are likely to be fuzzy.

The Role of Neighborhood

The neighborhood is a key element in one's experience of a city, since the arrangement of space in a neighborhood will influence the behaviors which occur there. Site plans can regulate the communication process between individuals and between groups. As Jane Jacobs (1961) pointed out, people do not like to cross "dead" spaces (large parks, freeways and very busy highways, swaths of industrial park, railroad tracks, etc.). The positioning of these activities will create barriers to communication

across them. Second, cultural groups are more likely to stay in areas which provide amenities which are important to them: Many ethnic communities use religion and worship as one expression of their identity (the synagogue, or a Ukrainian Orthodox church, or a Roman catholic parish with Spanish-language services, etc.), but there are other amenities which also help to anchor the community, like a kosher deli or a bocce court or a Vietnamese grocery. Third, the neighborhood—the site and the objects within it—acquire symbolic meaning and attachments over time. Gans (1959) reported how residents of Boston's West End resisted being moved from their neighborhood, in spite of the common perception of the area as a slum. For them, it was home and they had put a lot of effort into it.

The key issue in the effect of the physical neighborhood on the behavior of its residents is the impact of the site on communication. Festinger, Schachter, and Back (1950) explored these effects using the terms "proximity" (map-distance) and "propinquity" (path-distance, or distance-as-travelled). They found (as has been discussed above) that friendships develop based on recurring opportunities for people to interact with each other. This effect appears to depend on neighborhood homogeneity (especially *perceived* homogeneity), particularly in terms of family life-cycle. Families, at different stages of their growth, have different needs: Rearing babies makes different demands than rearing teenagers (or toddlers). The household without children has different needs and different activities than those with children. But if people have the opportunity to be physically and socially/psychologically close to each other, they will eventually communicate with each other. The effect of distances will wear away over time, as more opportunities to meet people who are farther away will occur, but the basic process still holds.

Communication in neighborhoods influences other issues, as well. Jane Jacobs (1961) pointed out that the safety of city streets depended on "eyes on the street." People like to watch people. If there are people watching what is happening on the street, and feeling secure enough in their neighbors that they trust them for backup, Jacobs argues that people will enforce the safety of their own streets. Oscar Newman (1973) applied Jacobs' ideas to the design of buildings and neighborhoods. He argued that space is safer if it is designed to maximize casual surveillance by the people who occupy this space. He tested his hypothesis on two housing projects in New York City, and found lower crime rates in the project which was more "defensible" in its design. The key, he found, lay in clearly defining ownership (he called it the "hierarchy of space"). If private and public space are buffered by a "semi-private" space, and if the semi-private space is designed so people can observe it from their private space, then people will police it. This principle can be applied to hallways, entryways, sidewalks and alleys.

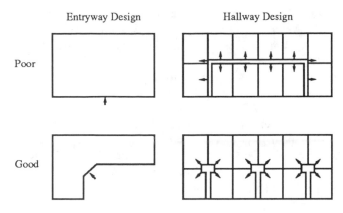

Entryway Design | Hallway Design

Poor

Good

Figure 5.9. Defensible Space

Neighborhood Perception

A constant theme through this entire chapter has been the differences in the way people perceive and react to space. This chapter ends with a consideration of two particularly important differences in perception.

Lower-class and poor people perceive their environment differently than the middle class, and these differences are generally not appreciated by social reformers (Saarinen, 1976). Marc Fried (1963), in his study of people relocated from Boston's West End, found that they experienced a deep sense of loss, both of spatial identity (being removed from all the places they have come to know) and group identity (losing all the people they used to know). The intensity of the grief was a function of the individual's feelings for the area; the better they knew the area, the greater was their sense of loss. This occurred in spite of the fact that the West Enders were relocated in housing and neighborhoods which were physically superior to those they left behind. Middle-class people, used to moving as part of occupational mobility, identifying with places and groups scattered throughout the city and often scattered throughout the nation and the world, are less tied to a local identity.

Second, as Appleyard (1969) points out, city planners and designers perceive the environment differently than other residents. Designers see the city in terms of its future. Their motives are diffuse and general. Residents are concerned with a particular neighborhood, their own specific interests, and their present circumstances. By themselves, these differences are merely a curiosity. The problem occurs when the designers forget that their perceptions are not necessarily shared, or (worse yet) blame the residents for not sharing the designers' values.

Summary: Space and the Strategy of Life

The key to designing for people is to understand how they perceive a place, and why. The perception of space is conditioned by both sensation and the social construction of that sensation—different people perceive the same thing differently. Everyone simultaneously inhabits three kinds of lived space—personal space, territory, and home range. These spaces are influenced by the individual characteristics of each of us, and by characteristics we share in common with others in our society. The city, as a type of space, has in its turn had an effect on society. It has supported upward mobility and has transformed the family. And living in cities creates a particular kind of experience, because cities are particularly large, dense, and diverse places. But it is in the neighborhood that most people come to terms with their city. The neighborhood has some particular effects on how people act within it, whether for well or ill.

Questions for Discussion

1. Design a room that encourages people to interact at a social distance (remember to use more than one of the senses). Design a room around intimate and personal distance.
2. Different groups need different things from their neighborhoods. How would you design a neighborhood for families with young children (say, an average of 3 children, aged 2, 4, and six)? How would you design a neighborhood for professional households (say, a couple with at most 1 child)? How would you design a neighborhood for elderly householders (say, people over 65 with about 1/3 widowed or widowers)?
3. Gans' "balanced community" is based on the concept of homogeneous blocks within heterogeneous districts. What particular problems of physical design does this raise? Problems of social policy?
4. Louis Wirth says that cities are large, dense, and diverse. What happens if a place is large, dense, and homogeneous? Or dense, diverse, and small? Or large, diverse, and spread out?
5. Historically, the city has had an impact on urban households. What new forms of household are emerging? What do you expect households to be in the 21st century?

Terms to Remember

personal space	cooperative housekeeping
perceived space	heterogeneity
proximate receptors	density
social construction of space	undermanning/overmanning
personal space	ning
personal distance	sensory overload
public distance	social density
home range	proximity
types of upward mobility	world of strangers
nuclear family	garden city

ordered segmentation	cult of domesticity
defensible space	social structure of the city
sense of place	large size
distance receptors	law of interaction
sensory space	anomie
lived space	physical density
intimate distance	crowding
social distance	propinquity
territory	balanced community
impact of urbanization	neighborhood unit
households	eyes on the street

References

Alexander, Christopher. (1967) The city as a mechanism for sustaining human contact, in Environment for Man, W. Ewald, ed. Bloomington, IN: Indiana University Press.

Appleyard, Donald. (1969) City design and the pluralistic city, in Planning Urban Growth and Regional Development, L. Rodwin, ed. Cambridge, MA: MIT Press.

Barker, Roger G. and Paul V. Gump. (1964) Big School, Small School: High School Size and Student Behavior. Stanford CA: Stanford University Press.

Bossard, James H. S. (1945) The law of family interaction, American Journal of Sociology, 50, 292–294.

Calhoun, John C. (1971) Space and the strategy of life, in Behavior and Environment, A. Esser, ed. NY: Plenum Press.

Cooper, Clare. (1972) The house as symbol, Design and Environment, 11, 30–37.

Chudacoff, Howard P. (1975) The Evolution of American Urban Society. Englewood Cliffs, NJ: Prentice Hall.

Desor, Jeanette A. (1972) Towards a psychological theory of crowding, Journal of Personality and Social Psychology, 21, 79–83.

Festinger, Leon, Stanley Schachter, and Kurt Back. (1950) Social Pressure in Informal Groups. NY: Harper.

Fried, Marc. (1963) Grieving for a lost home, in the Urban Condition, L. J. Duhl, ed. NY: Simon & Schuster.

Gans, Herbert J. (1959) The human implications of current redevelopment and relocation planning, Journal of the American Institute of Planners, 25, 15–25.

Hall, E. T. (1966) The Hidden Dimension. Garden City, NY: Doubleday.

Hayden, Dolores. (1984) Redesigning the American Dream: The Future of Housing, Work, and Family Life. NY: W. W. Norton.

Howard, Ebenezer. (1961) The Death and Life of Great American Cities. NY: Random House.

Jacobs, Jane. (1961) The Death and Life of Great American Cities. NY: Random House.

Kuper, Leo. (1953) Living in Towns. London: The Cresset Press.

Laumann, Edward O. (1973) The Bonds of Pluralism: The Form and Substance of urban Social Networks. NY: Wiley.

Lee, Terence. (1968) Urban neighborhood as a socio-spatial schema, Human Relations, 21, 241–268.

Lofland, Lynn. (1973) A World of Strangers. NY: Basic Books.

Loo, Chalsa. (1973) Important issues in researching the effects of crowding on humans, Representative Research in Social Psychology 4, 219–226.

Lynch, Kevin. (1960) The Image of the City.

Milgram, Stanley. (1970) The experience of living in cities, Science, 167: 1461–1468.

Newman, Oscar. (1973) Defensible Space. NY: Collier Books.

Perry, Clarence. (1929) The Neighborhood Unit. NY: Regional Plan.

Saarienen, Thomas F. (1976) Environmental Planning: Perception and Behavior. Boston: Houghton Mifflin.

Simmel, Georg. (1971) The Metropolis and mental life, in Georg Simmel: On Individuality and Social Forms, D. Levine, ed. Chicago: University of Chicago Press.

Stokols. D. (1972) A social-psychological model of human crowding phenomena, Journal of the American Institute of Planners, 38, 72–83.

Suttles, Gerald D. (1968) The Social Order of the Slum. Chicago: University of Chicago Press.

6
Design with Style

Like a piece of architecture, the city is a construction in space, but one of vast scale, a thing perceived only in the course of long spans of time.

Kevin Lynch
The Image of the City

Toronto City Hall (by author)

The human world can be divided into the built and the natural. The built environment of American cities has not been particularly notable for its design. In this chapter, we will discuss what it is that makes a city "well designed," what makes it a memorable visual and lived experience.

While many of the terms which follow are common to all of the design arts, there are two elements of urban design which make it distinctive. First, unlike paintings or even buildings, cities are never built all at once, nor are they built under the direction of a single person. The city represents the design decisions of many actors at many different times. Second, city design is a complex of nature, technology, and visual language. You must train your eye to notice the difference between dullness and beauty, blandness and excitement, formlessness and aesthetics.

Every place has the potential to carry a sense of place, of history, and of spirit. To realize this, we must perceive the character of the natural site, the situation, the interrelationships with other parts of the city, the appropriate scale, and the technology and the resources (including money) which are available.

Elements of Design

There are many systems for analyzing a design. Gordon Cullen (1961) has developed a very nice visual system; Grady Clay (1973) bases his system on language. This chapter focuses on four principal elements of urban design: space, scale, color and texture, and furnishings.

Space

Cities are full of space, but what is it? Until space is defined, it is nothing.

The primary element defining space is the dimension of **openness/closure.** According to Paul Spreiregen (1965), the perception of enclosure depends on the position of the viewer.

> If a building is as high as the distance from which it is viewed (i.e., if the relationship between height and distance is 1:1, or in other words, if the angle of vision is 45°), the feeling is one of full enclosure. One's field of vision is filled by the details of the facade.
>
> If the building is viewed from a distance which is twice its height (i.e., if the height-to-distance ratio is 1:2, or a 30° angle of vision), and building is at the upper limit of the field of vision and just barely gives a feeling of enclosure. One tends to focus on the facade as a complete unit.
>
> If a building is viewed from a distance which is three times its height (1:3, or 22°), the enclosure is minimal. One focuses on the facade in relation to its surroundings.

If a building is viewed from a distance which is four times its height (1:4 or 18°), the space completely loses any sense of enclosure. The facade of the building serves as an edge which defines some larger space.

Ratio	Angle	Closure	Field of Vision
1:1	45°	Full Enclosure	
1:2	30°	Enclosure	
1:3	22°	Minimal Enclosure	
1:4	18°	No Enclosure	

Figure 6.1. Enclosure and Viewing Distance

These relationships are very simple ones, derived from the physiology of sight. There are ways around these tendencies, of course. Transparent buildings give an illusion of both openness and closure. The sense of enclosure is weakened by gaps in the pattern of the facade or by strong variations or abrupt changes in facade.

A second element which defines space is **shade/illumination.** Dark objects against a light background recede, while light objects stand out against a dark background. Shade gives the appearance of great depth, while light gives the appearance of openness.

A third defining element is the play between **focal point/infinity.** Space can be completely enclosed and focused on itself (or on some objects within itself), or space can be only partially bounded, channelled to a "vanishing point" (that point, infinitely distant, where parallel lines meet). Focused space gives the feeling of stability; channelled space gives a feeling of movement.

Finally, space may be **monumental/intimate.** Monumental spaces are self-sufficient. They stand alone

Shade/Illumination—New York City (H. Roger Smith)

Infinity—New York City (H. Roger Smith)

and declare themselves as being the only important thing around. Intimate spaces are connected. They relate to each other, they lead from one to another, they lean on each other. Either extreme can be overdone, in which case it loses its impact and becomes boring.

Focal Point—Waterpark, Fort Worth, TX (by author)

Monumental Scale—City hall, Dallas, TX (by author)

Scale

Scale implies some yardstick, some rule by which to measure. There are many different scales which have been used, some very abstract. A common building scale these days is based on requirements for handling and shipping. Much of construction is designed around the 4x8 plywood sheet, for example—the standard size for a common construction material. In cities, whatever the scale, the measure should be human. The proportions should follow those of the human body and human experience.

One useful human yardstick for city design is based on **visual distances** (Spreiregen, 1965). In urban space, 3–10 feet is the range for conversation. Facial expressions cannot be seen much beyond 40 feet, nor facial features much beyond 80 feet. The maximum distances for recognizing gestures is 450 feet. Beyond 4,000 feet objects cannot even be recognized as people. Using these rules of thumb, one can divide urban distances (and, thus, urban scale) into three categories:

intimate scale (up to 80 feet)

urbane scale (80–450 feet)

monumental scale (400–4000 feet).

Automobile-scale detailing, Nicollet Mall, Minneapolis, MN (by author)

Pedestrian-scale detailing, Nicollet Mall, Minneapolis, MN (by author

Rhythm—Ghent District, Norfolk, VA (by author)

Scale is also a function of how we get around, or **circulation.** Appropriate scale for a pedestrian area is much finer, smaller, and more detailed than it is, say, along a highway. It is the difference between a store sign and a billboard. The more slowly one moves through a space, the more time one has to absorb details within the space. Conversely, the more rapidly one can move through space, the larger the design concept can be.

The apparent size of a building is also affected by the way the pieces are put together, by its **articulation.** Elements of similar size, repeated at regular intervals, create a feeling of rhythm and enlarge the apparent size of the structure. Too much rhythm is monotonous, however, and must be punctuated by other elements. Planting can be used to relieve monumental scale and soften the hard edges of otherwise grand structures.

Color and Texture

Both color and texture in city design are a function of light. The effect of **night versus day** in the city is totally different. Part of this difference is due to the brightness of available light, but part of it is due to the difference in the

Daylight Illumination—Jarvis Ave., Toronto, ONT (by author)

Nighttime Illumination—Jarvis Ave., Toronto, ONT. (by author)

source of light. At night, inside light sources play a major role in defining the buildings.

Different materials have different colors and suggest different textures. One of these is **"patina"**—the mellowing of the surface of an object which occurs with age or use. There is a charm, a subtle beauty that comes to a building which has aged in place. Each of the seasons has its own color: The environment takes on the color of the growing things. The time of day also has its own color. In a famous series of paintings, Claude Monet explored the changes over the course of a day in the color of light on the facade of the cathedral at Rouen in France. Strong light creates its own play of color through the shadows it casts. Shadows, in turn, create texture.

Texture is to the hand what color is to the eye. In the case of cities, one usually does not approach a facade to stroke it and feel the textures. In cityscapes, texture is usually revealed through the eye. Gold, crystal, and worked metal suggest richness. Patterns carved in stone or wood (or cast in metal) create texture. Stone also has colors of its own, as does water which provides constantly changing color and texture. If you look for it, you will discover that manhole covers, grates, and paving all create texture in the city.

Furnishings

Street furnishings serve a variety of functions in a city. They can be used to **give scale** to an otherwise abstract cityscape. They make the space appear liveable. When you see a park bench, you automatically assume a certain set of dimensions; when you see a set of windows and a doorway, you assume a certain set of dimensions. Designers can use these assumptions to play tricks. An oversized bench in front of a large building can make it appear smaller; and undersized bench can make a small building appear larger. The facade of St. Peter's Basilica was scaled to *appear* to be a three-story building.

Street furniture can provide not just scale, but also **identity.** A common practice these days in historic renewal districts is to replace contemporary street furniture with vintage pieces (or copies of vintage pieces). Shopping streets declare their unity by using common (and distinctive) street furniture. Even some residential neighborhoods maintain a sense of uniqueness by providing distinctive plantings, pavement, or lighting.

The problem with street furniture is **clutter.** Lampposts can become filled with signs. Add a mailbox, a trash receptacle, a bus stop sign, a bench for bus riders, a manhole cover, and a change of paving in front of the adjacent shops—too much of a good thing can keep the viewer from really seeing any of it.

Principles of Design

A design is more than a collection of elements. The elements must be combined in some coherent fashion. We turn now to three principles which are commonly used to organize the design of cities.

Functionalism

The battle cry of the modernist movement was "Form follows function." The form, or design, of any object was to be informed and shaped by the function it was serving. It was a natural extension of the arts and crafts movement: A good teapot had to be judged by how well it brewed and poured tea as much as by how pretty it looked. For a functionalist, a good building is one whose beauty comes from the structure itself—the way the rooms relate to each other and define the volume of the building—rather than from the application of decorative elements. Design was to be stripped of decoration, sparing in its use of elements, much like a well-designed machine. In fact, Le Corbusier (an earlier leader in functionalism) referred to cities as "*machines a vivre*" ("machines for living").

For a functionalist, design is **utilitarian.** There is a natural affinity between this approach and the design of cities, since a city is above all a "use object." While art collectors may pay millions for a single oil painting by Van Gogh or Picasso, none would spend that much for a building which could not be used (much less an entire neighborhood of such buildings). It was a short step from saying that building and cities had to work well to saying that how they work should determine how they look. The value of a design comes from its use.

Good design also implies **clarity** of use. Design is an organizing principle; if use is the organizing principle, then good design should make that use apparent. Functional buildings should "read" well, exposing the purpose of their spaces to the user. Stairwells should **say,** "Stairwell!" Entrances should say, "Enter here!" Confusion of function implies confused design.

Third, good design is **honest.** It is proud of the way it works, and exposes its clockwork for the admiration of the user. If value comes from how well things work, good design must expose the workings so they can be appreciated. Structural elements need not be buried behind veneer; they should stand as design elements of the facade. Stairwells need not be buried inside the volume of the building; they can be hung on the outside of the structure and hold their own space as a design component. The ultimate expression of this ethic is Philip Johnson's "glass house" which exposes almost the entire interior to outside view through the four glass walls of the building.

There are, of course, competing design principles which can be (and have been) used in place of functionalism. Certainly the fine arts do not focus on utilitarian values. Art can be purely **decorative.** In this approach, value comes not from use but from sensation; a

Structure as Design Element—Hancock Bldg., Chicago, IL (by author)

good design is one which delights the senses. One may work for layers of meaning, many of which might blend into each other so their cumulative effect may be one **mystery** rather than clarity of meaning. In the fine arts, good design may create a sense of **magic** and wonder by hiding their workings. This is, perhaps, the inspiration behind the Post-modernist movement in architecture which puts chippendale pediments on the top of skyscrapers and paints panels of bunting around office buildings. It remains to be seen whether the inspiration of Post-modernism will extend from architecture into the design of cities.

Symmetry

A second, and very powerful organizing principle for Western design, is **symmetry.** Symmetry carries with it the beauty of mathematics and geometry. It was a guiding principle in the design of the Egyptians, the Greeks, and the Romans and was restated in the great Renaissance designs of Michelangelo, Christopher Wren, and Palladio.

One of the elements of symmetry is **equilibrium.** What happens on the right is balanced on the left; a mass on the bottom is balanced on the top. Although the balancing is often accomplished by duplication—right and left are mirror images of each other—the balance can be created by variations on a common theme. This balancing of forces, this canceling of oppositions, results in a strong sense of stability. Symmetrical design is imbued with a sense of permanence.

Another element of symmetry is **regularity** of pattern. The requirement of balance, or course, encourages repetition of a pattern; repeating a pattern on both sides will balance them. But even when it is not required for balance, the regular recurrence of a pattern builds the stability of the design. It creates a sense of the "eternal recurrence" of a moment.

A third element of symmetry is **focus.** The eye is directed to the stable center of the design. Balance and repetition reinforce the centrality and stability of the point in the design where all forces are resolved. The forces are resolved, the eye and the spirit come to rest in the design. Stability is found in the cessation of movement, in a peaceful, restful eye.

Again, there are possibilities other than symmetry. Japanese design has been strongly influences by Zen, a religious philosophy which stresses the unity of opposites. Rather than stability, Japanese design strives for **dynamism,** an expression of the constancy of change. Designs are frequently asymmetrical, evoking a sense of movement. Dynamism is reinforced by the **unexpected** rather than regularity. Rather than focus on an equilibrium point in the design, Japanese design will carry the eye along a line and out sight, evoking a feeling of **movement** into the unknown. These elements of dynamic design can be found in Western work as well (Halprin, 1969; Ashihara, 1983).

Diversity

A third key principle of Western design, is **diversity.** The key to diversity is to express the range of each of the elements in a way that provides variety without tipping over into clutter.

Jane Jacobs (1960) describes the wonderful parade of people on city streets through the day—the paper carrier at dawn, the workers going off in the early light, followed by children on their way to school, domestic help (housecleaners, but also plumbers and general repair people) coming in shortly afterward, mothers with babies out for a noon stroll, the mail carrier on the rounds, the children coming home from school in the mid-afternoon, the domestic help going home shortly after them, followed by the workers' return, children playing outside in the early evening, adults going out for dinner or a movie and returning, the bar crowd at midnight, and the graveyard shift going to and from work in the wee hours.

If a city is to be alive, people must appear on the streets throughout the day. Usually it requires a **mixture of uses** to attract people at the various times of the day and night. It can be accomplished by providing different uses of the same facility (whether it be at the scale of a building or a neighborhood). It can also be accomplished with a variety of single-use facilities if different people have to use the same streets to get the them. It is important to provide a balance of uses over time. It does no good if everyone comes to use their different facilities at 9:00 A.M. and stays inside until quitting time at 5:00 P.M.

Mixing uses creates problems with maintaining compatibility of uses and providing some semblance of coherence. Many households with children will not welcome a bar on their corner, with its late-night activity. Business uses generate increased automobile traffic in the surrounding neighborhoods. Most people agree that auto body shops have to go somewhere, but preferably not in their backyard.

Short city blocks also provide diversity. They have more corners, which are attractive to businesses. And they provide a greater variety of paths which people can follow through the city. One of the pleasures of city living is the fun of being "creatively lost"—wandering in previously unexplored areas while still knowing roughly how to regain familiar landmarks.

Short blocks also have their disadvantages. More city land will be taken up with streets rather than income-producing (and tax-revenue generating) uses. The streets will require regular maintenance. And each additional corner creates an additional point of pedestrian/auto conflict.

A **mixture in the age of buildings,** a combination of new structures and "vintage" capital (as Jacobs, 1960, refers to it) also builds diversity. New buildings carry high overhead costs; their tenants must be established, relatively well-off users to be able to afford the extra cost. New ideas need old buildings. An entrepreneur with a new product or service can only afford low-rent space while the new idea is getting established and developing its market. Diversity in the age of building stock will help provide diversity of tenants, which in turn will attract a diversity of users.

Cheaper space is not an unqualified benefit, however. Older buildings embody older building technologies, which are frequently inadequate by current standards. Electrical wiring is usually inadequate for current loads, standards for fire detection and retardance were usually lower, energy insulation is frequently nonexistent or inadequate. The shell of an older building can, of course, be rehabilitated to current standards; but the cost can also be as much as a new construction in which case the price advantages to the renter would be lost.

Finally, diversity depends on sufficient **density,** or concentration of uses. Concentration supports diversity. This is the principle behind the shopping center and the downtown business district, although concentration by itself does not guarantee diversity.

A common objection to concentration is that high density means crowding, but Jacobs claims this is a false concern. Crowding means too many people in too little space.

"Too many people" depends on the definition of the situation. Fifty thousand people at a football game, while very dense, is not crowded. "Too little space" depends on the use of land. One hundred people living on one acre of land is very dense. It is crowded if they are living in single-story structures; it is quite spacious if they are living in a twenty-five story highrise.

As with the other two principles, there are alternatives to diversity. Traditional residential suburbs, for example, stress **simplicity** over diversity. Most of the space is dedicated to **single uses** rather than mixed use. Not only are the residential neighborhoods uniform in the type of housing they offer (one section may have large single-family detached houses, another may have mostly two-bedroom houses), but they tend to segregate shopping from offices and both from what few other commercial uses might be there. Rather than short blocks and the traffic they generate, residential suburbs favor **longer streets** in order to provide the maximum amount of land for residential development. Traffic is further discouraged by using cul-de-sacs and curving streets. Buildings in suburban neighborhoods tend to share a **common age,** and common buildings styles, rather than playing with the diversity of ages and styles common in city neighborhoods. And suburban areas stress **privacy and open space,** rather than the density of city life.

Levels of Design

The elements of design and the principles for combining them may be applied at various levels, from the individual structure up to the regional complex of the city and its "hinterland."

Buildings

The design of buildings—architecture—is an entire field of study in its own right. There are wonderful works on the history of architecture, such as Trachtenberg & Hyman's *Architecture: From Prehistory to Post-Modernism* (1986), and those which focus just on American architecture, such as Vincent Scully's *American Architecture and Urbanism* (1988). While these works focus on "high" architecture, the kind of work which was designed by an architect for a single client and fitted to a single site, there are also some good studies of "everyday" design, such as Carole Rifkind's *A Field Guide to American Architecture* (1980) and two field guides from the National Trust for Historic Preservation, Poppeliers *et alii, What Style Is It?* (1983) and Richard Longstreth's *The Buildings of Main Street* (1987). Although this chapter will not focus on this issue, Jim Kemp's *American Vernacular* (1987) is a good study of regional influences on the design of buildings.

There are nine broad periods of architectural styling which are commonly found in cities today:

Greek Revival—Minneapolis, MN (by author)

Greek Revival: Beginning with the 1830s and 1840s, Americans periodically rediscover the classical roots of their architecture. Greek revival buildings are most notable for their low-pitched roofs with triangular gables, reminiscent of the facade of the Parthenon. Frequently (although not always) the gables are supported by free-standing columns, making the appearance of a greek temple complete. The cornices are frequently decorated with dentil molding (a series of square blocks set in a row just under the roof line), and horizontal lines are emphasized throughout the building. The floor plan is rectangular.

Gothic Revival: Beginning around 1855 and continuing in various phases into the 1940s, much of Midwestern architecture drew on the inspiration of the Gothic cathedrals. The buildings have steeply pitched roofs, recalling the pitch of the gothic arch. The edges of the roof

Gothic Revival—Geneva, NY (H. Roger Smith)

were originally decorated with "bargeboards," boards which were pierced in lace-like designs, recalling the stone lacework of the cathedrals. Few of the original bargeboards remain, most of them having rotted away and never been replaced. The buildings have strong vertical lines, with long, tall windows (sometimes peaked at the top) and even vertical siding boards. The footprint of the building will commonly have a long main axis intersected by a short arm, recalling the transept of a gothic cathedral.

French Second Empire: After the Civil War, middle-class Americans began to travel abroad in increasing numbers. They brought back a taste for the architectural styles they found in Europe. In Paris of the 1850s, buildings were taxed by the number of stories they contained; an attic (the space above the roofline) was not counted as a story. So Parisians dropped the roofline below the top story of their buildings, avoiding some of the tax. This style was popular in America for twenty years after the Civil War. Its outstanding characteristic is the mansard roof, a roof which is almost flat on top but is steeply pitched on the sides and drops below the top row of windows. Often the windows project out from the wall in dormers. The roof is usually heavily embellished with railings on the top and decorative brackets underneath.

Italianate—Grand Rapids, MI (by author)

Romanesque: Not all American architectural styling of the late 19th century was imported. The American architect, Henry Richardson, developed a style which is often called "Richardson Romanesque." The buildings are massive stone structures of rough-hewn blocks. The Roman (round) arch is a strong design component, as are the small windows. The footprint of the building is frequently sprawling, with many angles, corners and nooks.

French 2nd Empire—Pittsburgh, PA (H. Roger Smith)

Italianate: Another popular style was based on the Italian country villa. It has low-pitched, sometimes almost flat, roofs with deep, overhanging eaves. The eaves are supported by ornate brackets. There are frequently bay windows and large porches ("loggia" in Italian), with thin, angular columns. The thin, tall windows are set close to the floor. Rising from the center of the roof, there is frequently a very ornate "belvedere" ("lookout," to Americans; in Italian, it means "nice view"), complete with pillars, brackets, and a flat roof.

Romanesque Revival—City hall, Minneapolis, MN (by author)

Victorian: Actually, there are many "Victorian" styles, too many for a simple introduction. They are all the result of the American genius for mass production. The houses are wood frame construction and are exuberantly decorated with every sort of mass-produced wooden millwork. What once used to be hand-carved from stone

Victorian Picturesque—Mankato, MN (by author)

Prairie Style—San Francisco CA (by author)

for the wealthy was now available to the middle-class in cheap reproduction. Victorian houses combine towers and bay windows, balconies and curved porches, using stained and beveled glass liberally.

Craftsman: This is the common, "everyday" housing of the first twenty years of the 20th century. Craftsman houses are small, 1 1/2 story bungalows. They have a low-pitched roof, frequently with a dormer on one or both sides. There is usually a generous porch, often integrated under the main roofline. The interior is simple and blocky, with simple woodwork.

Prairie: This style, popular into the 1930s, is closely identified with Frank Lloyd Wright, although there were others in this school. The style features flat or low-pitched roofs with wide eaves. The clean, angular lines of the buildings are strongly horizontal. Colors and materials

from nature, particularly from the local natural environment, are common. The buildings feature many windows and the floor plan is open.

Art Deco/Art Moderne: The 1920s and 1930s saw the triumph of the machine with the industrial assembly line and its products, like the automobile. Science and technology were promising to solve all of humankind's ills. In ar-

Art Deco/Art Moderne—Chrysler Bldg, New York City (H. Roger Smith)

Craftsman House—Mankato, MN (by author)

chitecture, as in the other arts, the machine and the manufactured were glorified. Buildings from this period are frequently simple boxes with highly decorative exteriors. The decoration is geometrical, using zigzags and streamlines curves. The colors are striking and contrasting, mating pink and black or pale green and black. Materials include glass block, chrome, and "vitrolite" (a glass tile which looks something like black marble).

Modernism: After World War II, the triumph of science and technology was complete. Architecture was stripped of all decoration in the name of functionalism. This style is mostly known for its skyscrapers, tall slabs of steel and glass which preach cost-effectiveness. The minimalism of the office tower has found expression in a few more modest buildings, such as Mies van der Rohe's townhouses (horizontal structures of steel and glass which are designed around the square and the cube). In everyday design, modernism expresses itself in the "rambler," a single-story collection of rooms strung together under a roof. The interior is simple and spare, with no millwork and little woodwork. The major architectural feature is the picture window.

Post-Modernism: The 1980s saw a reaction to the minimalism of modern architecture, but since it has no unifying point of view of its own, it is called by what it is not: non-modernism. Like the Victorians, post-modernists

Post-Modernism—Portland Bldg., Portland, OR (by author)

delight in decoration, incorporating references to many previous styles or architecture into a single building. Egyptian, Druid, Greek, Romanesque, and modern elements might all be combined in one piece. Like Art Deco, post-modernism delights in an artist's palette of colors, combining pastel blue with tan and rust and gray.

Neighborhoods

Urban design is more than the design of buildings. It must also deal with how the buildings relate to each other in their immediate context, in their neighborhoods.

Radburn, NJ, has been one of the most powerful inspirations for American neighborhood design. Designed by Clarence Stein and Henry Wright in 1928, it was based on English town planning designs but scaled to the neighborhood level. Detached, single-family houses faced into a common open space, almost a village green. Each house had its own private garden in addition to the common open space. Pedestrian and automobile were segregated, with automobile traffic coming to the back of the houses and a complete pedestrian circulation system coming from the front of the houses to the common open space. The open spaces were tied together with walking and bike trails, and pedestrian underpasses were constructed wherever the pedestrian and street system met. Both industrial and com-

Modernism—Piper Jaffray Tower, Minneapolis, MN (by author)

mercial districts were planned, but the Depression intervened and only a limited shopping district was constructed.

Radburn's design reinforced the concept of neighborhood as a close community of residents. The neighborhood turned in on itself and focused around common open space and recreational activities. Although the original design combined living and working, the employment elements of the design were never realized and often were not recalled in the imitations which followed.

The neighborhood as a residential unit was further refined by Clarence Perry's (1939) "neighborhood unit." Perry's neighborhood focused on childrearing. The center of the neighborhood was an elementary school, and the neighborhood extended 1/2 mile from it (the walking range of an elementary school child). Although Perry's plan used the conventional gridiron street plan, most traffic was routed onto arterial highways which defined the neighborhood boundaries. While perhaps appropriate in its time, Perry's neighborhood unit depends on a high density of children by contemporary standards. With smaller family sizes and a greater proportion of households with no children, many schools cannot draw enough children within only a 1/2 mile radius.

A third approach to neighborhood design comes from Jane Jacobs (1960). For her, neighborhoods serve two purposes: shelter and government. It is in the neighborhoods that the day-to-day work of governing happens. It is in the neighborhood that housholds work out their connection (and duties) with the rest of the city. If the neighborhood is to survive the inevitable processes of physical change and social mobility, it must be connected with the rest of the city to ensure that its interests are heard in the Council. This should be expressed in the physical design of the neighborhood. There should be lively and interesting streets, streets which are woven into the city network. Public facilities—parks, squares, public buildings— should reinforce this fabric. Barriers to the flow of people and traffic should be placed so they reinforce the neighborhood's connection to the city. If there are too many barriers, the neighborhood will strangle (and get strangled in the Council) for lack of visitors. Too few barriers, and the neighborhood will not be able to develop an identity and develop its own local leaders who identify with the neighborhood and go to bat for it in the Council.

Jacobs also describes a particularly important element of neighborhood design, the park. There are four elements which, she says, make a park successful: intricacy, centering, sun, enclosure. Intricacy is necessary to create enough interest that people will return. Intricacy can be created through the physical design elements and/or through the people who use the space. Centering preserves a sense of order and allows people to navigate the various elements of intricacy without getting lost. As a young child explores a new area by going out and returning to Mamma's knee, so people first come to the center of the park and ex-

plore our from there. Sunlight organizes the way people use the park, and without they will avoid it. Most of the year, open sun will be an attraction; for the few months of very hot weather, noontime shade—with a view of sunlit space—will draw. And, finally, enclosure provides the identity of a park. Space is nothing until it is defined; a park is undeveloped until it is limited.

Many of Jacobs' ideas were independently confirmed by a planner, Kevin Lynch. Lynch found that there are five elements which combine to build an "image of the city" (Lynch, 1960). The city is composed of **districts**, or identifiable units (much like neighborhoods). People usually deal with a city in terms of its districts rather than the city as a whole. The districts focus around a **node,** a focal point where there activity is more intense, and are defined by **edges,** boundaries and barriers which limit the district. The edges are stitched to the nodes by **paths** which are identified by **landmarks.**

Cities

At the level of the city, single structures—buildings or parks—are no longer the issue. They are elements which are used to create a much grander design (Barnett, 1982). There are three common designs which guide the growth of cities:

Satellite: In this design, a core city is ringed by satellites, each set off by open space (agricultural land, regional parks, etc.). This is an old design, in a sense one going back to the Greeks who limited the growth of their cities and sent out colonies when a town's population became too large. Ebenezer Howard (1898) proposed satellites (he called them "garden cities") as the solution to London's overcrowding at the turn of the century. In a satellite design, neighborhoods become literally freestanding; yet all are linked together in a common network around the central city.

Spread: In this design, the city spreads out from the center, maintaining fairly low densities as it grows. Los Angeles is the classic "spread city," but many cities in the midwest have followed the pattern (Dallas, Houston, Tulsa, and Omaha, for examples). The concept of a spread city was developed by Frank Lloyd Wright as "Broadacre City" (Wright, 1958). Each residence would have an acre of land, and the homesteads would be tied together with a freeway network. At regular intervals, there would be small factories, stores, offices, and churches. Residents would combine small-scale truck farming with professional occupations, thus "having it all"—the advantages of both city and country living. The key to Wright's plan was the transportation network; without high-speed travel, Broadacre city could not work. Los Angeles and Houston are finding, however, that freeways do not insure high-speed travel, especially at rush hour.

Radial: The third model design is radial. Growth extends outward along key axes, usually transportation arteries. Radial growth is more concentrated than spread growth but less focused than satellite growth. A leading exponent of this design concept was Le Corbusier, who proposed "*La ville radieuse*," or "radiant city" (Le Corbusier, 1946). In the radiant city, people would be concentrated in high-rise apartments strung out along a freeway system. This left a maximum amount of land open for recreation and agriculture.

Summary: How Cities Speak

The design of a city, the care with which the elements in a city have been juxtaposed on each other, speaks to us about the place and the people who made it. A "city functional," one which exercises great care in locating industrial and commercial activity while ignoring the visual impact of the structures which support commerce and industry, speaks of its disdain for people (and employees). The visual impact of city is built from a few basic elements—space, scale, color, texture, furnishings. The variety of designs comes from the principles by which the elements are combined and the level at which they are focused. In both cases, there are many design schemes which may reasonably be argued.

Questions for Discussion

1. What specific mixtures of uses might fit well together in a common facility (neighborhood or building) in ways that would promote urban diversity?
2. What sort of people would you expect to be most comfortable in a city built on functional lines? What sort of lifestyle goes with that philosophy, what sort of activities might it support? What differences would you expect from symmetry? Diversity?
3. How might you use the elements of design to reinforce Lynch's concept of the "image of the city"?
4. How would the use of design elements differ between a radial, spread, and satellite design for a city?

Terms to Remember

space	diversity
angle of vision	short blocks
field of vision	density
focal point/infinity	Gothic revival
scale	French Second Empire
circulation and scale	Victorian picturesque
rhythm	Prairie style
night/day	Modernism
texture	Radburn, NJ
functionalism	intricacy
utilitarian	sun
symmetry	path
regularity	edge

district	mixed uses
spread design	mixed-age buildings
openness/closure	Greek revival
height:distance ratio	Italianate
shade/illumination	Romanesque Revival
monumental/intimate	Craftsman style
visual distance scale	Art Deco/Art Moderne
articulation and scale	Post-modernism
color	neighborhood unit
patina	centering
furnishings	enclosure
"form follows function"	node
clarity	landmark
equilibrium	satellite design
focus	radial design

References

Ashihara, Yoshinobu. (1983) The Aesthetic Townscape. Cambridge, MA: MIT Press.

Barnett, Jonathan. (1982) An Introduction to Urban Design. NY: Harper & Row.

Clay, Grady. (1973) Close-Up: How to Read the American City. NY: Praeger.

Cullen, Gordon. (1961) The Concise Townscape. NY: Van Nostrand Reinhold

Halprin, Lawrence. (1969) The RSVP Cycles: Creative Processes in the Human Environment. NY: George Braziller.

Howard, Ebenezer. (1898) Garden Cities of To-Morrow. Cambridge, MA: MIT Press, reprinted 1946 and 1965..

Jacobs, Jane. (1960) The Death and Life of Great American Cities. NY: Random House.

Kemp, Jim. (1987) American Vernacular: Regional Influences in ARchitecture and Urban Design. NY: Viking.

Le Corbusier. (1946) Concerning Town Planning. London: Architecture Press.

Longstreth, Richard. (1987) The Buildings of Main Street: A Guide to American Commercial Architecture. Washington, DC: The Preservation Press.

Lynch, Kevin. (1960) The Image of the City. Cambridge, MA: MIT Press.

Perry, Clarence. (1939) Housing for the Machine Age. NY: Russell Sage Foundation.

Popeliers, John C., S. Allen Chambers, Jr. and Nancy B. Schwartz. (1983) What Style Is It: A Guide to American Architecture. Washington, DC: The Preservation Press.

Rifkind, Carole. (1980) A Field Guide to American Architecture. NY: New American Library.

Scully, Vincent. (1988) American Architecture and Urbanism, Rev. Ed. NY: Henry Holt & Co.

Spreiregen, Paul D. (1965) Urban Design: The Architecture of Towns and Cities. NY: McGraw-Hill.

Trachtenberg, Marvin and Isabelle Hyman. (1986) Architecture: From Prehistory to Post-Modernism/The Western Tradition. NY: Harry N. Abrams, Inc.

Wright, Frank Lloyd. (1958) The Living City. NY: Horizon Press.

Part III

Running the City

7

Governing the City

We will ever strive for the ideals and sacred things of the city, both alone and with many;
We will unceasingly seek to quicken the sense of public duty;
We will revere and obey the city's laws;
We will transmit this city not only not less, but greater, better, and more beautiful than it was transmitted to us.

from the Athenian Oath of Citizenship

Trajan, Roman Emperor (H. Roger Smith)

It is November. You are going to the polls to vote for, among others, Municipal Officers. The mayor is up for re-election, as are several of the council members. In the paper and on the news, the mayor has been bragging about her accomplishments. She points to all the new development which she has brought to town. She crows about the report from the State Department of Revenue showing that the city has lower residential property tax rates than all other cities of similar size in the State. Her opponent, a council member who is not up for re-election, complains about everything the mayor has not done. City streets are choked with snow in the winter, local housing is so expensive that working people cannot afford it, and the city's budget is a shambles. The three council members who are running for re-election have carefully avoided taking sides in the mayoral race, although for several years council meetings have been stormy events all around. People in several of the neighborhoods are upset with all of the incumbents, and have fielded a slate of "reform" candidates. Your friends tell you that it does not matter what you do because "they're all a bunch of crooks, anyhow."

What do you do? How do you sift through these charges and countercharges and vote for the best candidate? And how much of the praise and the blame is due to events outside the control of both the mayor and the council?

For most of us, when we talk about "how a city is run," we are thinking about its government. When we talk about the people who "run" the city, we mean the people who are elected to local government—the mayor and council. In this chapter, you will learn who these people are, and what they can (and cannot) do.

Forms of City Government

Cities, as municipal corporations, are constrained both by the general rule of law and by the specified limits in the "charter," or founding contract. One of the more powerful provisions in the charter is the type of city government which is specified.

Legal Basis of Cities

In the American system of government, the individual states "create" the cities, by granting them certain powers and authorities. Every city is a "creature of the state." The Constitution of the United States specifies certain powers which belong to the Federal government, and reserves all other powers to the individual states. Nowhere does the Constitution recognize a governmental unit called "city" or "municipality" or "town," in spite of the fact that cities and towns predate the Constitution.

The grant of authority from the state to the city is expressed in two ways. First, state statutes specify powers and authorities which are extended to cities. Frequently the statutes distinguish between types of cities, giving more autonomy to one category of city than to another.

The statutes usually treat larger cities and cities central to a region (sometimes called "cities of the first class," other times called "class A cities") as a different category than others. Second, charters grant specific powers and authority to individual cities.

Statutes cover a variety of topics and limit the powers of cities. In addition to specifying the scope of powers of the various classes of cities, most statutes require that local governments conform to certain standards of behavior such as, meetings and records must be public, elections must follow common procedures, certain officials must meet specified qualifications. State statutes are particularly detailed on matters of financial accountability, specifying debt limits and property tax limitations, requiring annual budgets and audits, and limiting the investment of idle funds. Other statutes will control the annexation of land and the arbitration of boundary disputes, or the conditions under which cities may exercise power outside their boundaries (called "extraterritoriality") or transfer some of their power to another government body.

Charters usually specify a number of things: The purpose of the city, its form of government, the duties of its officers, and procedures to follow (including procedures for changing the charter itself).

Charters come in three basic forms (although there are many variations among the 50 states):

Statutory cities are limited to only those powers which are expressly listed in state statutes, and no others. In a sense, whatever is not permitted is prohibited to them.

Home-rule charter cities may perform any function which is permitted in their own charter, which is locally adopted (and may be locally amended).

Home-rule grant cities may perform any local government function as long as it is not expressly denied by state statute. For these cities, whatever is not prohibited is permitted (see Weeks & Hardy, 1984).

Most cities are statutory cities, and most of the time they are indistinguishable from home-rule cities. But home-rule cities may act without prior legislative authorization, and home-rule grant cities may even act without prior authorization in the charter. This distinction may be important in times of rapid change. Suppose, for example, that a city realizes that it has a serious problem with flooding because people have been building upstream and this has increased the flood risk downstream. The city would like to impose a moratorium on new construction in flood-prone land while it drafts a new zoning ordinance to reduce the risk of flooding—a process which could easily take 1–2 years. A statutory city probably could not impose a moratorium, since most states do not specifically address it in their statutes. A home-rule grant city may impose one without question. A home-rule charter city may impose one only if the charter permits development moratoriums, or if the charter can be speedily amended.

Types of City Government

Cities can be classified based on statutory authority and based on their form of government. There is no necessary relation between the classification of a city and its form of government; cities of the same class may choose to govern themselves differently. There are four common forms of city government, their differences arising from the historical era in which they developed. They are the weak mayor/council, commission, council/manager, and strong mayor/council forms.

Weak Mayor Form: Early in this country's history, town government was styled on the English village. A group of "selectmen" shared the government among themselves as a civic duty and a public trust. As the towns grew into cities, the "mayor and council form"

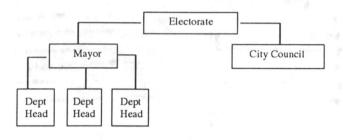

Figure 7.1. Mayor–Council Structure

developed. Since the council served without pay, it was generally composed of successful business people, usually merchants who worked in the center of the city. Each would take a turn and run for mayor. The mayor held little power, serving more as the figurehead for the city and "first among equals" on the council (the word *mayor* comes from the Latin *major,* which means "greater"). The council as a group appointed the administrative cabinet of the city and controlled the city budget. Over time, the mayor came to make day-to-day administrative decisions and, in virtue of greater familiarity with the workings of the city, was given power to veto decisions of the council. The mayor's veto was never absolute, since it could be overridden by a predominance of the council (e.g., a vote of 3/4 of the council). This form of city government is called the weak mayor/council form. Chicago, Illinois, still uses this form today.

As the social fabric and the American economic system were transformed by the Industrial Revolution and immigration, the old form of city governance proved inadequate. An elite of merchants and professional people could no longer govern "for the good of all." Instead, there arose a class of professional politicians, people who gained and maintained power by providing service to specific constituencies. This system was called "Machine politics" (Chudacoff, 1975). The Machine (some even had

names, like Tammany Hall in New York City) was led by a Boss (William Marcy Tweed of Tammany Hall, the Pendergast brothers in Kansas City, George Cox in Cincinnati, and in modern times Richard J. Daley in Chicago). The Boss coordinated the activity of ward bosses, who commanded a squad of precinct bosses. The Boss was not necessarily the mayor of the city—the real power was in being the party chairperson.

An old-time political machine worked something like this:

Bogdan gets off the boat (or train), a stranger in a strange city where everyone looks, talks, and acts differently. As Bogdan stands there, looking lost and wondering what to do, someone approaches him and asks (in Bogdan's own language!) if he needs help. After a bit of conversation in which the stranger determines that Bogdan has neither family nor a job in town, the stranger introduces Bogdan to Ivar and tells Ivar to take him down to "the Hall," and fix him up.

At the Hall, Ivar provides Bogdan with a hot meal. While they are eating, Ivar introduces Bogdan to Mr. Smith, who needs a laborer in his shop and will hire Bogdan. Then Ivar introduces him to Mrs. O'Leary, who has a room she will rent for a reasonable price. The next morning, Ivar shows up at Mrs. O'Leary's and takes Bogdan to Mr. Smith's and sees to it that Bogdan is settled into his new job. He picks him up after work and takes him to the Hall for another hot meal, and invites him to a party at the Hall this weekend. Ivar checks on Bogdan from time to time.

Soon March comes, and Ivar explains that it is election time (primary elections were more important to the Machine—that was when most of the smaller, functionary offices and ward and precinct chairs were decided) and he needs Bogdan's help. Bogdan, of course, will do anything for his friend. So Ivar explains that he wants Bogdan to vote in the upcoming election—he will arrange the voter registration for him—and, while he's at it, could he also vote for a couple of other people who would like to vote but can't be there (the fact that they are dead is beside the point).

Figure 7.2. Machine Politics Scenario

The Machine created a shadow political system which could control the formal system: The various bosses provided services to their constituents (jobs, housing, meals) who, in turn, provided votes for the boss on election day. In this fashion, the Machine was able to reward its workers by putting them into public office. Once the Machine was strong enough to control the local government, they also saw to it that elected officials were paid for their time.

The Machine provided, in effect, a welfare system at a time when there was no public welfare (the churches and some nonprofit organizations did provide private charity). But they had to find a way to finance all the services they were providing. There were two popular methods: "boodle" and "graft." Boodle was using inside information from the city government to benefit individual people who helped the Machine. Graft was extracting money from those who wished to do business with the city. Frequently they were used together: A Machine stalwart might receive inside information to win a lucrative construction contract with the city, and then turn part of the gain back to the Machine's coffers.

To some, it was a perfect system. The poor got jobs and food and housing, upward mobility was provided through the electoral process, elected officials made good money, and contractors got an inside line on projects. The problem was that the old power structure—the downtown merchants and the professional middle class—were left out of this loop, and were footing much of the bill through their property taxes.

The success of the Machine led to its own downfall. As more people moved into the middle class, the injustice of Machine politics became more burdensome. By the end of the Nineteenth Century there was a strong middle class movement for reforming the political system. "Throw the rascals out!" was their cry.

The reformers recognized, however, that the Machine worked because city government did not. The fractured lines of power and of responsibility made some form of informal power structure—the Machine—inevitable. If cities were to have honest and efficient government, it would have to come under a different system.

Commission: The Reform movement in city government was part of a larger societal shift toward centralized, bureaucratic control whether in government or business. Rationality, which meant efficiency and economy, was the battle cry. Politics should be removed from local government and "good business" principles applied. At-large elections were to replace of the ward system, to break the power of the Machines. Home rule charters were urged, on the grounds that all the powers of a city should be specified at the outset and removed from political interference from the Statehouse. When the Reform movements went national, they developed into the Progressive movement, which advocated nonpartisan local elections (hoping to further distance local government from politics) and short ballots (most city jobs became professional appointments rather than political offices).

Two new forms of government came out of the Reform movement, the Commission and the council/manager

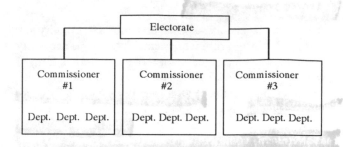

Figure 7.3. Commissioner Structure

forms. In 1900, downtown Galveston, Texas, was destroyed by a hurricane and tidal wave. The existing government proved incompetent for the emergency, squandering disaster relief funds without rebuilding the city. The state intervened, suspended the charter and established a commission of business people to run the city during the emergency. They divided the city departments among themselves: One took police and fire, another took streets and public property, a third sewer and water, and one took finance and revenue. The fifth, the mayor, coordinated the activity of all and handled anything that was not already covered. It was a style with which the downtown business people were comfortable, not all that different from the way the Chamber of Commerce operated. Conceptually, there was a problem with this commission arrangement, since it combined the legislative (policy making) and the executive (administrative) functions into one body. It also had the weakness of rule by committee—the responsibilities of government were fragmented among the Commissioners rather than being commanded by a single person. On the other hand, it worked, at least in smaller cities. Over time this new form, the Commission form of city government, spread slowly across the country. In 1988, 3% of cities used this form, including Tulsa, Oklahoma, and Portland, Oregon.

Council/Manager: In 1910, Dayton, Ohio, suffered a disastrous flood, and again the local government could not respond. This time the city's business community was dominated by corporate people who were used to the model of a chief executive officer and a board of directors. They borrowed an idea first tried in 1908 in Staunton, VA, and hired a professional manager to run the city with policy guidance from the city council. The manager was hired by the council, and can be fired at any time by a majority of the council. This provided strong oversight of city administration, something which was lacking when the executive was elected. The council/manager form quickly spread to other large cities in Ohio and elsewhere, and became a common form of government for smaller cities and suburbs. It has the advantage of maintaining a formal distinction between the legislative and executive functions. In practice, however, especially in larger cities, it proved very difficult for the manager to run the city

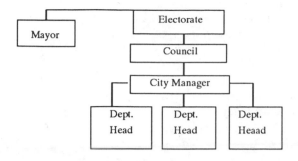

Figure 7.4. Council–Manager Structure

without being able to make policy. Faced with difficult choices, a manager following his or her professional conscience could risk being fired. The alternative was to avoid conflict, but serve ineffectively. In 1988, 50% of American cities used this form, including Dallas, Texas, San Diego, California, and Grand Rapids, Michigan.

Strong Mayor/Council: As the weaknesses of the Commission and manager/council forms became more apparent, and as the economic crisis of the Great Depression put particular stress on the larger cities, a fourth form of city government was developed. It was called the strong mayor/council form, and combined the strengths of the manager and weak mayor forms. The mayor was elected by the city at large (even if the council was elected by wards), and had sole responsibility for the management and administration of the city. The mayor prepared the budget and hired the department heads. The council approved the budget and made city ordinances and resolutions. The mayor could veto council actions (but the mayor's veto could be overridden). In effect, the strong mayor form combined the accountability of the manager form with the political and policy base of the weak mayor form. In 1988, 41% of American cities used this form, including Detroit, Michigan, San Francisco, California, and St. Paul, Minnesota.

Problem Solving and Decision Making

In cities the ultimate authority to make policy, to decide what should be done and how it should be done, rests in the hands of elected officials. This means that solving problems and making decisions is, in the end, a political issue involving conflict and compromise.

Problem Solving: Avoid Making Enemies

The first rule in a political environment is to avoid making enemies. It is almost a rule of thumb that people will remember any harm you do them ten times longer than any good, so avoid doing harm at almost any cost. This has a profound impact on the way problems are perceived in city government. Any problem lacking a clear consensus for its solution is automatically a difficult

problem. Elected officials use a variety of strategies to address such problems.

Occasionally, a politician will take an unpopular stand on an issue because of a deep **conviction** that a stand must be made. Like Martin Luther before the Diet of Worms, occasionally a politician might say *"Ich stehe hier, Ich kann nicht anders"* ("Here I stand, I can do no other"). And, like Martin Luther, they frequently find themselves excommunicated from the others as a result. For obvious reasons, most politicians strive mightily to find some other solution.

A common tactic is to **postpone** any action. Perhaps with more time the problem will solve itself. Or maybe it will go away. Certainly with the passage of time a number of alternative solutions will fall away, no longer workable in the time that remains. With fewer alternatives remaining after a delay, even though the problem might be more severe at least the alternatives will be more clearly differentiated. And perhaps, with fewer alternatives to choose from, a consensus might arise. The problem with this approach is that it does not often work as one might hope. Frequently, the alternatives which became unworkable were the less expensive and less disruptive ones. The passage of time can polarize the issue rather than muddling toward a consensus.

Another common tactic is to **defer to experts.** If the solution does not work, the blame can be shifted to the experts. If their advice does work, then one can take the credit for one's perspicacity in recognizing good advice when it was offered. And there is no denying that, for some problems, experts can use their specialized knowledge to produce a solution which no one had considered previously. But most of the interesting problems do not rise or fall on technical issues which experts control. Most of the interesting problems come from the clash of different values which every community embodies. For these problems, no outside expert can help.

The final approach is to **seek consensus.** As with postponement, one can eliminate options; the difference is that in consensus-seeking one tries to eliminate undesirable alternatives before more desirable ones become unworkable. Another technique is to carve out a compromise in which all sides get something (and, usually, no side gets everything they wanted). A skilled politician will try to work out a consensus before the public meeting, getting together with members of the various sides, sometimes on the phone, sometimes over coffee, sometimes at formal meetings, always probing for a workable compromise. The public meeting (whether a city council meeting, a commission hearing, or a special community meeting) can serve to publicly ratify what was arrived at privately. Sometimes the intended consensus fails to develop at the public meeting—maybe there was a miscalculation, or perhaps someone brought in some new information.

Making a Decision

Given that problems will have to be resolved in a political climate, there remain several other key issues for local government decision making.

One of the first questions to be resolved is the primary **role** of local government. What is the proper business of the city? Some would argue that the city should provide *only* the traditional services of streets, water and sewer, fire and police protection, and general administration (which may or may not include planning and zoning). Anything else, they argue, is either an inappropriate intrusion of the public sector or is more efficiently done by the business or nonprofit sectors. Others would expand the range of services to include parks and recreation, libraries, public transit, etc. They argue that cities must go beyond the bare minimum and enhance the quality of life for all. Others would include economic development programs, arguing that cities must actively promote and develop the employment base of their community. Finally, some see the city as a primary forum for arbitrating among conflicting interests in the community. The role of city government, they argue, is as much to foster a process of democracy as it is to provide tangible services. There is no single correct choice among these roles; in many respects, the process of making the choice is more important than which choice is made.

Once a city agrees on which services to supply, they then must decide **how much** of each service to supply. Take, for example, planning for a freeway through town. If the road is designed to carry the "average" flow of traffic, then it will be used beyond designed capacity about half the time. On the other hand, if the road were designed to meet "peak" demand there would be unused capacity most of the time. Public services are supported by tax dollars; over-supply of services generates tax bills which are larger than necessary. Under-supply of services makes people wait, and time spent waiting is called a "dead-weight loss"—nobody can make use of that time, it is a wasted opportunity. The trick is to find a balance between wasting city resources by providing more than is needed and wasting citizens' opportunities (in terms of time, stress, quality of life, etc.) by failing to provide enough.

Another part of the puzzle of service delivery is the **scale** at which it should be delivered. Providing a service city-wide may not meet the needs of the neighborhoods, while other services are not well-provided on a piecemeal basis. In the case of the arts, for example, an Art Institute cannot be located in each neighborhood. The cost would be too great, and the use of each facility would be too small. Yet a "central" Institute (no matter where it is located) will not flourish if the arts are not fostered in each of the neighborhoods. There are other examples of purely local services, such as garbage collection, which can easily be organized on a neighborhood basis. Police and fire protection, while closely tied to the neighborhood, need the support of a city-wide (and even regional) system for those occasions when the problem is more than the local unit can handle.

Besides the neighborhood/citywide issue of scale, there is also a question of the balance between the public and private sectors. To what extent is the city a public institution, to what extent a private venture? Early in American history, local government was an extension of local business. "Boosterism" advertised real estate and the downtown businesses as much as the city being boosted. Clearly, the fate of the city and of the businesses which provide employment for its citizens are intimately connected. In recent times, this has been expressed as **"public/private partnerships,"** mutually agreeable arrangements which are intended to provide public benefits and private gain simultaneously. For example, the city of Philadelphia entered into a partnership with a hotel chain which was building a major conference hotel in the heart of the city. The hotel chain got tax breaks and low-cost land, which made the project workable. The city got new jobs and a boost for downtown, and an equity partnership in the hotel. But the ghost of the political Machines haunts these arrangements; the public is generally suspicious of businesses which do "too well" with public money.

This fear of private involvement in public affairs is basically an issue of fairness. But how does a city decide what is fair? A business corporation knows what it is about; its purpose is to make a profit. The corporation then manages its resources to make as much profit as possible.[1] Knowing *what* to do is called **"effectiveness."** Doing it with as few resources as possible is called **"efficiency."** The purposes of a city are more diverse, and not as easily measured as corporate profit. Much of the debate in city affairs is about what should be done in the first place. It is entirely possible to do the wrong thing very efficiently. But people trained in business, which focuses on efficiency since it already knows what effect is desired, often criticize cities for being inefficient—for not operating like a business.

The fairness issue is further complicated by uncertainty, which implies a certain amount of risk. Some things are inherently unknowable, because they are not determined beforehand. A winning lottery number is inherently unknowable (at least, if the lottery is fair). Others could be known, if one had the wisdom and foresight to pick them out of the welter of apparently extraneous factors which surround an issue, but for all practical purposes one is rarely certain that all the relevant dimensions of an issue have been considered.

1. Actually, contemporary discussions of corporate responsibility recognize that the situation is more complicated than just maximizing profit. Returning a profit discharges the corporate responsibility to the equity shareholder; the corporation also has a responsibility to other stakeholders (employees, customers, the community) and may reasonably limit profit to meet its responsibilities to these other stakeholders. Nonetheless, all the discussions recognize that returning a profit, over the long run, is essential: Without profit, there will be no corporation.

Garret Hardin, in **"The Tragedy of the Commons,"** tells a tale which underscores the importance of incomplete knowledge (Hardin, 1968). In Medieval England, the yeoman farmers grazed their animals on a common field in the center of the village. Every farmer in the village had the right to graze all of his or her animals on this land, called the "Commons." In the sixteenth century, a technological advance in weaving began to destroy the Commons. A new type of loom permitted weavers, working in their homes, to produce high quality woolen fabric at a much greater rate than before. Yeoman farmers could weave wool from their own sheep at home and sell it for a good price in the export market, thus freeing themselves from subsistence farming. This encouraged farmers to graze increasingly larger flocks of sheep on the Commons. When the Commons was first established, most of the grazing was done by horses and cattle—cows and oxen—which nip the tips of the grass but leave the roots undisturbed. Sheep, on the other hand, eat the grass down to the roots; sheep pasture must be left fallow if it is to recover. The farmers, seeking the economic security of an outside income, overgrazed the Commons until it died. They lost their farming income as well as their weaving, since the draft animals lost their pasture along with the sheep.

There were probably few farmers who recognized the risks they (all) were running. But even supposing one of them recognized the danger before it was too late, what could s/he do? If one farmer refused to put more sheep on the Commons, it just left room for the others to put more on, and the self-sacrificing farmer would be left to face the coming crisis without the additional income that the last few sheep would have brought. Logic would only seem to push the farmers more quickly to their common doom.

The logic of such public choices has been called **"The Prisoner's Dilemma,"** after another story (Schelling, 1978). Suppose you are picked up and interrogated by the police. The detective informs you that they know you and your buddy have been burglarizing houses in the neighborhood, and they have enough evidence to send you both away for 3 years as it is. But they are particularly interested in closing the file on the job they suspect you two of having done last night. If you turn State's evidence and testify against your partner, you'll get off with 1 year (your partner will get 10 years). If you remain silent and your partner talks, the sentences will be reversed. If you both talk, then you'll probably go up for 7 years each.

What do you do? Suppose you can trust your buddy not to squeal on you. Then if you stay silent you will spend the next 3 years in prison, but if you talk you can walk out in 1 year. Suppose your buddy **does** talk. Then if you stay silent you will spend the next 10 years in prison, while if you talk you only get 7 years. Clearly, either way you come out ahead by talking—the rational choice is to betray your partner. Since your partner is also rational, you can expect that both of you will talk. The result is that you will both go to prison for 7 years instead of the 3 years you would have gotten had you not been so "rational." This information, however, does not help; no matter what your partner chooses to do, your self-interest is best served by talking.

The model which underlies the Prisoner's Dilemma explains a great number of apparently irrational choices. It explains why the farmers overgrazed the Commons. It explains why landlords allow their buildings to turn into slums (Davis & Whinston, 1961). It can explain why industries pollute watersheds and airsheds and why commuters persist in creating gridlock. It represents probably the single greatest challenge to making decisions in local government.

Local Government Coordination

The art of politics is to create a coalition from disparate interests; in a word, coordination. There are two major focuses of local government coordination, the internal constituency and the larger context of the other units of government.

Local Actors: Public Participation

Any action between two actors or two groups of actors automatically divides everyone else into three groups: Those positively affected, those negatively affected, and those unaffected (Dewey, 1927). On almost any issue, the vast majority of people will be unaffected. The "public" are all those people who are positively *or* negatively affected by the actions of some third party. Note that this definition implies that publics are **"polycentric."** There is not one public ("monolithic public"), or one public good, but a whole host of publics, each created by a different set of relationships. An individual may be now in one public, later in a different public. The art of politics is holding together a coalition of publics. In a sense, politics is the art of **creating** the public.

The people who hold these coalitions together are said to have **"power."** Their power is in proportion to the size of the coalition they can muster. In this sense, power is the ability to influence decisions that shape the future of the city. Some of these leaders are elected to office, some exert their influence through other means.

There is, in fact, a longstanding debate about the nature of political power in local communities. When scientists asked people, "Who influences the way public decisions

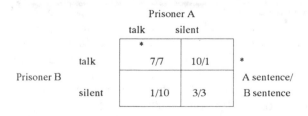

Figure 7.5. The Prisoner's Dilemma

are made in this community?'', they found a **"reputation-al elite,"** a few people whose names were mentioned repeatedly (Hunter, 1953). Some concluded that power was held by a local **"power elite"** composed mostly of the wealthy, the business leaders, and certain elected politicians (Mills, 1957). When others examined, instead, which people were actively involved in the public debates on a range of major local issues, they found a great number of people and little overlapping leadership—a **"pluralistic"** base of leaders (Dahl, 1961). While the research has not succeeded in reconciling these different findings, it appears that the everyday exercise of power is shared among a plurality of actors. Some actors, for example junior corporate executives performing community service, are particularly responsive to the interests of the reputational elite. These few do not need to be actively involved in the trenches; they send their lieutenants instead. At the same time, the popular perception of the power of the elite is perhaps overstated.

The opposite side of power elites is citizen participation, the sharing of power among the masses rather than concentrating it in the few. But, as Sherry Arnstein (1969) pointed out, there are many forms of citizen "participation." At its most cynical, the process can be little more than manipulating the masses into playing their part in a charade which has been scripted from the beginning. Arnstein uses the metaphor of a "ladder of citizen participation" and calls this rung **"nonparticipation."** It includes strategies such as outright manipulation ("You can have anything you'd like as long as it is what I am offering"), therapy ("What is wrong with you that you can't get behind this project?"), and informing ("Let me tell you what we are going to do"). A less manipulative, but still not empowering, rung on the ladder is called **tokenism.** This includes consultation ("This is what we want to do; will you go along with it?") and placation ("You can't have what you want; what will you take instead?"). The **full participation** rung includes strategies of partnership ("Let us reason together"), delegation ("In this specific area, you may choose as you see fit"), and full control ("The choice is yours"). Arnstein recognizes that full control is not the only authentic possibility: A community conditioned to non-participation will not be able to operate at the level of full control, and even the most empowered community will not wish to exercise full control over all matters. But she sees citizen control as the ideal type of citizen participation, the goal toward which all other forms point.

Others have pointed to some assumptions in Arnstein's work. Just as the "elite" are not a homogeneous power bloc, neither are the "have-nots." Arnstein's ladder is mono-dimensional, but community power is pluralistic. Nor does Arnstein's analysis discuss the roadblocks to participation—resistance to the redistribution of power, inadequate information to counter elite interpretations, and even simple inertia. In fact, it is not at all clear that the have-nots **should** want to participate.. From a rational, self-interested point of view, most of the public policy debates will not put bread on the table nor clothes on the children. Certainly the immediate return to the individual will almost never equal the cost in time and effort of getting involved. Further, the elite have spent a large part of their lives training themselves to deal with issues on an abstract level, and frequently are expert in the very issues under discussion. Is it worth it for the have-nots to train themselves to a similar level, given all the competing demands for their time? The great community organizer, Saul Alinsky, recognized the importance of this question when he advised community advocates **never** to go into a community unless they are invited in.

Regional Coordination

Any action taken by a city imposes constraints or offers opportunities to the surrounding cities and the countryside (counties, townships, and region). It will affect taxation policy, service provision, private ventures to the extent that the draw on public facilities (particularly true for theaters and nightclubs). Further, urbanization transforms the environment (air, water, climate, raw materials) and returns it into the surrounding environment (in the form of polluted air and water, garbage, etc.).

It is apparent, then, that local governments need to find some way to get along together, even as they compete for residents and industry. Cooperation may be economically more efficient, but the resulting loss of individual prerogatives could be costly in political power. Over the years, three approaches to regional coordination have been developed (Bollens & Schmandt, 1975).

The **centrist** approach coordinates by combining the units of government in a metropolitan area into one super-unit. Annexation is a centrist approach; so is consolidating the city and the county into a single unit of government, as has been done in Baton Rouge, LA, Nashville, TN, and Indianapolis, IN. The problem with the approach is that it does not necessarily do away with multiple municipalities, since usually it is the central city and the county which consolidate, leaving the suburbs standing off. Also, bigger is not necessarily better. When Indianapolis consolidated with Marion county and thus expanded its tax base, the minorities in the central city found that their political power was diluted and they had less say than before.

The **federationist** approach leaves the local units intact for local affairs, but creates an overarching unit for certain, specified functions which have metropolitan significance. Examples of this include the Metropolitan Council (Minneapolis/St. Paul, MN), the Metropolitan Service District (Portland, OR), the Comprehensive City/County Plan (Miami/Dade County) and the Metropolitan Toronto Federation. The federal approach can avoid some of the disadvantages of large size if it takes only those functions which require metropolitan coordination. The difficulty lies in deciding which are those problems.

The **polycentrist** approach avoids the pitfalls of large size by preserving all the local powers. On a case-by-case basis, local governments enter into contracts, with other units of government or with private suppliers to obtain what they cannot provide themselves. For example, Lakewood, CA, provides no services itself but contracts with surrounding cities, the county, and private suppliers for all of the services normally provided by a city. Many cities enter "joint powers" agreements, which is a contract to provide a common service for a specified period of time—an airport, perhaps, or a water district. Another common approach is a "mutual aid" agreement, by which local units agree to come to each other's assistance in the case of a fire or police emergency, for example. The polycentrist approach has the advantage of flexibility. It has the disadvantages of impermanence and fragmentation.

Summary

This chapter began with the question of how do you evaluate the skill with which a city is governed. The answer began with a review of the constraints within which local government must operate, constraints which are both legal and historical. The discussion then turned to the two key issues on which a local government will rise or fall: The skill with which decisions are made and issues resolved, and the level of empowerment which is fostered. Frequently these two issues conflict with each other. Issues are resolved through technical expertise and with an eye to efficiency. Empowerment is messy and inefficient and means letting the amateurs into the act. But the conflict is more apparent than real. Those local governments which are held up as models seem to have found a way to transcend this polarization and treat issue resolution as an exercise of empowerment, and empowerment as a process of making the community more expert in the exercise of its own affairs. And, to return to the original question, that is a standard to which local elected officials could be held accountable come election time.

Questions for Discussion

1. Would people in your city today subscribe to the Athenian Oath of Citizenship? Why not? In what ways are we better off (as "people of a city") than they were? In what ways are we diminished?
2. Obtain the charter for your city or town. What type of city is it? What form of government does it have? Who are the chartered officers, and what are their responsibilities?
3. Is there a "best" tactic for public problem-solving? Why or why not?
4. Build a case in favor of one of the four roles for local government. Are there other roles which the text does not consider?
5. What do you think is the proper relation of the city government to business interests?
6. How can you resolve or avoid a "Prisoner's Dilemma"? What changes in values/philosophy/worldview are required to implement your solution? What are the barriers to the changes you would wish to implement?
7. What could "the public good" mean within a polycentric definition of "public"?
8. How would you influence a city council decision if a "power elite" were in your city?
9. What is the source of political power in local government? What traits must a leader have, given these constraints? What would characterize a *good* leader in such a system?
10. Why should the average citizen get involved in local public issues?
11. In local governance, is bigger necessarily better?

Terms to Remember

Athenian Oath of Citizenship	mutual aid agreement
home-rule charter city	statutory city
weak mayor/council form	home-rule grant city
manager/council form	commission form
Machine politics	strong mayor/council form
Progressive movement	Reform movement
act on conviction	postponing a problem
seek consensus	defer to experts
peak vs. average demand	4 roles of local government
public/private partnerships	scale of service provision
effectiveness	equity
risk in decision-making	efficiency
prisoner's dilemma	incomplete knowledge
polycentric publics	tragedy of the commons
power	monolithic publics
reputational elite	power elite
ladder of citizen participation	pluralism
tokenism	non-participation
centrism	full participation
polycentrism	federationism
	joint powers agreement

References

Alinsky, Saul. (1971) Rules for Radicals. NY: Random House

Arnstein, Sherry. (1969) A ladder of citizen participation, Journal of the American Institute of Planners *35,* 216–224.

Banfield, Edward C. and James Q. Wilson. (1963) City Politics. Cambridge, MA: Harvard University Press.

Bollens, John C. and Henry J. Schmandt. (1975) The Metropolis, 3rd Ed. NY: Harper & Row.

Chudacoff, Howard P. (1975) The Evolution of American Urban Society. Englewood Cliffs, NJ: Prentice Hall.

Dahl, Robert A. (1961) Who Governs? New Haven: Yale University Press.

Davis, Otto A. and Andrew B. Whinston. (1961) The economics of urban renewal, Law and Contemporary Problems *26*, 105–117.

Dewey, John. (1927) The Public and Its Problems. NY: Holt.

Hunter, Floyd. (1953) Community Power Structure. Chapel Hill: University of North Carolina Press.

Lowi, Theodore. (1964) At the Pleasure of the Mayor. NY: Free Press.

Mills, C. Wright. (1956) The Power Elite. NY: Oxford University Press.

Schelling, Thomas C. (1978) Micromotives and Macrobehavior. NY: W. W. Norton & Co.

Talbot, A. (1969) The Mayor's Game. NY: Harper & Row.

Weeks, J. Devereux and Paul T. Hardy. (1984) The legal aspects of local government, in Small Cities and Counties: A Guide to Managing Services, J. Banovetz, ed. Washington, DC: ICMA.

8

Managing the City

The Master said, ''Guide them by edicts, keep them in line with punishments, and the common people will stay out of trouble but will have no sense of shame. Guide them by virtue, keep them in line with the rites, and they will, besides having a sense of shame, reform themselves.

Confucius
The Analects

Infrastructure Repair (H. Roger Smith)

95

Public Employment and the Bureaucracy

"Bureaucracy" comes from two words—*bureau* and *kratos*. *Kratos* comes from Greek and means "power" or "strength," and is found in words like "democracy" (rule by the *demos*), "aristocracy" (rule by the *aristos*), and "technocracy" (rule by *tekne*). *Bureau* comes from French, and means "writing desk" or "chest of drawers." So, "bureaucracy" means "rule by desks"— or, in modern idiom, "rule by pencil-pushers."

Bureaucracy takes its name from the administration of government under Louis XIV of France. While Louis was away at Versailles, keeping the nobles at court with him and away from the administration of his government, he left behind in Paris an army of functionaries to manage the everyday affairs of France. When people came to do business or plead a cause, they found themselves addressing not the decision-makers (the members of the Court, who were in Versailles), but nameless clerks who took copious notes at their desks and sent memos back to Versailles. The decision, made at a distance, was again committed to paper and returned to Paris where it was delivered by another clerk at another desk. It did not take the Parisians long to dub this a "bureau-cracy."

Yet for all of its drawbacks, bureaucracy is a reasonable response to complexity (Weber, 1946). The usual examples of bureaucracy are the Federal government ("a bunch of bureaucrats") and the Army ("there are three ways to do anything—the right way, the wrong way, and the Army way"). For all their failures, the Federal bureaucracies did build the TVA, extend electricity to rural America, put a man on the moon, and tie the nation together with interstate highways. Nor is bureaucracy synonymous with government: IBM, General Electric, and General Motors are very successful bureaucracies. So is the Catholic Church (which preceded Louis XIV's system by many centuries).

A bureaucracy—whether or not it is effective—has three characteristic elements: **compartmentalization, hierarchy, and policy.**

In order to deal with complexity, a bureaucratic organization is broken into smaller units, each responsible for one (and, ideally, only one) function. In this way, everything that must be done is the clear responsibility of one person or group of people—everything has its own place, or compartment, or "bureau."

While separating functions into bureaus establishes responsibility, it does not provide coordination. So a cadre of managers are designated to coordinate the activity of several bureaus. If the organization is complex enough, no single manager will be able to coordinate all the bureaus ("span of command" is usually limited to no more than 10 people or functions), so another cadre of managers will coordinate the coordinators, and so on until there is an "executive" cabinet of manageable size who, in turn, advise the chief executive. This is the classical model of a "hierarchical" organization (the term is taken from the organization of the Catholic Church). In a hierarchy, each person reports to one and only one person; information is passed up the chain of command and orders are passed down.

If the hierarchy is to coordinate the activities below it, and if the managers are to have confidence that their desires are being met as they intended, activities must be carried out in "standard" form. Information must be processed into standard reports which can be compared across functions; actions must be performed in a standard fashion which is known to produce a desired result. A set of rules—"policy"—are developed which enunciate the standard expectations of the organization.

Ethics and the Public Sector

While there are a great many similarities between private-sector and public bureaucracies, there are several key differences. One of them is the values which each embody.

An investor-owned organization exists, first, to make a profit. While a private corporation can (and should) do a lot more than simply turn a profit, if it is not profitable it will not survive. Private corporations will shift their emphasis or even leave a business entirely if they cannot make a profit at it. Ford Motor Company, synonymous with automobile manufacture, now derives a major part of its profit from aerospace and investment activities. The 3M Corporation, once called Minnesota Mining and Manufacturing, is no longer in the mining business.

A public organization, especially a government, exists, first, to serve the public good. Whatever else they do, cities must provide common services for their residents and must protect the common welfare. While they can (and should) manage their affairs as efficiently as possible, they must above all secure the life, liberty, and opportunities of those within their domain—even at a net loss, if need be.

This has implications for the rules of behavior which public and private bureaucrats will follow. No one is ever encouraged to behave unethically, whether in private, non-profit, or government service. But in private organizations, discipline is maintained through profit—what is not profitable will be divested, eventually if not immediately. Employees may do anything that is not illegal or unethical in order to return a profit. In the public sector, discipline is maintained through public confidence—since the "public good" is not directly measurable, public confidence that their good is being served must serve as its proxy. This is a very fragile commodity, so public employees must do nothing which might weaken it. People in the public sector must not only avoid illegal or unethical activity, they must avoid *even the appearance* of impropriety.

For example, it is common in business to exchange gifts or to offer "incentives" to preferred customers. A vendor might offer to fly a buyer (and his/her spouse) to a trade meeting, say in San Francisco, to see the company's latest products and to pay the buyer's expenses while s/he is there. This is considered an appropriate business practice. But a public employee, faced with a similar offer, must refuse it and attend the trade meeting at his/her department's expense. This difference between public and private ethics was highlighted in the Reagan administration. A great number of his appointees were drawn from the corporate world, and had little government experience. It was not that they were dishonest (although in some cases the Court found that they were) as much as it was that they failed to appreciate that different rules of behavior were in play. The result was the infamous "sleaze factor."

Civil Service

The differences between the public and private sector are also reflected in the rules of employment. In the days of the Machine politics, one of the ways a Boss could reward a lieutenant for services rendered was to put him (or her) on the public payroll. When one party wrestled control of the city from another, the old employees were fired so their jobs could be given as rewards to those who worked for the new power holders.

One of the first reforms to city government was to insulate city employees from political favoritism. This system, called the "civil service," was styled after earlier reforms of the federal system. Under civil service rules, the hiring and firing of most local government employees are strictly regulated. A vacant position must be advertised publicly and widely, and the qualifications for the position must be determined beforehand. An applicant's qualifications are determined in some formal fashion—usually a combination of experience (determined by the resume) and knowledge (determined by a written or oral examination, and often both). The applicants are ranked by their performance on the formal examinations, and usually the top few are interviewed for the position. This screening system was designed to eliminate favoritism in the hiring process.

Once an employee completes a probationary period of employment, s/he may then be fired only "for cause." It is not easy to establish that there is a justifiable cause for firing someone: S/He must be given a verbal warning first. If the failing recurs, a written warning is given, along with specific steps which can be taken to remedy the situation. If the failing persists, the employee is notified and given a limited time in which to overcome the problem. Only if the problem is still not resolved may the employee then be fired.

Not all public employees are civil service employees. The system recognizes that a new chief executive needs to bring some trusted advisors with her/him. The system could not work if a chief executive (be it a mayor, a city manager, or a city administrator) had to set up the office

and depend on the advisors to the former executive. The civil service regulation allows a limited number of managerial positions to be designated as "exempt"—appointed positions which are exempt from the usual civil service procedures.

Service Delivery

It is through the delivery of local services that most people interact with the management of a city. Most of the time, the "city" is invisible to its residents. But when the trash is not collected, or the streets crumble into one massive pothole, or the water suddenly runs a muddy orange—then you call city hall.

Issues

There are three major issues in the provision of city services: Determining how much of what service to provide, providing it as efficiently as possible, and paying for the services which are provided.

Probably the single most vexing problem of service management is the issue of "coverage." How much of which services should the city provide? The answer to the question has four parts.

In the first place, it is not self-evident that a city should supply *any* services. There is a difference between making the decision to provide services and the actual production of those services. Choosing among alternative bundles of services—decision-making—is an essential role of the city, usually part of the policy-making of the city council. But it is possible for some other agency or business to implement the decision, to actually supply the intended service. The City of Lakewood, California, for instance, contracts for all of its services from surrounding governments (especially the county) and from private contractors (like garbage haulers). This frees the city from having to purchase the initial capital equipment (garbage trucks, sewage treatment plants, etc.) and gives the city the flexibility to "rent" the latest techniques as they become available without being locked into the previous technology. Of course, the suppliers of the service must charge Lakewood for administrative and overhead costs, and private suppliers must include a reasonable profit, so the unit-cost might be a little higher than what it would cost Lakewood to provide the service itself. But as long as there is competition among suppliers, competition will keep the "overhead" charges to a minimum. Lakewood also surrenders some of the control of service provision during the life of the contract. The contract must be carefully written to specify all of the performance criteria which must be met, because the contractor is under no obligation to provide (at no additional cost) anything that was not agreed beforehand.

Whether a city decides to provide a service itself or to contract out for it, the scale of the service must also be determined. The larger the project, the more "economies of scale'' can be realized. Just as large department stores can purchase (and sell) goods at a volume discount, so many city services can be more efficiently (less expensively) delivered as more households or neighborhoods are served. A police dispatcher can serve a large precinct as well as a small one; a city bus line is less expensive to run when the seats are full than when they are half-empty. It is, however, more difficult to individualize service at large scales. While a single dispatcher may serve a large precinct, the service in the smaller precinct is likely to be more personal. While full busses are more efficient, they are perhaps less comfortable. Larger systems generally require more standardization, which in turn means less flexibility and variety of choices.

Third, the decision to provide a service must balance current need and future capacity. If at all possible, one wants to provide enough surplus capacity to meet future growth and satisfy changes in demand (assuming, of course, that the city *is* growing). But who will pay for the surplus? Current users have no interest in paying for what they do not use so that someone maybe someday might use it. Future new users are not around to pay for it today. The result is usually some sort of compromise—less future capacity than might be desirable, but perhaps a bit more than would be allowed just for increased demand from current users.

Not only is future capacity slighted, it turns out that current demand is usually not fully met. Consider the freeway as an example. If the downtown freeway were designed to carry *all* of the current demand, it would have to be wide enough to move all the traffic through at fifty-five miles an hour at 5 P.M. on Friday afternoon of Memorial Day Weekend (traditionally the highest volume traffic hour of the year). A freeway that wide would be virtually empty at 4 A.M almost any night of the year. Almost any other time of the year, there would be a significant amount of unused capacity. Unused capacity is a wasted resource, and to make matters worse it costs a lot of money to provide it. In a very few circumstances, one might decide to meet peak demand, usually in life-and-death circumstances. A hospital emergency room is usually designed to handle the largest flow of critical cases that can be anticipated (barring a disaster); a fire protection plan is designed to handle the worst outbreak of fires.

Most of the time, one plans for less than peak demand; the problem is to decide how much "less" is still enough. It has to be greater than "average" demand. By definition, meeting the average demand for service will result in inadequate capacity half of the time. Even the Chicago and Los Angeles freeways are not so under-designed (although sometimes it seems that way). When a service system is under-designed, it forces the users to line up— "queuing," as the British call it. The line at a movie theater, a rush-hour traffic jam, the wait at the county welfare office are all examples of queuing. The problem with queuing is that it is a "deadweight loss" (Stokey & Zeck-

hauser, 1978). In a normal business transaction, one person's loss is another's gain—the money I pay for a loaf of bread is the shopkeeper's gain (part profit, part expenses). But no one gains from the time lost in queuing. The time spent waiting in the theater line can be used neither by me nor by the theater owner. Providing less than peak capacity creates deadweight losses; providing more than average demand creates unused capacity. Neither is desirable.

There is no rule-of-thumb for balancing all these issues of coverage. But there are some general principles to apply. Areawide service delivery is called for when the scope of the project or the expense of the project exceeds local capacity. For example, air and water pollution, while aggravated by local behavior, are rarely purely local issues. Service should be delivered to an entire district (a neighborhood, the city, or a region) when the cost of the service is related to spatial coverage. For example, a sewer system or a TV cable system are least expensive when a single trunk line serves as many installations as possible. Service should be delivered on an individual-by-individual basis when the cost of the service is related to the volume of service output rather than to spatial saturation. For example, public housing need not be concentrated in any one area but can be delivered effectively on a case-by-case basis. In any event, whenever possible local decision-making should be retained, even if the actual production of the service is city-wide or even regional.

A second issue central to local government service delivery is "productivity." Productivity is the measure of value produced by labor. In business, it is the price of goods divided by hours of labor to produce them. There are two problems managers of local government face as they try to increase the productivity of their organizations: assessment and labor enhancement.

Any product can, of course, be produced at different levels of quality. Presumably, a $60 sweater is of higher quality than a $25 sweater. It is difficult to assess the productivity of local government since so many of the goods and services provided by local government have no market price. What is the value of repairing a pothole? Of patrolling a neighborhood? Of waiting for a fire to break out? The streets get fixed, the police patrol the neighborhood, the fire department stands ready; but in the absence of a pricing mechanism it is very difficult to determine how *well* each of those tasks is being performed. The result is an emphasis on resources and process which are used ("inputs"), rather than results achieved ("outcomes"). It is entirely possible to go "by the book" without wasting any resources (to be "efficient," if you will) and completely fail to achieve an overall goal (to be "efficiently unproductive," as it were). The road crew could patch all the potholes while overlooking the rotting structure of a key bridge; the firefighters could put out all the fires while ignoring fire safety and prevention.

The second issue, enhancing the productivity of available labor, has two components, automation and motivation.

If the effort of producing a good or a service can be shifted from people to machines, then by definition the remaining people will be working more productively. The same amount of goods or services would be produced with less labor, since capital (the machines) has taken over some of the work of producing the goods or services. One person operating a backhoe, for example, can dig a much longer trench for a sewer line in one hour than one person working with a pick and shovel; one secretary working on a wordprocessor can produce many more public hearing notices in an hour than a secretary working on a typewriter. Sometimes automation replaces workers; more often, automation is introduced slowly and allows the work accomplished to expand without increasing the number of workers. Unfortunately, many city services do not lend themselves to automation. The police and fire dispatch and record-keeping functions may be automated, but it still requires human judgment on the scene to fight the fire or apprehend the criminal. Sometimes automation, while increasing "efficiency" and lowering costs, can result in less service. Police patrols were "automated" when the police officers on the beat were replaced by cars on patrol, and the precincts saved money, but community relations and neighborhood security were also lessened.

Even goods and services which cannot be automated can be produced more productively if the producers are motivated. Employees who are satisfied with their working conditions (Follett, 1941; McGregor, 1960) and who feel they are producing something worthwhile (Drucker, 1974; Peters & Waterman, 1982) work more productively. The problems of managing productive working conditions are basically the same as those in any organization, although senior managers will have to deal with political constraints which might not be present elsewhere. The thornier issue is motivating workers to produce *results,* when so much of public sector work does not produce measurable results and when multiple goals are being served simultaneously. It is difficult to reward employees for achieving results when it is not clear what the "results" should be, nor how well the results were achieved.

The third issue in local government service delivery is finance. How should services be funded? Traditionally, the cost of services has been spread among all the residents of the city through the "general fund" of a city. Much of police and fire service are provided this way. It is also possible to fund services through specific grants, a technique popular with Federal housing programs in the 1960's and 1970's. Finally, some services are funded through fees charged for the use of the service. Operation of public recreation facilities such as golf courses and swimming pools are often funded in this way.

Each method has its problems. The general fund is largely fed by tax revenues; but since there has been a "tax revolt" across the land, many local governments are restricted in how much they can raise from taxes. Grants are usually made by the State or Federal governments (private foundations, a third source, have minuscule resources compared to the other two). They also get their funds from taxation and are seeking ways to cut their expenses, and giving money away is an easy target for trimming. Fees have the advantage of tying payment to services received and could even introduce some market-like accountability into public service delivery; but fees will likely exclude people with limited income, the very people who most need public services.

Today cities are experimenting with a variety of "nontraditional" methods of funding their activities. The experiments include public/private partnerships, where the city takes an equity position in a private project in return for special services. For example, in Philadelphia, the city has taken a (small) partial ownership in a downtown hotel in return for special street and utility improvements which the city provided during construction. Other cities are taking a page from the nonprofit sector, and developing sophisticated volunteer systems to maintain neighborhood parks or provide crossing guards for school children. None of these experiments has developed yet into a major source of city funding.

Common Services

Cities traditionally provide a wide variety of services to their residents, although each city will have its own twist on how it is done and will likely provide at least a few services not listed here.

Streets are probably the oldest city service. Even before there was a bucket brigade to fight fires, there was a crossroads along which the first residents settled. The primary purpose of the street system is transportation of goods and people. The automobile has certainly helped to meet this need. But the contemporary emphasis on the automobile to the exclusion of other transportation modes causes problems. The automobile is an intensive use of resources: As such as 30% of a city's land can be devoted to the automobile and its service (streets and driveways, parking, gas stations and repair shops, etc.). The automobile is a major contributor to air pollution and a major consumer of fossil fuel. The capital investment in streets can be enormous, both in the cost of construction (a two-lane blacktop road will cost over $300,000 a mile, not counting drainage and other site improvements) and in repairs (at least $50,000 a mile for resurfacing). The biggest problem with streets is congestion, but widening the roads and providing more parking only aggravates the problem. Finding more parking and more traffic lanes, drivers who were discouraged by the previous congestion will return in large numbers. The solution, if there is one, lies in a balance between the auto, mass transit, and walking.

In America, fire protection is almost as ancient a city service as streets. In pre-Columbian Europe, "urban renewal" occurred when the great cities were burned to the ground. London was rebuilt thanks to a fire in 1189. Colonial Boston had an ordinance requiring that every household must keep by the door a bucket filled with water. When the fire alarm was sounded, everyone grabbed their bucket and formed a bucket brigade from the town well to the fire. Modern firefighting is qualitatively different in large cities and small towns and residential suburbs. Fire departments in large cities must be trained to fight fires in tall buildings which cannot be reached by ladders (some even have helicopters for firefighting), and to fight fires in factories and warehouses which contain hazardous chemicals and chemicals which become toxic when heated. It is a full-time job for professionals. Many small towns and even some residential suburbs can provide fire protection with only a volunteer force, or a combination of volunteer and professional firefighters. Fire protection is probably the "most local" of all the city services. The local government is most familiar with its own needs and the service is easily staffed by locals, whether professionals, volunteers, or by contracted service.

The first major public waterworks in America was built in Philadelphia in 1793. Water was not piped to the poorer neighborhoods, since they could not afford to pay for it and continued to rely on local wells. Public water systems became more frequent as scientists began to establish the link between water and disease (in ancient times, it was held that diseases were transmitted through "humors" on the air; water was not seen as a vector of infection), especially the epidemics of typhus and cholera. City wells, contaminated with human and animal waste which was simply emptied onto the ground, were identified as a major source of disease. Since water piped into the city had to be removed, it was an easy step to make the waste water also serve as the sanitation system. Today central cities usually own and operate their own water and sewer system. Suburbs usually depend initially on wells, which in time become contaminated with the by-products of their own growth and the growth of surrounding communities. When that happens, they usually switch over (at no little expense) to the central city's system or build their own. Many suburbs also initially used septic systems to treat the waste water drawn from the wells. As these systems age and as more of them are put on the land, eventually they contaminate the surrounding water system. Central sewage systems may alleviate the problem locally, but if untreated or minimally treated sewage is dumped into nearby rivers it will contaminate the water systems downstream. There are Federal laws which are attempting to eliminate this (and other) contamination of waterways.

Another piece of the waste removal puzzle is garbage disposal. Garbage may be collected by the city or by private collectors, and each has its merits. The current concern is with disposal of what is collected. In 1988, a garbage scow from New York City spent almost six months at sea trying to find some place to unload its cargo. Everywhere, suitable sites for dumps are becoming scarce as environmental protection authorities are setting stringent requirements for soil and groundwater protection. Incineration pollutes the air, and the remaining ash is concentrates toxins. Recycling materials at the dump is not cost-effective, and recycling at the source (whether a household or a business) is considered burdensome.

The first salaried police officer was hired in Boston in 1838. Prior to that, citizen "night patrols" provided some semblance of public safety. The police force are the most visible public personnel in a city, and crime is frequently listed as the most important social problem. The police serve both the criminal justice system and a variety of miscellaneous services like traffic control, parking enforcement, funeral escorts, and safety education. The administration of a police department has traditionally been a local function, but enforcement frequently spills over into other communities (criminals have a way of ignoring municipal boundary lines). In fact, there are significant scale economies which can be realized areawide in functions such as communications, record-keeping, training, and laboratory facilities.

The provision of recreation as a public responsibility is a relatively recent addition to city services. The first public park was New York City's Central Park, designed by Frederick Law Olmstead and Calvert Vaux in 1858. As cities grew (in 1790, there were only 3 cities with more than 25,000 people; by 1860 there were 35 and 1880 there were 77—and New York was over 1 million!) more land was urbanized and less land was available for recreation. While neighborhood parks may be primarily local, large parks tend to serve an entire region. The States began to offer grants so cities could afford to construct large recreation areas, and now parks are maintained at the Federal, State, and local levels.

Housing, while primarily the domain of the private market, is increasingly becoming a local government service. One of the innovations of Roosevelt's New Deal was the entry of government into the provision of low income housing. Over the years, the Federal government has experimented with direct provision of housing, both by the Federal and by local government (the infamous "housing projects" of the 1950's and 1960's), with subsidies to private developers for the construction of low income rental housing ("Section 236" housing), and with grants to local government to write down the cost of renting market-rate housing to low-income households ("Section 8" housing). None of the schemes has been completely satisfactory. Part of the problem is that these subsidies are paid (through taxes) by working- and middle-class taxpayers, who have complained if they felt the poor were living as well as they were. As a nation, we are deeply ambivalent about the treatment of poor people. Part of the problem is that concentrating the poor into one or a few areas increases the strain on other service delivery systems. Part of the problem lies among the poor themselves, with that portion of them who abuse the help that is offered. In any event, when the poor are not housed, they find places to live in the city anyhow, as the homelessness problems of the 1980's demonstrated.

There are a variety of other services which cities provide, and some which are central to city life but are not provided by the city. Schools and libraries are examples of this latter group. Public education is *not* a responsibility of the municipalities, although it is clearly a significant factor in the quality of city life. Public schools are independent of the municipality and are governed by their own boards. Public education came from a mid-nineteenth century reform movement which focused on the civic and cultural enlightenment of the poor and working classes. Compulsory school attendance was legislated in the 1870s and 1880s. Later reforms focused on increased efficiency, including graded schools, centralized policy making, standardized curriculum, and vocational programs (an outgrowth of the arts and crafts movement of the 1920s and industrial trade training). Prior to the public education system, and continuing parallel to it since then, have been the private schools—the upper-class boarding schools, the church-affiliated middle-class and working-class schools, and the adult outreach programs of a variety of social service agencies.

The library movement in this country began in the last half of the nineteenth century as a natural outgrowth of universal literacy. In the beginning, libraries were private, subscription clubs. Late in the nineteenth century, Andrew Carnegie endowed public libraries all over the country and established the tradition of free and public libraries. Most cities either operate a library of their own or subscribe to an independent (often regional) library system. Modern libraries see themselves as community centers for information, more than as a repository for books. They now stock films, records, videotapes, and computer software; they loan audio and video recorders; and they provide meeting space for lectures and community groups.

Infrastructure Problems

A particularly difficult, and increasingly significant, problem of cities is infrastructure maintenance. "Infrastructure" is the accumulated capital investment in a city—the roads and the sewers and waterlines under them, sewage treatment plants and water towers, bridges and highway overpasses, and streetlights. Most of the time we take the infrastructure for granted. But when a city well becomes contaminated and a new one must be drilled, when a highway bridge collapses and seven people are killed, when an arterial road erupts in springtime potholes

that bend rims and snap axles—then the importance of city infrastructure becomes clear.

Most of the city's budget goes to current operations (more than 70%) and only a relatively small amount to capital projects (just over 15%). But these small outlays, over time, build to a considerable value—and a considerable expense. There are three central issues in the provision of city infrastructure: maintenance, timing, and budgeting.

The capital cost of a major infrastructure component is high; but the maintenance and operating costs, over the life of the project, can come close to the construction cost. A $300,000 stretch of highway will cost another $50,000 for resurfacing, $8,000 for sealing (which should be done 5 times in the life of the road), plus the annual expense for repairing potholes as they appear. In other words, the decision to invest in a capital improvement carry with it not only the cost of the improvement but the certainty that, over time and especially at certain key times further expenses will be incurred.

Timing is also an issue with capital projects. Most capital projects are "lumpy": they cannot be phased in a little at a time as needed, but must be provided in hunks which will have to work for a significant time to come. Normally, one cannot add an office or two onto city hall every year or so as the need arises. Instead, one shoehorns people into janitor's closets until every available nook is filled, then an annex is built which is larger than needed. For awhile, there is surplus space until, gradually, the operation grows into all the usable space. If one waits too long to add new infrastructure, the overuse of existing facilities will lead to inefficiency, both because of the strain it puts on individual behavior and because of the strain it puts on the physical capital itself. If one adds new infrastructure prematurely, the surplus capacity will be wasted.

The third issue is budgeting. City budgets are set in a political environment. Unlike corporate managers who are evaluated on a single, quantifiable basis (profit) by stockholders who voluntarily invest in the company, city managers and city councils are evaluated on a complex, qualitative basis (public good) by taxpayers who are legally constrained to contribute every year to the public purse. In such an environment it is easy to defer maintenance (or settle for lesser maintenance). While this plays well at the next election, it also leads to premature replacement of the infrastructure. Any capital project has a "life expectancy," a period of time beyond which one can reasonably expect to replace it. A city should also have a "sinking fund," a "savings account" for replacing the infrastructure as it ages beyond repair. When money is short, this fund is easily raided and rarely replenished. Again, short-run concerns, especially public concerns over taxation, too easily outweigh fiscal prudence.

Any capital project carries operating, maintenance, and replacement expenses, in addition to the cost of construction. Like any industry, cities must reinvest in "factories and equipment" if they are to remain productive.

Finance and Budget

Revenue		Expenditures (Functional)	
Grants	24.3%	Operations	
Property Tax	15.9	Police	9.0
Sales Tax	9.4	Fire	4.9
Income Tax	7.0	Streets & Sewer	15.1
Fees & Licenses	21.1	Water System	6.9
Revenue	17.9	Parks & Recreation	3.6
Investments	4.4	Housing & Development	3.6
		Transit System	2.4
		Libraries, Airports, etc.	19.1
Expenditures (Categorical)		Other Revenue Business	11.8
Current Operations	70.9%	Administration	
Capital Outlay	15.3	General Administration	5.4
Intergovernmental	2.4	Interest on debt	10.6
Other	11.4	Other	10.6
* * * *		Insurance Trust Expense	3.4
Salaries & Wages	34.3%		

Figure 8.1. Local Government Revenue and Expenditures, 1985. *Source*: *Statistical Abstracts of the United States, 1988*

Financing the Public Interest

Cities derive their revenue from a variety of sources and expend them for a range of purposes. Taxes have traditionally been the major source of revenue for cities.

There are several sorts of taxes which cities use. The most common one is the property tax. Dating back to Colonial times, it is based on the belief that cities provide service primarily tied to property (and therefore which increase the value of the property), and that property owners are particularly able to pay for those services. Currently, commercial and industrial property is taxed at a higher rate than residential, and investment residential property is taxed more highly than owner-occupied property. Many cities are also authorized by the State to levy a sales tax. There are several reasons for this. It can be argued that ownership of residential property is no longer a major source of wealth, as it was in agricultural times. A sales tax, since it is based on consumable income, may be a better way to draw money from those who can afford it. In addition, if a city attracts many people from beyond its boundaries (whether for work or play), they can enjoy a city's services without paying for them. A sales tax is one way of drawing revenue from tourists and commuters. If there are a great number of commuters, some cities have even won the right to impose a flat tax on income. In

1985, about 1/3 of the average city's revenue came from taxation.

Grants constitute a second major source of revenue (over 24% in 1985). Both the State and the Federal government make grants to cities, and occasionally private foundations will, too. Some State and Federal grants (called "entitlements") represent payments from those units to meet obligations imposed on the cities. For example, most states share highway funds with the cities to help maintain the arterial streets within city boundaries. Other grants (called "categorical") are given for specific projects, such as a low-income housing project or a bridge renovation.

A growing source of city revenue is from fees (21% in 1985). There are a variety of fees which cities levy, from park and pool passes to parking meters. In addition, cities sell licenses for animals and permits for construction. And, finally, cities levy fines for failing to pay appropriate fees or licenses. As taxpayers vote against additional levies and the State and Federal government find their purses equally pinched, cities are finding more ways to charge for what they used to give away.

Cities are also learning to operate in a more businesslike manner. They are being careful to invest available funds in interest-bearing accounts, for example. Large amounts of money, even if invested for only a week, can return a substantial sum of money. And cities are running "businesses" which generate their own revenues—water, sewer and utilities being common ones.

Cities may also borrow money. Although this does not generate additional funds (in fact, it will cost something), in the short run it provides "new" money. There are three major types of borrowing which cities use. "General obligation" (GO) bonds pledge the faith and good will of the city to repay them. In other words, the city promises to use its tax revenues to pay back the bonds. If current revenues are inadequate, the city will have to raise its tax rates. "Revenue" bonds pledge the revenue produced by the project they fund to repay the bond. Should the project fail to produce the expected revenue, the bondholders have no recourse to the city's tax base. Revenue bonds are commonly used for water and sewer projects. A third, "tax increment financing" (TIF), is a type of general obligation bond. The city uses the funds from the bond to redevelop a district and is permitted to reserve the increased taxes from improved property values to pay off the bond. In effect, the city is speculating on the increased values it expects will result from the project. However, should the project fail to perform as predicted, the city is liable to repay the bond from the rest of its tax base. There is no limit on the amount of revenue bonds a city may float. Cities are generally limited, however, in how much general obligation debt they may incur. In Minnesota, the debt limit for cities is 6.6% of total assessed value in outstanding general obligation debt (including TIF bonds).

Although every city is unique in the services it provides and the way it structures its budget, there are also some common patterns in the way cities spend their revenue. Larger cities tend to spend more of their resources on basic services like fire and police protection and park maintenance. Central cities spend more of their budgets on operations and on social programs, while suburbs are building the infrastructure which the core cities already have in place. Because of the heavy capital investment program, suburbs tend to spend more per capita than the core city. Although tax *rates* are often higher in the central city, it is more densely populated (so the tax *per person* is lower), and the value of housing in the suburbs is frequently higher.

The Budget

The budget serves two purposes, planning and control. As a tool of control, it helps the city manage its resources and control its costs. As a planning tool it is the embodiment of the council's determination of the city's objectives and their allocation of resources to achieve them.

The control function of a city's budget is the most familiar. Like a household budget, it sets annual targets and tracks the "actual" versus "budgeted" expenditures and revenues over the course of the year. In the case of a city, there are generally several funds which must be accounted separately (this is called "fund accounting"). A city budget will commonly include accounts for:

General Fund (the city's all-purpose checkbook)

Special Revenue funds (each categorical grant usually requires separate accounting of its own funds)

Capital Projects fund (for the big-ticket, long-lived projects the city is planning)

Debt Service fund (for paying the bonds which were floated for those capital projects)

Special Assessment funds (when property is assessed for road or sewer replacement, or if businesses are assessed for a common public parking ramp, the city must demonstrate in each case that the revenue from the assessment was used for the assigned purpose).

Within each fund there will be a series of items among which the revenue in the fund is distributed. These items, called "line-items," usually include

personal services (wages, salaries, fringe benefits and other "add-on" personnel costs)

supplies (office and operating supplies, including small tools and repair supplies—generally, the kind of equipment which is either low-cost or will be consumed in the year)

services and charges (consultants, telephone, transportation, rentals, utilities, etc.)

capital expense (current year's share of the cost of long-lived items, such as automobiles and trucks)

debt service (current year's share of the interest paid for purchasing capital assets)

Since the city is a creature of the State, and the State can be held responsible for debts which a city incurs but cannot repay, cities are generally required to file their budgets annually with the State. The State of Minnesota in 1983 published a "Uniform Chart of Accounts" which cities must follow in filing their budgets. Minnesota's chart of accounts is a line-item budget which includes the previous year's performance and the current year's estimates.

There *are* other types of budgets than line-item budgets. Beside the desire to control costs (which underlies the line-item budget) there is also the need for guidance in allocating resources (Key, 1940). The key question for these other approaches is not how to stay within the resources allocated, but how to decide how much resources should be allocated. In the best of all possible worlds, perhaps every program could be funded to the full extent necessary; but in practice there are never enough resources to go all the way around. This is a difficult problem to resolve analytically—the intrinsic merit of each program or project must be determined, and then some way must be found to compare the different programs in order to divide the available resources among them. The budget director must determine not only how much it should cost, for example, to inspect 100 building sites and to patrol one neighborhood, but then must balance building inspection against neighborhood patrol to decide how much of each can be funded.

"Performance budgeting" focuses on the intrinsic merit of programs, comparing the work produced to the cost of producing it. This results in a "unit cost" calculation. Unit costs can be compared over time for the same program to determine how efficiently it is being managed, and similar programs might even be compared. Performance budgeting, however, is not particularly suited for comparisons across programs, since the meanings of "unit" will differ. "Zero-based" budgets try to extend performance budgeting by comparing the efficiency of alternative ways to perform the work and to build in some cross-program comparisons. These two are management tools, focusing on the efficiency of the work which is performed. The next two are planning tools, focusing on how well the program achieve benefits which have been targeted by the policymakers. "Program" budgeting focuses on the goals to be achieved (rather than the work performed), and calculates the ratio of benefits from a program to the cost of getting it. This results in a "rate of return" calculation. As with performance budgeting, this is well suited for monitoring changes in program performance, but is not particularly suited for comparisons of different programs. "Planning/Programming/Budgeting

Type of Budget	Measures Used	Criterion
Line-item Budget	Expenditures	Economy
Performance Budget	Unit Cost	Efficiency
Zero-Base Budgeting	Alternate Unit Costs	Efficiency
Program Budget	Rate of Return	Effectiveness
Program-Planning-Budgeting-System	Alternate Rates of Return	Effectiveness

Figure 8.2. Summary of Types of Municipal Budgets

System'' (PPBS) compares the rate of return of alternative methods of achieving the desired benefits, and permits some cross-program comparison (Lehan, 1981).

Why have States relied on line-item budgets, even though scholars have expressed dissatisfaction with line-item budgets since at least 1940? There are at least three reasons:

It is difficult to obtain useful measures of efficiency and rate of return, especially in a governmental setting which is not oriented to a single product (profit) and which must serve multiple ill-defined goals simultaneously (the common good).

City services commonly serve overlapping goals and provide services which have benefits beyond the department's and the city's boundaries. It is difficult to partition work effort or benefits across such a diversity of cross-cutting goals and constituencies.

A budget is not just an accounting tool. It is also a political process. By focusing on comparisons (internal and cross-program), these other budgets may surface the political conflicts in too central a fashion. Line-item budgets may allow political accommodation without loss of face.

Summary

Throughout this chapter, there has been a comparison between cities—government corporations—and private business corporations. In many ways they are similar—perhaps in all the unimportant ways. Like a business corporation, cities have managers and employees. Like businesses, they provide goods and services and struggle with issues of marketing. Like businesses, they have revenues, expenses, and budgets. And cities have often been called upon to run themselves in a "businesslike and orderly" fashion. But unlike businesses, cities are expected to provide what is not profitable to produce. Unlike businesses, cities must be concerned not only with the corporate good but also with the common good. Unlike businesses, cities are not in a single business (nor are they a conglomerate of businesses) with clearly defined objectives. Cities are—and must be—imbued with political, civic concerns. And managers of cities must perform this feat for an electorate who are, overwhelmingly, more familiar with business affairs than with civic affairs.

Questions for Discussion

1. Communication in a hierarchy is time-consuming at best. And information is frequently lost as it is passed from hand to hand. Why put up with hierarchical communication? (Hint: What happens in a bureaucracy if bureaus communicate outside the formal chain of command?)

2. Policy is established to provide uniformity within the organizations. What (if any) are the weaknesses of enforcing standard behavior?

3. The civil service was established to insulate the management of local government from local politics. What problems does such a system create, in turn? How can these negative impacts be minimized?

4. What can you do to mitigate the negative effects of unused capacity? Of deadweight loss? How would *you* choose between them?

5. One of the principal ethical commands for public employees is to "serve the public good." What is the public good? How does an employee know what it is?

6. How else might a city fund its services besides general fund, State and Federal grants, fees, public/private partnerships, or volunteers?

7. Times change, and with them needs change. Are any of the traditional city services no longer needed (as *city,* as opposed to private or non-profit or Federal, services)? Are there new services which changing times will be requiring cities to provide?

8. Under what conditions (and to what extent) would you use a goal-directed budget system? What information would you need that is not present in a line-item budget? How would you get it?

Terms to Remember

bureaucracy	garbage disposal
hierarchy	recreation
"serve the public good"	schools
civil service	infrastructure
rules of firing	infrastructure timing
"exempt" employees	sources of revenue
decision-making vs.	sales tax
production	entitlement grants
scale economies	general obligation bond
future capacity	tax increment financing
average demand	central city/suburb
productivity	expenditures
productivity enhancement	budget control
motivation	general fund
general fund	capital projects fund
fees	special assessment fund
streets	performance budget
water	program budget

compartmentalization
policy
"appearance of
   impropriety"
rules of hiring
"for cause"
coverage
Lakewood, CA

current demand
peak demand
deadweight loss
productivity assessment
automation
financing services
grants
common city services
fire protection
sewers

law enforcement
housing
libraries
infrastructure maintenance
infrastructure budgeting
property tax
income tax
categorical grants
revenue bond
debt limit
budget planning
fund accounting
special revenue funds
debt service fund
line-item budget
zero-based budget
planning/programming/
   budgeting

References

Adams, R F. (1965) On the variations in the consumption of public services, Review of Economics and Statistics, 400–405.

Bish, Robert L. (1971) The Public Economy of Metropolitan Areas. Chicago: Markham Pubs.

Drucker, Peter F. (1974) Management: Tasks, Responsibilities, Practices, NY: Harper & Row.

Follett, Mary Parker (1941) Dynamic Administration, ed. H. Metcalf & L. Urwick. Harper & Row.

Hirsch, W. (1964) Local vs. areawide urban government services, National Tax Journal, *17*

Key, V. O., Jr. (1940) The lack of a budgetary theory, American Political Science Review, *34*, 1138.

Lehan, Edward A. (1981) Simplified Governmental Budgeting. Chicago: Municipal Finance Officers Association.

Lindblom, Charles. (1959) The science of muddling through, Public Administration Review, *10,* 79–88.

McGregor, Douglas M. (1960) The Human Side of Enterprise. NY: McGraw-Hill.

Peters, Thomas J. & Robert H. Waterman, Jr. (1982) In Search Of Excellence. NY: Harper & Row.

Rapp, B. W. & F. Patitucci (1977) Managing Local Government for Improved Performance. Boulder, CO: Westview Press.

Stokey, Edith & Richard Zeckhauser. (1978) Queues, in A Primer for Policy Analysis. NY: W. W. Norton.

Weber, Max (1946) Bureaucracy, in Max Weber: Essays in Sociology, ed. H. H. Gerth & C. W. Mills. NY: Oxford University Press.

9

Planning the City

Do you see, Arren, how an act is not, as young men think, like a rock that one picks up and throws, and it hits or misses, and that's the end of it. When that rock is lifted, the earth is lighter; the hand that bears it heavier. When it is thrown, the circuit of the stars respond, and where it strikes or falls the universe is changed. On every act the balance of the whole depends. . . . But we, insofaras we have power over the world and over one another, we must learn to do what the whale and the wind do of their own nature. We must learn to keep the balance.

Ursula LeGuin,
The Farthest Shore

Minneapolis, MN (H. Roger Smith)

City planning is not one of the world's oldest professions. Many cities grew without any plan; others were ordered to fit some impersonal, Imperial pattern. In the United States, the roots of city planning lie in the landscape design movement of the mid-nineteenth century. The founders of the "parks movement"—the landscape designer, Andrew Jackson Downing, the designer of New York's Central Park, Frederick Law Olmstead, and Calvert Vaux—were the precursors of modern city planning.

Park planning led planners and others to the realize that people could determine how their cities would look. Daniel Burnham's "White City," created for the Columbian Exposition of 1892, focused attention on the need for public buildings and grand open spaces. It anticipated the urban renewal movement which came fifty years later. In 1902, the Macmillan Commission produced the first American comprehensive plan, this one for Washington, D.C. In 1909, Daniel Burnham wrote a comprehensive plan for Chicago under a commission from the Chicago Commercial Club. This early Master Plan had many of the components of contemporary comprehensive plans, including a focus on a "well-ordered, convenient, and unified city," a section on improved transportation, another on accessible areas for public recreation, and provisions for controlling growth (Schlereth, 1981).

The modern public planning movement took shape during the 1920s and 1930s. The Sociology department at the University of Chicago, led by Robert Park, Ernest Burgess, and Louis Wirth, pursued a systematic study of urban problems. They focused on the relations between people and their environment, founding a "human ecology" movement. Clarence Stein, Henry Wright, and Lewis Mumford found the Regional Planning Association of America. They developed designs for neighborhoods and cities which self-consciously sought to ameliorate the physical and social environment of cities. Building on the work of the Englishman, Ebenezer Howard, they planned "garden cities," planned communities of limited population and surrounded by open space. One of America's most famous garden cities, Radburn, NJ, was built in 1928 and still exerts a powerful attraction in contemporary planning. During this same period zoning, a new technique for regulating the development of land, was imported from Germany. Comprehensive planning, the extrapolation of long-range community trends and responses to those trends, was also popularized during this period.

Definitions

"Planning" is an ongoing attempt to guide future development and redevelopment of a neighborhood, community, or region in order to create and maintain a desirable environment and to promote the public health, safety, welfare, and convenience (Isberg, 1986). There are several key terms in this definition which must be defined

further. Planning is "ongoing," which means it is a process which builds on itself. It is not satisfied by producing a document which gathers dust on a shelf. Planning "guides future development," which means that its focus is on past trends and current opportunities as they shape what is to come. Land use regulation and building code enforcement, although important tools for planning, are important less for their control on current development than for their impact on future possibilities. Planning aims to "maintain a desirable environment," which is both an issue of the carrying capacity of the physical environment and the quality of life in the social environment. Planning promotes "public health, safety, and welfare," which are the three justifications for planning specified in the enabling statutes passed by most state legislatures. Planning also promotes "convenience," although this is not part of its legal mandate. One of the traditional assumptions of planning is that the physical environment has a direct impact on human behavior and the quality of life.

Planners generally work with land and its uses. It would be useful, therefore, to define everyday terms in the way planners might use them:

1. **Acre:** Land area is usually measured in acres (hectares, in the metric system). There are 43,560 square feet in 1 acre, or 4,840 square yards. This is a square slightly less than 209 feet (just under 70 yards) on a side.

2. **Lot:** An average city lot may range from as little as 5,000 square feet (50 x 100 feet) to as much as 8,000 square feet (60 x 135 feet). Some suburban areas specify lots as large as 20,000 square feet (almost half an acre).

3. **Block:** There is no standard size for a city block. In cities laid out in a regular gridiron plan, a square mile (640 acres) is frequently 8 x 16 blocks (128 blocks of 5 acres each). Each block includes not only housing lots, but also right-of-way for streets. Each 5-acre block could support 24 lots of 6,750 square feet (50 x 135 feet), or 20 lots of 8,000 square feet (60 x 135 feet).

Name	Measure	Common Units
Acre	43,560 sq. ft. 4,840 sq. yds.	@ 209 ft. on each side @ 70 yds. on each side
Lot	5–8,000 sq. ft.	50 x 100 ft. to 60 x 135 ft.
Block	@ 5 acres	24 lots of 6,750 sq. ft. 20 lots of 8,000 sq. ft.
Street	60 ft. R. O. W. (right-of-way)	2 traffic lanes, 2 parking lanes
House	1200 sq. ft.	2 bedrooms, one-story
Garage & Driveway	300 sq. ft. 800 sq. ft.	15 x 20 ft. 10 x 80 ft.

Figure 9.1. Common Planning Units

4. **Street:** To a planner, "street" means not only the roadway for passage of traffic, but also space at the side of the road for parking and the public space next to the curb which includes the boulevard and the sidewalk. A standard residential street, with parking on both sides, requires a 60-foot right-of-way. In a 5-acre block, over 1.25 acres is dedicated to streets and sidewalks.

5. **House:** Houses come in a variety of sizes and shapes, but a common "footprint" for a modest city lot is just over 1200 square feet (30 x 40 feet) on the first floor. This permits a kitchen, living room, dining room, bath, and two bedrooms on the first floor, plus stairs to a basement and second story, if needed.

6. **Garage and Driveway:** A single-car detached garage takes about 300 square feet (15 x 20 feet). A ten-foot driveway from the curb, past the house, into the garage will typically cover another 800 square feet.

There are, of course, many variations on these "typical" plans. If you are interested, you might look at a book like *Urban Planning and Design Criteria* (De Chiara & Koppelman, 1975).

Basis for Planning

The practice of planning rests on three legs: legal, economic, and organizational. In one sense, public planning is an exercise of the power of the sovereign in its region. In another sense, the authority of planning depends not on the coercion of law but on the necessities of economics. And, finally, planning can be seen as an organizational support, mediating between the community and city hall.

Legal

From one point of view, the Law is the basis for all planning. The purpose of planning is to promote the common good (the "public interest," if you will). The law provides guidance for arbitrating different opinions of what the common good might be. The law, in other words, provides a basis for determining what is to be allowed, and what is forbidden—both to the planners and to those for whom they plan.

Planning derives its legal authority from the "police power" which resides in any sovereign, be it a city, a county, or the State. The police power is the authority to regulate the domestic order to insure the general welfare, and extends from the beginning of English Common Law. In planning, the police power is expressed in the regulation of land, usually through zoning and subdivision regulation. The roots of zoning controls can be found in the Law of the Indies, promulgated by King Philip II of Spain to regulate the development of towns in the new

world. The Law of the Indies specified street layouts, lot sizes, and public health measures which must be maintained. Although the English colonies were not subject to the Spanish regulations, the early towns usually established fire codes and similar ordinances to control dangerous uses within town borders. Towns also passed ordinances limiting "nuisances," another strand of the police power which came to be embodied in planning law.

While there are strands in legal theory which could support the regulation of land use, for more than 100 years United States courts refused to recognize zoning as a constitutional use of the police power. Private property rights were held to be more important. In the 1920s, Alfred Bettman wrote the Standard State Enabling Act for Zoning, at the request of the Department of Commerce. Ohio adopted the Act, and in 1926 the United States Supreme Court found, in the case of *Village of Euclid vs. Ambler Realty Co.,* that zoning was a constitutional use of the police power when delegated to a local community by the State. Since then, zoning has been one of the standard tools in a planner's repertoire.

For zoning, or any other application of the police power, to be legal, it must meet three tests:

1. It must promote a public purpose.
2. It must be reasonable and fairly applied.
3. It must be capable of amendment.

In the case of zoning, the public purpose has been defined in the law as "public health, safety, or welfare." Welfare has been interpreted to include economic well-being, such as the preservation of property values. The fairness rule requires that acts may not be "capricious or arbitrary" (i.e., there has to be some good reason for every regulation) nor may they be applied to some and not others who share similar circumstances. So, for example, the Courts have generally not approved of zoning regulations which attempt to control the color of paint on buildings, on the grounds that there is no good reason of public health, safety, or welfare which would justify such a rule. The Courts have also struck down entire zoning ordinances when too many exceptions (called "variances" and "conditional uses") had been granted to general rule, on the grounds that the ordinance was no longer being applied fairly. At the same time, the Court will not recognize an ordinance which is so inflexible that it cannot accommodate unusual circumstances nor change with the times. Any law must be capable of amendment. All zoning ordinances include provisions for amendment, and some flexibility in their application through variances and conditional uses.

Cities also enjoy another power of the State which is often confused with the police power, called "eminent domain." Eminent domain is the principle that the common good is superior to individual benefit (*not* individual rights, but *benefit*). Under the principle of eminent domain, the sovereign may take private property for public use, under two conditions. The intended use must serve a *public* purpose (a city cannot deprive an individual of property solely to benefit another individual), and the party whose property is taken must be *compensated* for what is taken.

The difference between these two powers are subtle, but important. A city may use the police power to demolish a building that is unsafe; this is regulating a threat to public health and safety. Since the building was unsafe for human habitation, nothing of value was taken in the demolition. But the property remains in the hands of the original owner. A city may *not* use the police power to demolish a sound building to clear a right-of-way for a highway expansion. The demolition would "take" from the owner the remaining economic value in the structure, and the construction of the highway would "take" from the owner any other use of the land. This "taking" is an exercise of eminent domain, and the city would have to compensate the owner—pay for what was taken. In some cases, nothing need physically change hands for eminent domain to have occurred: Some Courts have ruled that rezoning a property from a higher (and therefore more valuable) use to a lower (and therefore less valuable) use without the consent of the owner is a "taking" (called "inverse condemnations") and must be compensated. If this were done in a neighborhood with, say, 1,000 properties and the average property loss were, say, $3,000, a city could face a bill of $3,000,000! For this reason, cities are very cautious about "downzoning."

Economics

From another point of view, economic values are the basis for all planning. The uses of land are developed primarily through private speculation. At the same time, these land uses are the base in the community which provides the income that permits all the other activities in the city, both in terms of the public tax base and in terms of the local employment base. Thus, private activity plays a critical role in public wellbeing, whether the public is thought of as individuals or as a "commonwealth."

As a result, most of the effort in planning is devoted to dealing with development crises. Much of zoning is devoted to preventing incompatible uses from lessening the value of existing land in the city. Planners are regularly asked to advise on proposed locations for shopping centers or other economic activities. In addition, planners devote considerable effort to retaining existing major industries and to attracting new ones.

The irony of the situation is that public planning, in attempting to protect the community's investment in the land, must in the end depend on the private sector to implement the plans. Public planning may propose, advise, and regulate; rarely does a city take a direct role in the actual development of its land.

Organizational

A third basis for planning is its staff role within the municipal corporation. In this sense, planning serves both a managerial and a political function.

There is no single common location for a municipal planning department in the city structure. In some cities, planning is a "staff" function, and serves as an advisor to the chief executive officer (be it the mayor or the manager). This model seems to be particularly favored in organizations which stress strategy and change management. In others, planning is a "line" department, equal with the water department and the streets department. These organizations tend to stress the land-use management (zoning) function of planning. Other cities place planning as a subdivision of one of the major departments: Sometimes planning is located in an Engineering department; some place it within an Economic Development department; some even place it within the Public Safety department. In this case, "planning for the future" is usually a function of all the departments, and a formal "Planning" (i.e., land use regulation) function is treated as an adjunct to other purposes.

No matter where planning is placed within the formal structure of a city's bureaucracy, there is a common pattern in the way its power is exercised. The **City Council** has the ultimate authority to regulate the use of land in a city, and the Council may not delegate that authority to another body. Therefore, the council approves the zoning ordinance and subsequent amendments, and the comprehensive plan.

On the other hand, regulating land use is a volatile situation. Americans do not like being told they cannot do anything they want with their own property. And when voters get unpleasant news they are likely to vote you out of office. Thus, the **Planning Commission** was invented. The Planning Commission is a body of local citizens who are appointed by and advise the Council on matters of zoning and planning. Since the Commissioners represent the common citizen, the Council can trust their advice to represent the community's will on land use issues. Besides, if the community takes exception to a planning or zoning decision, the Council can pass the blame to the Commission. Although the Planning Commission provides an administrative function (implementing the zoning ordinance), its members are appointed by the Council.

Since the Planning Commission is composed of common citizens, they cannot be expected to be expert in matters of planning and zoning. They depend for technical advice on the **Planning Department** which is composed of one or more professional planners. These people have trained themselves to think in terms of the future impacts of the present use of land—not an everyday concern for most people. While the planning department provides technical support for the Planning Commission, the members of the department are usually hired by the chief executive officer of the city.

The ultimate authority for planning, however, resides in the **Community**. There are two faces to this authority: The Council is accountable to the community, and may be removed from office by the community. If the community believes that the city is poorly planned, the Council can expect to pay for it at the polls. Perhaps more importantly, the planning is a profession in service to the "public good." At its best, planning captures the spirit and the aspirations of the community—it "etches them into the ground," to paraphrase Chombart de Lauwe (1960). To the extent that planning fails to capture the community, it fails to achieve its goals.

Planning Process

For some, planning is a document or set of documents which will guide the future development of a city. For others, it is a process by which the future of a city is developed. No matter which perspective is taken by a public planner, ultimately the fate of the plan will be in someone else's hands.

No matter how they go about it, all public planners have to resolve four key issues as they go about planning:

Mandate to plan: The authority for planning must come from some source other than the planner. A consulting planner must be at least not displease the client; a city planner must at least not displease the council. The source of one's authority will influence how the planning task is defined and will clarify the nature of the problem at hand.

Problem definition: The problem at hand comes from a confluence of conditions and resources. If there are no problematic conditions, there is no problem. If there are problematic conditions and no resources, there still is no problem—there is nothing to be done, and if there are no alternatives there is no need to plan. The definition of the problem must embody assumptions about the nature and causes of the problematic conditions, and must project the future state of those factors (if the problem will go away by itself, there is no need to act). The generation of alternatives—in some respects the heart of planning—flows directly from the statement of the problem.

Policy formulation: Choosing between alternatives is to make a policy. Whatever choice is made, it must be done in a way that grants legitimacy to the choice. This means, in practice, that the choice is made by the same authority that provided the original mandate to plan. There are many bases for making a choice; usually the key issues are ones of value ("Are the impacts of the project fair? Is this something we *should* be doing?") and economics ("Are the benefits worth the cost?").

Feedback: No implementation of a plan is perfect. Even if the project were perfectly designed, the world in which it will be placed is not. What was planned may not have been built. Or maybe everything went according to script, but everything around you changed in the meantime. Consequently, every implementation of any plan must be monitored so that mid-course corrections can be made. When the project is completed, the final impact must be compared to the intended impact.

Process

The process approach to planning stresses the community-building role of planning activity. When Portland City Commissioner Margaret Strachan began work in 1984 on the new central city plan, she envisioned a plan developed entirely under the direction of citizen volunteers (Oliver, 1989). The purpose of such a planning process is as much to build a community consensus as it is to arrive at a workable solution. Process planning, even at its best, is not without controversy: Although Strachan was given a distinguished leadership award by the American Planning Association for her efforts, opponents criticized her for failing to focus the community's efforts and her successor abandoned the process she had initiated.

Typically, a process-planning approach will proceed through a series of steps, although there is no formal system to which all process planners subscribe. The process begins with a meeting or meetings between the planner and the community. Jointly, they agree on the purposes they wish to accomplish, and a ranking among the purposes—what *must* be accomplished, what is highly desirable to accomplish what would be good to accomplish. The community then decides on the major objectives which the planning process will achieve. Alternative approaches to meeting the objectives are proposed, and the community selects the desired alternatives. An implementation plan is developed, and the community sets the schedule for implementing it. The planner monitors performance of the implementation plan, and necessary mid-course corrections are made. If the community is not satisfied with the results, the planning process is initiated again and the cycle repeats. Several "schools" of planning fit into this mold (Davidoff, 1965; Hoch, 1984; Harvey, 1975).

Community	Planner
Jointly ⟷	1. Identify purposes for planning
Jointly ⟷	2. Develop hierarchy of purposes
Community Decides ⟶	3. Establish Objectives
Jointly ⟷	4. Develop major alternatives
Community Decides ⟶	5. Select best alternative
Jointly ⟷	6. Develop recommended solution
Community Decides ⟶	7. Set implementation schedule
Planner Facilitates ⟷	8. Monitor performance
Jointly ⟷	9. Follow-up changes
Community Decides ⟶	10. Begin new planning cycle

Figure 9.2. Steps in Process Planning

Product

Other planners focus on the end-product of their efforts—whether it be a document like a comprehensive plan or a zoning code, or a brick-and-mortar project like a shopping mall or an industrial park. For them, planning is the application of one's professional expertise to the solution of the city's problems. For example, a 1987 national planning award for best project was given to *Hamlets of the Adirondacks*, a series of studies performed by a consultant for four counties in New York. The project produced a report which outlines the history and prospects of hamlets in the region, and a resource manual which presents eight redevelopment strategies for the area (Henderson, 1987). It is not that community involvement is not sought or used. But in the end the project is the planner's and community input is one of the many sources of information s/he may use.

A typical product-oriented approach to planning will usually follow six steps. From an original statement of the problem, the planner analyzes the current situation which produces the problem and predicts how the problem will appear in the future. This may lead to a redefinition or a refinement of the problem statement. Once the problem is correctly stated, the planner prepares a list of project alternatives which are feasible in light of social, political, and economic realities. The client (usually a city government, although many planners work for private developers) selects from the alternatives the one to be implemented. The planner then prepares a plan for implementing the choice and monitors the process. If all goes as planned and if the predicted impacts occur, the process is complete. If the project is not implemented as planned, or if the predicted impacts fail to materialize (either because the predictions were faulty or because unforeseen change transforms the analysis of the problem), then the problem is restated and the planning cycle is repeated. Several "schools" of planning fit this mold (Kent, 1964; Altshuler, 1965).

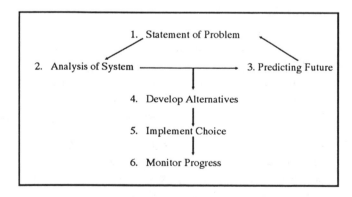

Figure 9.3. Steps in Product Planning

Implementation

In practice, planners combine both of these approaches if they are to succeed. The 1988 Outstanding Planning Project Award of the American Planning Association was awarded to Chicago's River North Urban Design Plan (Zotti, 1988). The Plan was developed by Patti Gallagher, a public planner with the city of Chicago, and Bill Martin, a planner for a business group, the Chicago Central Area Committee. While they were the "experts," they worked closely with their respective employers and held weekly meetings over the course of a year with the major businesses in the area. Howe & Kaufmann, in their survey of the role choices of contemporary American planners (Howe & Kaufman, 1980), found that there are two dominant dimensions on which planners divide: a technical focus and a political focus. Among the planners surveyed, they found that roughly 26% favored a technical role and 18% favored a political role—but more than 50% favored a combination of both.

It is not enough to draw up a plan; one must develop a way to get there from here. Yet the public planner is at a distinct disadvantage when it comes to implementation. Public planning is concerned with the use of land in the city. Yet most of the land in a city is owned and controlled by private individuals, and they enjoy constitutional protections in their use of it. Planners may propose a pattern for the growth and development of a city, but usually it will be realized only if the city can convince the private owners of the land to go along. Planners may prefer to locate a major retain center for the city in a certain location, only to see the plan fall apart because the landowners want to construct an office park. Most of the time, planners are limited to regulating other people's use of land; more positive guidance is limited to those occasions when the city is paying for a project.

Tools for Planning

Most of the tools available to a public planner involve regulation and/or suggestion. Public planners may guide, but they cannot direct the future development of their cities. Planners generally bring two assumptions to these tools: First, planners assume that the use of land should be geared to the population that it can carry. If land is overused, quality of life will be lessened (American Public Health Association, 1948). Second, the design of physical spaces is assumed to shape the social behavior which occur in those spaces. As Churchill once said, "We shape our buildings, and afterwards they shape us."

Land Use Inventory

Curiously enough, one of the most powerful tools a planner has is a simple inventory of what land is available and how it is being used. When a business considers a new location, it needs to know where suitable land is available.

A land use inventory can provide the answer. When a developer considers a site for development, s/he needs to know what the soil and underlying geological formations are likely to be. A land use inventory can provide that answer, too. When the city considers the location for a new park or a school, a land use inventory can inform that choice.

A land use inventory, in its final form, is simply a set of maps which display all of the parcels of land in the city and their uses, the streets, the location of utilities (gas lines, water lines, sewer lines, etc.), and the suitability of land for development. Underlying those maps are file drawers of data, including field surveys, soil and geological surveys, official maps, and building permit data.

Almost any land use inventory will include categories for agricultural, residential, commercial, industrial, recreational, public uses, and vacant land. If the land use inventory is to be useful, it should display as few categories of land use as possible while still showing the character of the city. Too many categories make the map confusing and difficult to read. Too few categories oversimplify and misrepresent the community.

Zoning Ordinance

Zoning is the legal regulation of the use of land, controlling the use of property and the shape and bulk of buildings on the land. Zoning is an exercise of the police power, and may be invoked to prevent incompatible uses (or, to maintain the harmony of uses), to stabilize property values, to maintain the level of demand for services and utilities, and to enhance community aesthetics (Babcock, 1969).

Zoning is accomplished through an ordinance and an official map. The ordinance defines the various uses of land and what will be permitted in them. The map displays all of the land which is covered by the ordinance, and where each of the uses may be located. The zoning plan may be modified in three ways: amendment, variance, and conditional use.

An amendment is a permanent modification of the ordinance and/or the map and requires action by the city council. Since it is a formal motion by the council, a zoning amendment requires a public hearing and two readings (that is, it is proposed at one council meeting and disposed at a second).

A variance is a departure from the dimensional standards set in the ordinance for setback (the minimum distance a structure must be placed from the lot lines), lot size, or bulk (the maximum height, length, and breadth allowed for a structure). A variance may be granted if the Board of Zoning Appeals or planning commission finds that adhering to the standards would create an "unnecessary hardship" for the parcel in question. A variance should not be used to permit a nonconforming land use (e.g., it should not be used to permit an apartment building in a single family district); its purpose is to allow for un-

usual characteristics of a parcel of land (uncommon shape, nonstandard size, unusual topography) while maintaining the essential character of the intended land use.

A conditional use permit is a permission to use land in certain specified ways, as long as certain conditions are fulfilled. The permitted uses and their conditions are specified in advance in the zoning ordinance for each category of land use. Usually, the permitted uses are ones which serve a particular community need but are not extensive enough to demand their own zoning classification. An electric transformer station might be a conditional use in a residential zone because of the safety issues they create; many cities now treat churches and schools as conditional uses because of the parking and traffic problems they generate.

As with land use categories, zoning categories should be as few as possible while still guarding the character of the neighborhoods in the city. Zoning categories generally specify the uses which are allowed and the minimum standards which must be met. Common categories include:

✳ **Agricultural:** Land available for commercial farming; frequently housing is limited to one unit per 40 acres.

✳ **Residential:** Dwelling places. Residential land is usually divided into single-family and multi-family; frequently finer distinctions are made (low- and medium-density single-family residences; duplexes and triplexes; medium- and high-density multi-family), depending on the character of the community. A single-family moderate density zone might specify a minimum of 7,000 square feet per lot.

✳ **Commercial:** Wholesale and retail sales space. Sometimes office space is combined in this category. Common standards include a requirement of 50 feet of frontage per 100 persons, or 6 parking spaces per 1,000 square feet of floor space.

✳ **Industrial:** Manufacturing space. Frequently this category is divided into light- medium- and heavy-industrial based on the amount of noise, smoke, vibration, or dust which the use creates.

Running through these descriptions of zoning standards is the concept of **performance standards.** Increasingly, land use is being categorized on the basis of its impact on surrounding land rather than assuming that certain uses always produce certain impacts. Zoning categories are looking beyond density and are considering the carrying capacity of the land and its improvements. In addition to the noise, vibration, and dust standards used for industrial zones, examples of performance standards include:

✳ **F. A. R.:** Floor-to-area ratio, which is a form of height and bulk regulation. The floor-to-area ratio limits the development of land to some ratio of the area of the lot. Typically, residential areas are limited to a fraction of the area of the lot (FAR of .25 or .5); commercial and office zones frequently specify FARs which are multiples of the lot's area (FAR of 4, 6, or even 14). An FAR of 1 means

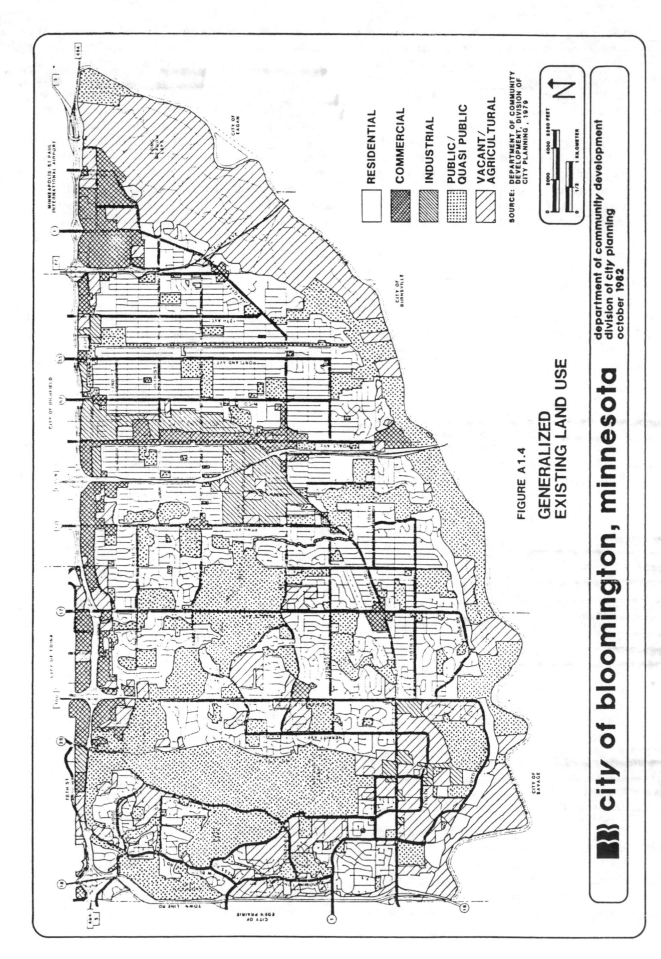

RESIDENTIAL

COMMERCIAL

INDUSTRIAL

PUBLIC/ QUASI PUBLIC

VACANT/ AGRICULTURAL

SOURCE: DEPARTMENT OF COMMUNITY DEVELOPMENT, DIVISION OF CITY PLANNING, 1979

FIGURE A1.4

GENERALIZED EXISTING LAND USE

city of bloomington, minnesota

department of community development
division of city planning
october 1982

Figure 9.4. Land Use Map

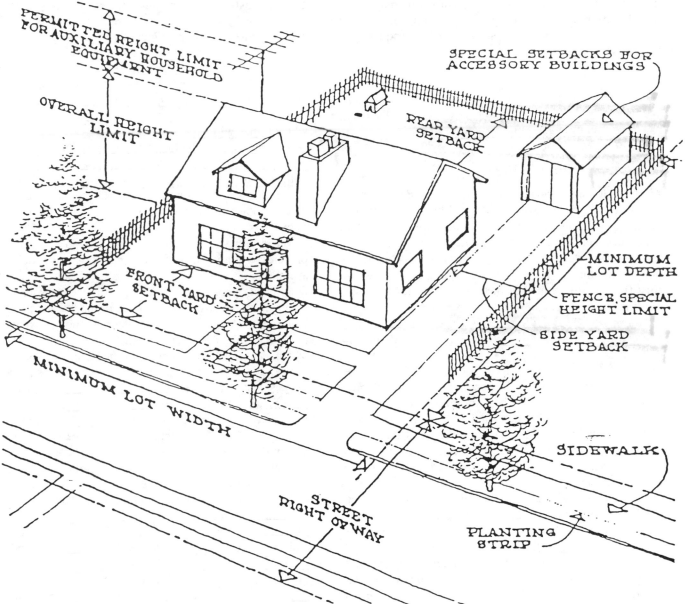

PERMITTED HEIGHT LIMIT
FOR AUXILIARY HOUSEHOLD
EQUIPMENT

OVERALL HEIGHT
LIMIT

SPECIAL SETBACKS FOR
ACCESSORY BUILDINGS

REAR YARD
SETBACK

MINIMUM
LOT DEPTH

FRONT YARD
SETBACK

FENCE SPECIAL
HEIGHT LIMIT

SIDE YARD
SETBACK

MINIMUM LOT WIDTH

SIDEWALK

STREET
RIGHT OF WAY

PLANTING
STRIP

Figure 9.5. Typical Residential Lot Plan
Source: Zoning Ordinance, City of Blaine, MN

that one may build a one-story structure over the entire surface of the lot, a two-story structure on half the lot (2/2), a three-story structure on one-third of the lot (3/3), and so on (Leary, 1968). Generally, FAR is not used alone, so some open space is assured on every lot.

A. L. O.: Angle of light obstruction limits the height of a building by a maximum angle of sight from the lot line to the top of the structure. An ALO of 45 degrees would require that the highest point on a building be located that same distance back from the lot line (so an imaginary line from the top of the building to the lot line would fall at a 45 degree angle); an ALO of 66 degrees would permit a building twice as tall as its distance from the lot line; and so on (Leary, 1968).

T. D. R.: Transfer of Development Rights allow local variations in the density of development while maintaining the overall density of a district (Woodbury, 1975). In this system, a low-density development may sell its "air-rights" (the remainder of development which the property is permitted but which has not been used) to another property in the same district. Once the rights have been transferred, the seller has surrendered the right to develop the property later to a higher density. TDR is commonly used in historic preservation where low-density historic buildings are saved by allowing them to sell their unused air rights.

Parking supply: An increasingly common performance standard is parking supply. Many zoning codes establish minimum off-street parking requirements which

115

must be met by various land uses. Apartments may be required to provide 2 parking places per unit; retail stores may be required to provide 6 spaces per 1,000 square feet of floor space.

Other Regulations

In addition to zoning, there are two other applications of the police power which planners commonly use: subdivision regulation and building codes.

Subdivision regulations control the way larger lots of land are subdivided into smaller parcels for sale or development. Subdivision regulations generally specify minimum lot sizes and access requirements. Each lot must be serviced by necessary utilities and by a street built to certain specifications. Most communities also require that large subdivisions make appropriate provision for parks and schools, or dedicate land or money so the community can provide them. The person who is subdividing the land must file a certified map of the site which shows the survey lines for each parcel which has been created.

Building codes specify the standards to which a structure must be built. There are different standards for different classes of buildings. A public building must meet very high standards of safety, for example. Wiring in walls must be armored or in conduit; all stairwells must have fire doors; there must be a minimum number of fire exits, and each must be identified by an illuminated sign of certain dimensions and characteristics; exit doors must open out and be fitted with "panic bars"; and so on. High-rise buildings are generally required to be fitted with sprinkler systems to combat fires. Residential buildings must have smoke detectors. Building codes usually specify the structural requirements (maximum distance between studs in the wall; load-bearing ability of floors; minimum opening in the wall per wall area; etc.), standards for electrical service (minimum service to the unit; gauge of cable used for wiring; minimum number of outlets per run of wall space; etc.) and plumbing (size and type of pipe used for water and for sewage; minimum drop per foot of run of waste line; etc.). Building codes are designed to protect the people who will use a structure, and combine issues of engineering, public health, fire safety, and hazard prevention. They are usually extensive and very detailed.

Comprehensive Plan

Planning is future-oriented. If zoning is the tool by which planners attempt to shape the future of the city, the comprehensive plan is the blueprint they are following. In fact, zoning is seen as an application of the comprehensive plan and some courts have ruled that a zoning ordinance must be grounded in a comprehensive plan if it would avoid the charge of being a capricious and arbitrary use of the police power.

The comprehensive plan appears under several names, each carrying a slightly different connotation (Cornish,

1987). **Master Plan** is generally a privately-commissioned plan for anything from an individual lot to an entire region. **General Plan** is a publicly sponsored plan which focuses on land and its uses. **Comprehensive Plan** is also a public plan, expanded to include not only land use but also social and economic issues in the development of a city. **Policy Plan** focuses on community goals and objectives, but usually does not address the specific issues of where things will happen.

Besides an introduction and summary, a comprehensive plan frequently has four major sections: basic policies, current setting, land use plan, and implementation. It is not uncommon for these four sections to be combined in some fashion, or for one or more of the sections to be broken into several pieces.

Basic Policies: There is no single way to create a comprehensive plan. Different communities have different aspirations, begin at different stages, face different challenges and opportunities, and enjoy different resources. It is the job of the city council to determine the direction the city intends to pursue, and that determination is expressed in the Basic Policies section of the plan.

Current Setting: Any plan for the future is constrained by the present, which is an expression of choices made in the past (that is one of the differences between describing utopias and designing cities). The comprehensive plan must take inventory of what the community has to work with. Part of this work might already have been done in the **land use inventory.** In addition, the comprehensive plan should also survey and analyze **population** trends, **physical and natural resources,** existing **public utilities,** current **traffic** capacity and trends, and the local **economic** environment.

Land Use Plan: This is the pivot of a comprehensive plan. Based on the analysis of the current setting and expected trends, the planner describes the nature and pattern of current and future development. Using community standards for various uses of land, the planner can estimate, from projected population and employment growth, how much land will be needed to support that growth and the secondary growth which will come from it. Drawing on the basic policies of the council and professional standards for land-use performance, the land use plan can specify how much of what kind of activity the community needs to prepare itself (Chapin, 1965).

The land use plan section of the comprehensive plan is usually divided into sub-sections. The **Working-and-Living Areas** section focuses on the future demand for residential, commercial, and industrial uses in the city. The **Community Facilities** section focuses on the public land which will be needed to service the working-and-living area land uses (parks, schools, libraries, etc.). The **Civic Design** section specifies how the city as an integral unit should grow into the future—where should growth go, where will the neighborhood centers be, how should the buildings relate to each other. The **Circulation** and the

Utilities sections each focus on how the growth of the city will affect transportation, sewer and water, electric and gas service, and other utilities.

Implementation: The land use plan lays out the vision for the future. The Implementation section explains how to get there. Part of the implementation section should include at least a discussion of the zoning plan and the other regulatory systems (subdivision regulations, building codes, etc.). In addition, the Implementation section will frequently present a land acquisition program for community facilities and a capital improvements program for public projects.

Capital Improvements Plan

The capital improvements program is a planned schedule of public investment to meet present and future development and maintenance needs. It influences private developers and investors by setting the allocation and timing of public improvements. Capital improvements are projects like streets, sewers, libraries; they may also include major refurbishing of existing buildings and replacement of large-ticket stock like snowplows, garbage trucks, and buses. Because these long-lived investments also tend to be big-ticket items, it is very important to plan ahead to insure that the city will be able to afford them when the time comes.

One of the principal functions of capital improvement planning is to control the sequence and timing of large expenses which the city can foresee. These decisions have implications for the city's ability to maintain or improve the service which it offers its citizens, and that in turn has political implications (more than one mayoral campaign has been waged over the issue of potholes).

The second principal function of capital improvement planning is to control local development. The cost for providing public capital services (sewers, streets, utilities) to a residential lot can run to $10,000 or $15,000. It is obviously to a developer's advantage to wait until the city supplies those services rather than attempting to provide them oneself. In the Minneapolis/St. Paul metropolitan area, the Metropolitan Council has controlled the location and timing of suburban development through its capital plan for extending sewer lines. Developers are free to build in areas which are not yet served by public sewer lines, but in most cases the cost of providing private sewers is prohibitive.

Summary

In this chapter, you have seen how planning is grounded in legal principles, economic necessity, and organizational structures. You have looked at planning as a process and as a product. You have developed a familiarity with the way planners think about land and its uses, and the tools they use to guide the development of land.

Yet there is one final question to be raised: Why plan? We know we can do it. We know that, in at least some cases, it affects how cities grow and develop. But *should* we do it? Should the community invoke its right to impose its standards on an individual's enjoyment of her/his own property? The issue is complex. As you have seen, the planning process is not purely technical; there are political considerations at every point. You have also seen that the planner is in at best a weak position, reduced to suggesting and guiding but not controlling the development of the city. And, as anyone who has planned a tight schedule knows, attempting to predict what will happen even tomorrow is an iffy proposition at best.

What is the alternative? What happens if we do not plan our cities? There might be no comprehensive plans. Maybe there would not even be any zoning. But there are some cities in the Union which do not use zoning even today to control the use of land (Houston, TX is the usual example). The real loss, it seems to me, would not be the lack of plans, but the lack of planning. Planning provides us the opportunity to think about the future of our city, to create the vision which can lead us to its realization. If we do not know where we are going, we are unlikely to get there. In the end, perhaps it *is* the process of planning—which means the *community's* process of planning—which is the heart of the process. Perhaps that is the meaning of the "public good" which every planner strives to serve.

Questions for Discussion

1. The Standard Enabling Act for Zoning defines the public purpose as "public health, safety, or welfare." Isberg's definition of planning includes a fourth term, "convenience." Should the law be amended to include convenience as a public purpose protected by power of the State?

2. How much land is devoted to transportation in a typical neighborhood subdivision? Does the ratio of housing to transportation land use seem appropriate? Could anything be done to lessen it?

3. Suppose a developer approaches the city, asking them to condemn a group of properties so the developer can build a shopping mall. Under what circumstances is this a legitimate use of the power of eminent domain?

4. Does the location of planning in the organizational structure of a city make any important differences?

5. What impact would the membership of the Planning Commission have on planning policy in a city? What sort of appointments might favor the business community? the development community? the residential community?

6. What are the differences between process planning and product planning in the way they handle the four key issues for planning?

7. How does one balance the regulation of the use of private land against the constitutional protection of private property rights? How well do the current planning tools achieve this? What further criteria might future tools try to meet?

8. Is comprehensive planning worth the time and effort it takes to perform? What are the alternatives to it?

9. If a person's property were zoned R-1 (only single family housing allowed) and s/he wanted to construct a duplex, how would one go about getting a change in zoning classification? What would be a good justification for the change?

10. You are involved in writing a comprehensive plan for your home community for the year 2010. What are 4 major goals that you think should be included in the plan?

11. How is the role of the city planner different when he implements process planning than when s/he implements product planning?

Terms to Remember

Andrew Jackson Downing	Frederick Law Olmstead
Calvert Vaux	Daniel Burnham
Robert Park	Ernest Burgess
Louis Wirth	Clarence Stein
Henry Wright	Lewis Mumford
garden city	acre
lot	block
street	house
garage	zoning
comprehensive plan	planning
police power	eminent domain
Law of the Indies	Euclid vs. Ambler
inverse condemnation	a "taking"
legal basis of planning	economic basis of planning
organizational basis of planning	managerial function of planning
political function of planning	City Council
	Planning Department
Planning Commission	Mandate to plan
Community	Policy formulation
Problem definition	10 steps in process planning
Feedback	
6 steps in product planning	land use inventory
zoning	zoning amendment
variance	conditional use
agricultural zone	residential zone
commercial zone	industrial zone
performance standards	FAR
ALO	TDR
master plan	general plan
comprehensive plan	policy plan
basic policies section	current setting
land use plan	implementation
capital improvements plan	

References

Altshuler, Alan. (1965) The goals of comprehensive planning, Journal of the American Institute of Planners, *32* 186–196.

American Public Health Association. (1948) Planning the Neighborhood. Chicago: Public Administration Service.

Babcock, Richard F. (1969) The Zoning Game. Madison: University of Wisconsin Press.

Chapin, F. Stuart, Jr. (1965) Urban Land Use Planning, 2nd ed. Urbana, IL: University of Illinois Press.

Chombart de Lauwe, Paul. (1960) Famille et Habitation. Paris: Editions du Centre National de la Recherche Scientifique.

Cornish, Robert. (1987) Notes on the master plan: Coming to terms, Planning *53* (September), 16.

Davidoff, Paul. (1965) Advocacy and pluralism in planning, Journal of the American Institute of Planners, *31*, 331–338.

De Chiara, Joseph & Lee Koppleman. (1975) Urban Planning and Design Criteria, 2nd ed. NY: Van Nostrand Rheinhold Co.

Harvey, David. (1975) Social Justice and the City. Baltimore, MD: John Hopkins Press.

Henderson, Harold. (1987) Top of the line, Planning, *53* (April), 7–8.

Hoch, Charles. (1984) Doing good and being right: The pragmatic connection in planning theory, Journal of the American Planning Association, *50*, 335–345.

Isberg, Gunnar, (1986) Local and Regional Planning in Minnesota, 2nd ed. St. Paul, MN: Minnesota League of Cities.

Kent, T. J., Jr. (1964) The Urban General Plan. San Francisco: Chandler.

Leary, Robert M. (1968) Zoning, in Principles and Practice of Urban Planning, W. I. Goodman & E. C. Freund, eds. Washington, D.C.: ICMA.

Oliver, Gordon. (1989) Portland goes for broke, Planning *55* (February): 10–15.

Schlereth, Thomas J. (1981) Burnham's *Plan* and Moody's *Manual:* City planning as progressive reform, Journal of the American Planning Association, *47,ID 70–82.*

Woodbury, Steven R. (1975) Transfer of development rights: A new tool for planners, Journal of the American Institute of Planners, *41*, 3–14.

Zotti, Ed. (1988) River North Urban Design Plan, Planning *54* (April), 9–10.

10

Summary: Future of the City

Optimism and pessimism are not arguments. They are opposite forms of the same surrender to simplicity. Relieved of the burden of complex options with complicated consequences, both optimists and pessimists carry on without caring about the consequences of their actions. Convinced of a single course for the juggernaut of history, whether malignant or benign, both optimists and pessimists allow themselves irresponsible actions because they believe that individual actions have no significant consequences. . . .

Real power can accrue to people who understand the limits of human nature, old and new, and who therefore measure their preferences against an understanding of what can and cannot be accomplished in a day or a decade.

Paul Hawken
Seven Tomorrows

Milwaukee, WI (H. Roger Smith)

119

Two thousand years ago, a Roman senator named Seneca wrote to a young friend who was discouraged about the lack of opportunity in the city in which he was living, *"Animum debes mutare, non caelum. . . . Tecum fugis"* (You should change your attitude, not your location. . . . You flee with yourself)(Summers, 1962). Cities have their problems, but they are people-problems rather than place-problems. Playing frontiersman by packing up and starting a new city someplace else merely transports the problems to a new location, perhaps giving it a different face. Any city can be a "good" city, given a common will, and no matter how "good" a city may look it bears the seeds of its own destruction if it does not contribute to the growth of its people, both singly and as a public.

The Good City

The search for a "good" city has led thinkers to attempt to describe such a place. These attempts are usually called **"utopian literature."**

The first utopia, written by Plato, was called *The Republic*. He began by asking how justice was possible, and proceeded to describe what a truly just city would look like. St. Augustine, in *The City of God*, despaired of ever finding a good city on earth, and reserved it for Paradise. Sir Thomas More, Chancellor England under Henry VIII, returned to Plato's question and wrote a short book called *Utopia* (from the Greek for "no place" and for "good place"). His book gave its name to this whole family of writing. More's utopia was a place where people's physical needs were all satisfied; everything was held in common and shared equally, and the spirit of private ownership was foreign.

In the nineteenth century there were attempts to build practical utopias, real communities where people lived in harmony and without class distinctions. Communities were built at New Harmony (by George Owen, the English industrialist), Amana, Economy (by George Rapp), Sylvania (by Horace Greeley, following the ideas of Charles Fourier), and Salt Lake City (by Brigham Young). While some of these towns still exist, none of them continue as a philosophical community. Those which survive today have done so by growing away from their founder's ideals.

The nineteenth century also saw a flowering of stories describing hypothetical utopias: *Erewhon* and *Erewhon Revisited* (a fanciful place in the Andes where money was the religion and banks were the temples), *News from Nowhere* (a non-city utopia where people had returned to a village life), and *Looking Backward* (a surprisingly accurate prediction of what Boston might be like in the year 2000). *Erewhon* ushered in a new type of utopian story, the anti-utopia or **"dystopia,"** which uses irony to describe, as if it were ideal, patterns which were extensions of all that was considered wrong in society.

In the twentieth century, this theme continues in the dystopias of *Brave New World* (where the search for pleasure and comfort is taken to extremes), and *1984* (where political repression and surveillance are extreme). The utopian tradition continues in *Walden II* (an ideal society based on the psychological principles of instrumental conditioning) and *Ecotopia* (an ideal society based on environmental principles).

All of these utopias reflect the beliefs of their writers— they are strong on abstract generalizations, weak on individual differences. They describe a single point of view, and fail because they fail to create concinnity (and so fail to support a good city).

Urban Trends

The future of the city depends in part on what its people want the city to be, in part on the press of events and forces. Present trends will not determine the future; the future will be created from the response of a city's people to those trends and to unforseen events. Even though trends will not *predict* the future, at least they provide some ideas of the arena in which future events will be played out.

Megatrends

In 1982, John Naisbitt published what he considered to be the ten major trends which were already shaping the future. He called them **"Megatrends"** (Naisbitt, 1982). There was, and has continued to be, much debate about his choice of trends and about the accuracy of his descriptions and predictions. Whether they are occurring exactly as he predicted, at least they provide a structure to work against:

Information Society: Work in society, according to Naisbitt, is shifting from an industrial economy to an information economy. People are working more with their brains than with their backs. This puts increased strains on the ability of our educational systems to prepare people (*all* people, not just the most able) to work in the system. And it puts increased strain on each of us to process the continually increasing flow of information to which we are exposed. The computer revolution can help us manage

1. From Industrial to an Information society
2. From "Forced" Technology to High Tech
3. From National Economy to World Economy
4. From Short Term Business Planning to Long Term Planning
5. From Centralization to Decentralization
6. From Institutional Help to Self-Help
7. From Representative Democracy to "Participatory" (Direct) Democracy
8. From Hierarchies to Networking
9. From North to South
10. From "Either-Or" to Multiple Option Life Style Possibilities

Figure 10.1. "Megatrends in U.S. Society
Source: John Naisbitt, *Megatrends* (1982)

the flow of information, but it cannot substitute for the human ability to process and understand what the computer is producing.

High Tech: As society depends more and more on technology—automated manufacturing, computers, artificial hearts and other medical prostheses—there is a counter movement to what Naisbitt calls "high touch." People who work at a computer terminal all day could do it at home as well as at an office, but they choose not to. As we come to depend more on sophisticated mechanical devices, we come to realize how much we also need human contact. Naisbitt does not predict that, like the Luddites, we will go around smashing our high-tech machines; no one wants to outlaw pacemakers or coffee makers. But as we spend more of our time interacting with machines, we will want to spend more of the remaining time interacting with other people.

Global Economy: Driven in part by technological advances, people are living their lives on an increasingly global scale. Americans drive Japanese (or Korean or Yugoslav) cars, wear Italian shoes, watch French movies, eat Mexican food, consume Saudi oil, collect Nigerian art, dress in Chinese and Indian textiles, and vacation in the Caribbean. A Ford Motor car may have an engine built in England and a chassis designed in Germany. The Pillsbury Doughboy is owned by a British conglomerate and American shopping malls and office towers are owned by Japanese and Saudi investors. America is no longer an island in isolation; the price of tea in China will come back in the price of pop-tarts on your breakfast table.

Long-Term Planning: To compete in the global market, to manage a high-tech (and highly expensive) operation American business must shift from short-term to long-term thinking. The Japanese, it is said, have beat the American at their own game by working for long-term returns; they will accept five years of losses to gain, twenty years from now, a dominant market position. It is not clear, however, that corporate America is as convinced of this trend as Naisbitt was. Since 1982, we have seen a frenzy of "leveraged buy-outs" of corporations and stockholder insistence on high quarterly returns. Both of these are short-term strategies which focus on capital accumulation rather than productivity enhancement.

Decentralization: The information revolution and the shift from "forced" technology to high technology have both led to decentralization. It is no longer necessary for people to live in high concentrations in central cities; inexpensive automobile transportation allows us to live in suburbs. The flexibility which advanced technology and information bring is moving the focus of national policy toward the states and the regions, rather than Washington, D.C., according to Naisbitt. But as the farm towns empty out and rural Americans move to the big cities—the outskirts, perhaps, but still away from the farm—and as the global economy is concentrating more power in New York and London and Tokyo and Paris, it seems that Naisbitt's prediction may have been premature. The central places may be less dense, they may look different than previously, but they have not evaporated.

Self-Help: Naisbitt predicted that American society would move from dependence on institutional help to self-help. The country which once depended on church schools, community barn-raisings, and volunteer fire departments may once again discover the satisfaction of "doing it my way." But information needs and high-tech equipment both militate against self-help. An old Volkswagen Beetle was simple enough that an only moderately handy owner could maintain it. A contemporary Volkswagen requires German-trained mechanics to be serviced. Millions of people use computer wordprocessors; very few of them could repair them. In the old days, if a community organization needed support, someone went to the local businesses and asked for some money. Today they need professional fundraisers who talk to the corporate giving officers at the corporate office of the local retail outlet.

Participatory Democracy: Along with the move to decentralization, Naisbitt predicts that power will be returned to the people. We will move toward participatory, rather than representative, democracy. Using cable TV, every home can participate in city council or national town meetings by watching the meeting on television and voting through a terminal attached to the TV cable. Tally boards could instantly calculate the will of the people and display it on the screen. But, again, the ability of people to process information may work against this trend. Many issues are very complex, and most people will not have time to study them (there are those that claim that national defense issues are so complex that even the average Congressperson does not understand them). Other issues are very emotional, and may not be well served by popular debate (How much light, for example, has the abortion debate shed on the issue?)

Networking: Naisbitt predicted that hierarchies would give way to networking, and certainly the word has come into common currency in the 1980s. He cites as evidence the move toward "quality circles" in manufacturing industries. On the other hand, a global economy works against networking simply by the constraints of distance. A few people in a corporation may "network" internationally, but even they will do it only infrequently.

Sunbelt: In 1982, it looked like the nation was moving south in search of the sun. The Rustbelt cities were dying, the sunbelt cities were booming. Since then, the population decline in the North has slowed and even halted, and growth in the South has stalled in many cases. In the late 1980s, New England has started to grow; the central Plains never really declined. Cleveland no longer has a flammable river, and Pittsburgh has changed its image from steel mills to corporate offices. Meanwhile the housing and the office development industries in Denver and Houston have stagnated badly.

Multiple Options: Decentralization, information flows, high technology, networking, self-help and democratic participation will all combine to provide a variety of options for people. Rather than take-it-or-leave-it, either/or options, the trend of the future is for "have it your way." Provided, of course, the resources do not run out and assuming that one has the money to pay for it. There is no question that cities today support a wide diversity of lifestyles; there is also no question that a formerly unemployed auto worker who now works at McDonald's has fewer lifestyle choices than formerly. It takes two middle class people to earn an income with the buying power that one middle class wage-earner enjoyed in 1970.

Problems

Others have attempted to structure the future around problems, rather than opportunities. Rather than focusing on the continuity between the past and the future (the "trends") they focus on *dis*continuity, on the issues which must be resolved if future growth is to occur.

In 1974, one futurist listed eight issues which would be central in the coming years: Education, the generation gap, race, crime, health, solid waste and litter, transportation and the city, and underdeveloped countries (Ackoff, 1974). Ten years later, Richard Lamm (former governor of Colorado) listed his eight issues: The economy, health care, pensions, immigration & integration, crime & terrorism, urban decay, education, and law & lawyers. Five of the issues are common: Education, health care, crime, race (restructured as immigration and integration), and the generation gap (now redefined as a problem of the elderly). Concern about crowded rush-hour traffic has been replaced by concern for the crumbling roads on which rush-hour traffic idles. Concern about the economic inequalities between us and poorer nations has been redirected to the weakness of our own economy.

More recently, Rushworth Kidder of the *Christian Science Monitor* interviewed 22 thinkers throughout the world, asking them to reflect on the major issues which would face humanity in the 21st century (Kidder, 1987). Six major issues emerged. As with the other two futurists, the need for a fundamental restructuring of the education system was noted. Kidder's interviews also pointed to a breakdown in public and private morality, which is cognate to the "crime" issues already listed. As did Ackoff, Kidder noted the importance of the gap between the developing and industrial world and the degradation of the global environment. Kidder also found his people concerned about the threat of nuclear annihilation and the danger of overpopulation.

The point all three authors make is that the specifics of the issues are less important than making an early start at finding solutions. As Lamm put it, "We did not take steps early enough, so now there are fewer choices left" (Lamm, 1985).

Roles Cities Play

Whatever the changes the future brings, a city may choose to play its role in different ways. Theodore Hershberg proposed four roles for Philadelphia as it faces its future (Hershberg, 1982):

Conservator: In this role, the city maintains its physical and social infrastructure. The city provides a baseline of services, but depends on others (non-profits, corporations) to provide discretionary items. In this role, the city sees itself as protecting and preserving the resource base which it represents. Most of the city's activity is regulatory, providing the opportunity for private interests to compete on equal terms and preventing the unnecessary destruction or decay of existing structures and utilities.

Innovator: In this more active role, the city sees itself as providing a structure for individuals and enterprises to maximize their potential. Not just protecting what is handed on from the past, in this role the city is aggressively structuring a future. The risk, of course, is that the city is also putting itself in the position of favoring some individuals and groups over others, or "picking the winners," an uncomfortable position for any public body.

Mediator: In this role, public officials serve as brokers allocating limited resources among competing groups. This role is less one of backing a winner than one of providing a common meeting ground, using its good offices to actively build a commonality of interests, a "common weal." Such a role is a tricky one to manage for elected officials, since election often depends on perceived good will rather than justice.

Enhancer: Finally, the city can take it upon itself to provide a high quality of life. How else is a city to attract the best and the brightest, except by convincing them that this is a great place to live? Cities compete with their suburbs and with each other for corporate offices, retail malls, and taxpayers. Since cities offer essentially the same basic services, it is the "extras," the quality of life they offer, which will distinguish them from their competition.

These roles are not contradictory, nor even necessarily in conflict. It is, at least in principle, possible for a city to pursue all four simultaneously. Most cities, though, will be distinguished for pursuing one more than the others.

Strategies for City Futures

In their book on the future, Paul Hawken and his colleagues stress what they call **"voluntary history"** (Hawken, *et alii*, 1982). They present seven scenarios of possible tracks for the future, depending on choices which people make. By drawing out the future implications of present choices, they intend to assist people to make responsible, intelligent choices.

The scenarios begin with an analysis of the forces of change, both environmental and human, which are likely to be the **"driving trends"** of the future. Hawken and his colleagues selected five: energy, climate, food, economy, and values. For each trend, three or four **"dispositions"** are developed, ranging from optimistic to pessimistic, depending on the choices people make. From the combinations of trends and their dispositions (there are 125 combinations of 5 trends with 3 dispositions each), the most likely ones are developed into "scenarios," or stories, which explore the interaction of human choice and the forces of change.

The focus of voluntary history is not on the outcomes, but on the process which led to them. "Human choices make a difference," they state, "because human history is partially the product of choices among alternative possibilities" (Hawken, *et alii,* 1982, p. 4). The future is neither predetermined—the choices people make will determine what happens—nor entirely of human making—we must live with the consequences of previous choices and with forces which are outside our control. The future is **contingent.**

The future of the city, the future of the place where most Americans will spend much of their lives, is contingent on the choices made today by the people who live in them.

Questions for Discussion

1. Most of the work on future trends focuses on national or international issues and trends. These will, of course, affect the cities; but they do not capture the future of the cities. What forces do you see as driving the future of the cities? What scenarios might you construct for the future of cities, based on these forces?

Terms to Remember

utopia	*Republic*
City of God	*Utopia*
New Harmony	Sylvania
Erewhon	*News from Nowhere*
Looking Backward	dystopia
Brave New World	*1984*
Walden II	*Ecotopia*
10 megatrends	Conservator
innovator	Mediator
Enhancer	voluntary history
scenario	driving trends
dispositions	contingent future

References

Ackoff, Russell L. (1974) Redesigning the Future. NY: Wiley.

Hawken, Paul, James Ogilvy, & Peter Schwartz. (1982). Seven Tomorrows: Toward a Voluntary History. NY: Bantam Books.

Hershberg, Theodore. (1982) A Philadelphia Prospectus. Philadelphia: University of Pennsylvania.

Kidder, Rushworth M. (1987) An Agenda for the 21st Century. Cambridge, MA: MIT Press.

Lamm, Richard D. (1985) Megatraumas: America at the Year 2000. Boston: Houghton Mifflin.

Naisbitt, John. (1982) Megatrends: Ten New Directions Transforming Our Lives. NY: Warner Books.

Summers, Walter C. (1962) Select Letters of Seneca. NY: St. Martin's Press.

Appendices

Projects for Experiencing the City

Neighborhood Awareness Tour

The purpose of this "Awareness Tour" is to expand on your understanding of cities, and their component parts or systems. This "Awareness Tour" is designed to lead you through a neighborhood via bus and walking. The "Awareness Tour" will take approximately two hours.

A. Obtain a map of the city beforehand. Locate your neighborhood on the map, and note the boundaries, landmarks, and likely paths through it.

B. Catch the bus and ride through the neighborhood. Take note of the people and places you observe, both in the neighborhood itself and in the adjacent areas.

C. Get off the bus on the edge of your neighborhood, and walk back through the neighborhood. Follow the major pathways, but also explore areas off the beaten path (alleys, dead-ends, etc.). Pay particular attention to:

1. General appearance of the neighborhood, including street, trees, houses, etc. (This may be hampered by winter conditions; however, a lot of things are not hidden to the keen eye by snow.)

2. Housing types—wood frame, brick, one or two story, style of the housing stock, etc.

3. Housing quality with standards such as Substandard, Moderately Well Kept, and Well Kept. Also, is there plenty of parking space for cars and what is the condition of any outbuildings?

4. Age of Housing—often told by the style. For example: two-story wood with high peaks, gables, and porches is most likely pre-1900 (and may in some cases be the original farmstead for the neighborhood).

5. Demographic characteristics of the neighborhood: general age of population (look for clues—bikes, toys, and playground equipment along with fences and stationwagons might indicate a young family population. The condition of houses, cars, streets, etc. might yield clues to the "economic" status of the residents.) Also would you say the neighborhood is racially mixed?

6. Conditions of streets, sidewalks, and other public areas. Even in winter, the condition of these "Public Facilities" can be guessed pretty accurately by the way in which they are maintained. Have trees been planted in the boulevard to replace lost elms and what kind of public street lighting is available?

7. Density of population: The average family is approximately three persons per family/dwelling unit. By looking at a particular block or set of blocks, you can quickly determine the population density of an area.

8. Diversity—Single family houses, duplexes, apartments, and non-residential uses such as businesses, warehouses, etc. Is there a mixture of business and is there evidence of rehabilitation, reinvestment, and are there new businesses? Has the rehabilitation (if any) been sensitive to both neighborhood characteristics and the original architecture of the building?

9. Traffic—In addition to the quality or physical condition of the streets, what is the traffic system designed for? Is there a rational layout of streets?

10. Signage—What kind of signage exists for both public and private purposes?

11. Topography and Drainage—Is the neighborhood on high or low ground, protected by dikes, storm sewers, etc?

12. Are there public and private places for people to meet? Are there pedestrians on the street? Does this appear to be a cohesive neighborhood? Are there parks in the neighborhood—either municipal—for the whole city—or neighborhood in orientation and if so, do you think the design incorporates the four criteria for good design: sun/centering/intricacy and enclosure? Also consider location, accessibility, posted time of operation,etc.

13. Schools/churches and other community buildings: What are they? Where are they? Do they appear to fit in?

14. What boundaries are there to the neighborhood? How significant are they?

15. What changes are taking place in the neighborhood?

D. Write a 3–5 page, typewritten report on your field trip: Pretend you are on an advisory panel for the neighborhood. Your charge is to develop a plan for improving the neighborhood. Based on this awareness tour, what are the neighborhood's strengths? What are its weaknesses? What would you recommend for improvements? [In developing your recommendations, be sure to incorporate ideas mentioned in lectures and/or readings.]

1. a. In my back yard; 10 years old

   b. see neighbors houses trees

   c. more houses and a creek

   d. hear cars going up and down closest street

   e. grass, pine trees

   f. feel the cool air and the cool green grass and the sun hitting my face

   g. I love this place

The City of the Mind

1. Think back to your first memory of your home environment
    a. Where are you? How old are you?
    b. What do you see in the "near" field of vision?
    c. What do you know you would see in the "far" field of vision?
    d. What sounds do you hear?
    e. What scents do you smell?
    f. What perceptions do you feel with your skin?
    g. How do you feel about this place?
2. Draw a picture or a map of this place. Indicate the scale of the map you are drawing. On the back of the map, please list
    a. name
    b. present age
    c. age at time of memory
    d. location (urban, suburban, rural)
    e. size of family
    f. did you like or dislike this place?
3. Repeat this same exercise for the place where you live now, and for the kind of place you would like to live in.
4. Write a 3–5 page, typed essay comparing the three drawings:
    a. What sort of elements did you use in each one? (People? What sort? Animals? What sort? Nature? Streets? Churches? etc.)
    b. Are there elements which show up in all three drawings? Elements that are prominent in one and not in the others? Can you develop some general statements about these commonalities and differences?
    c. What conclusions can you draw from your comparison about the relationship between the "city of the mind" and satisfaction with where one lives? Phrase your conclusions in such a way that you could (if you chose) repeat this study with some of your friends to test your conclusions.
    d. Go back to your drawing of where you'd like to live. Is it possible for the city to continue to exist if everyone lived as you wish to? What implications do you draw from that?
    e. Include your drawings with the report.

Environmental Autobiography

1. Describe the interior and exterior of the place you live in *the day after* you moved in. If you have been living in the same place for more than a few years, describe what it looked like when you started college (or, if that was eons ago, what it looked like four years ago).
   a. You may do part of the description by sketching or drawing it.
   b. At least part of the description should be written.
   c. Record the names and ages of all household members (include information for guests who stay with you a week or longer).
2. Each week, describe any changes that occur:
   a. Changes in interior space and/or its use. Include decorative changes as well as changes in types of activities.
   b. Changes in structure or decoration to exterior.
3. Three weeks before the end of the term, write a 3–5 page report based on a review of your journal.
   a. Summarize the changes.
   b. Account for the changes. (Why did they occur?)
   c. Look for patterns in the changes.
   d. Draw conclusions: What does this tell you about your preferences for a place to live? About the preferences of other members of your household?
   e. Attach whatever sketches or drawings you think are appropriate.

Urban Environment

1. Pick 3 locations going in a straight line out of town:
   a. One near the center of town
   b. One on the edge of town
   c. One outside the town, in the open country.

2. Sketch a map of each location. Note (on the map or in the margin)
   a. Thermal and solar conditions
   b. Wind, and evidence of prevailing winds
   c. Dust
   d. Evidence of precipitation
   e. Vegetation—type and condition
   f. Evidence of animal life.

3. Note on the map any transformation of the natural environment by urbanization.

4. Write a 3–5 page report based on your field survey. Discuss the suitability of each location for further development from the point of view of designing *with* the environment. What are the advantages of the site? What disadvantages would have to be overcome? What techniques might be used to overcome those disadvantages?
   Include your maps with the report.

Urban Wildlife

1. Pick a partner. Find an empty lot (@ 100' x 50') in a residential block.
    a. Map the block-face (i.e., both sides of the street), showing the location of streets, sidewalks, & buildings
    b. On a separate piece of paper, map the empty lot
2. Survey the block-face from the sidewalk only (do not attempt to go into people's yards); survey the empty lot in detail.
    a. Note the location of all the different types of plants
    b. Note the approximate location of the various vertebrate animals (different birds, reptiles, mammals)
    c. Look carefully for different insects, and note their location (you need not dig into the ground)
    d. Note any signs which different plants or animals might have left as clues to their presence.
3. *From your survey,* write a 3–5 page, typed report.
    a. What is the most common urban plant? bird? mammal? insect?
    b. Do you find that some plants & animals are usually in the same place?
    c. What could be done to promote diversity of urban wildlife?
    d. Include your maps with the report.

5 councils
1 police
1 fire
1 parks + rec
1 streets
1 over sewers

| 17 people should b |

- recorder lists the gever
- mayor said reading of the minutes of the last meeting which means that they went over it last time
- mayor's in charge of room (and 1 police officer)
- issues are decided either openly open with talk from public council decides after listening to public concerns and they voted in front of everyone
-

```
    1 1
18 ) 20 0
     18
     20
     18
      2
```

```
   2 2
    8
   9 6
   6 0
  156
```

Governing the City

1. Attend one of the public meetings of one of the units of local governance.

2. Arrive 1/2 hour before the meeting begins. Sketch a plan of the room.
    a. Walk to the front of the room: How are the chairs set up for the officials? How will they view the meeting room? How will they be viewed by those attending the meeting?
    b. How are the chairs arranged for the general public? Are any provisions made for the public to address the meeting? How many people can the meeting hall contain?
    c. Sit somewhere (to the back or to the side) where you can get a clear view of both the officials and the public. How many people come to the meeting? When do they arrive? Where do they sit?

3. Pay attention to the public meeting.
    a. How many issues are raised at the meeting?
        —Of these, how many do the public officials consider to be important? How could you tell?
        —Of these, how many do the public consider to be important? How could you tell?
    b. How is the meeting run?
        —How is order maintained?
        —How is ''power'' demonstrated and used?
        —How are issues decided

4. Write a 3–5 page, typed summary of the experience.
    a. What is the public process of local governance?
    b. Is there a ''private process'' in local government? What clues to its existence could you find at the meeting you attended?
    c. Include your sketch/plan with the report.

Miniapple City Council Game

Welcome to a meeting of the Miniapple City Council with the class serving as the city council persons. Like any city council, you are divided into factions based on the areas of the city from which you have been elected and whose point of view you represent in the council.

Miniapple is divided into six wards. Each ward has unique socio-economic and physical characteristics which can be described as follows:

Ward I

The old deteriorated downtown and residential slum. The CBD is in bad shape needing new investment in the form of loans for new businesses and improvements of infrastructure. The people who live around the CBD occupy old apartments and single family homes converted into rooming houses. The residents are primarily elderly and low-income families. The majority of the public housing units in the city are in Ward I. Obviously, there is a need for housing rehabilitation, better schools and services, and playgrounds.

Ward II

Blue Collar (Joe Sixpack) neighborhood that includes the major factory in the city. The factory is a real stinker that pollutes the air in Ward II and causes constant noise. The housing in the ward is single family detached but is old and deteriorated. Ward II has a large number of public housing units, second only to Ward I. There are inadequate schools, parks, and the streets need repair.

Ward III

Incumbent Upgrader neighborhood with a mixture of middle class and working people. They are very proud of their housing and have spent large amounts to fix them up. Most of the housing is single family and was built after World War II. Their main concern is "keeping the neighborhood" nice and improving a neighborhood commercial district.

Ward IV

Gentrification Neighborhood. Young professionals have moved back to the city and are fixing up old historic homes. They have put a lot of time and energy (not to mention dollars) in preserving the city's only historic district and they want to protect their investment.

Ward V

Upper Middle Class Neighborhood consisting of businessmen. This ward has new homes (built in 1950's and 1960's) with large yards and well maintained. The schools are very good and most of the city parks are in this area.

Ward VI

Upper Class Neighborhood. Inhabitants are doctors, lawyers and bankers with big bucks! The homes are all over one acre and are very luxurious.

Physical Characteristics of Miniapple

Miniapple is a river town. The eastern side of the river (Wards I, II, & III) are in the flood plain while the western side (Wards IV, V & VI) are either on the bluffs or on top of the bluffs above the flood plain. The original settlement of the city was in Ward I and IV. Ward VI has the best views of river valley while Wards I & II have the most problems with flooding.

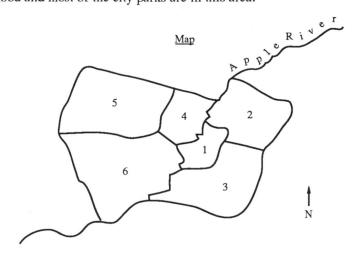

Issue before the Council

Today, you are attending a special meeting of the Council to consider the Fair Housing Plan developed by the Planning Dept. and to decide whether to accept the plan as proposed or to modify it.

The Fair Housing Plan

The U.S. Dept. of Housing and Urban Development has notified Miniapple that it will not receive any more housing and community development funds unless it develops a plan for allocating low-income family housing throughout the city. The HUD guidelines require that these family units be duplexes and 4-plexes and that they be "scattered site" or located in these wards that have not previously had an subsidized housing. Since all of the public housing now exist in Wards I and II, the Planning Dept. devised the following "fair share plan" for the 200 units HUD allocated the city:

Ward I—no units	Ward IV—35 units
Ward II—25 units	Ward V—50 units
Ward III—40 units	Ward VI—50 units

Presentations at the Council Meeting

Following the presentation of the *Planning Director* of the Fair Housing Plan, the next person who got up to speak to the Council was the *Mayor*. The Mayor lives in Ward V and he understands the strong pressure that is being applied against the plan but he endorses the plan because it is the "best we can get" and calls on all his "friends" in Ward V who he helped get elected to support this plan. The next speaker was the *union president* from Ward II—he thinks this is a good plan because it will make wards 5 and 6 take a share of public housing because up to now it has all been in ward 1 and 2. Finally, the representatives from the powerful *neighborhood organizations* in each ward get up and present their positions on the plan:

Ward I—Thinks the plan is great! Too many poor people are concentrated in this ward and "they have a chance to enjoy the fresh air and good schools out in wards 5 & 6."

Ward II—Support the plan because other wards will not be forced to take public housing but will oppose it if "through wheeling and dealing, wards 5 & 6 do not have to take their 50 units each."

Ward III—Oppose the plan because they believe 40 units is too much for their neighborhood. They have put in a lot of money fixing up the housing in their area and fear that this large number of units will "lower property values and discourage other folks from fixing up their homes."

Ward IV—They oppose the plan because they want to save the historic homes in their area and do not see how you can build 35 units and still do this.

Wards V and VI—Strongly oppose the plan! They have hired an attorney who argues it makes no sense to build public housing in these wards where land costs are so expensive and where low-income would be too far from jobs and social services. They threaten to sue the city if plan is adopted.

Council Task

The council decides to break into ward caucus meetings. Each ward must consider the information it has heard and decide on three things: 1. Is your position in favor or in opposition to plan, 2. If you oppose, what is your alternative allocation plan? What are you willing to "give" to the other wards to get them to accept more units? 3. If you favor the plan, what will you do to convince others to accept it or what would you expect in return for accepting more units in your ward? CONSIDER STRATEGIES AND TRADEOFFS.

After your ward members meet for 15 minutes, be prepared to report out to the council on your position on the above 3 points and to take a vote on the plan or a modification of the plan.

Urban Impact Analysis

You are a member of a planning team assigned the task of analyzing the impacts of a proposed residential development in Des Moines, IA.

Proposal

Exxon Development, Inc. has proposed that a currently vacant 600 acre site in Southeast Des Moines be developed into "Happy Acres" a new-town-in-town consisting of 6,000 units. The breakdown for the units by housing type and number of occupants is:

Single family-detached	3,000 units	9,000 persons	(average 3.0 persons/unit)
Townhouse	2,000 units	4,000 persons	(average 2.0 persons/unit)
Apartments	1,000 units	2,000 persons	(average 2.0 persons/unit)

The single family units will be on small lots, sell for an average price of $70,000 and have a total market value of $210 million ($70,000 x 3,000).

The townhouse units will sell for $50,000 each and have a total market value of $100 million ($50,000 x 2,000).

The apartments will rent for $300 per mo. and have a total market value of $3.6 million (1,000 x 300 x 12).

Attached you will find 3 maps to illustrate the nature of the development.

1. "Existing Facilities" map identifies the location of the site near the central business district and adjacent to the Des Moines River, a single family residential neighborhood, a shopping center, railroad tracks, and Jackson School.
   On the site, you will notice a few sewer lines, a small park, a few roads, and a sewage lagoon across railroad tracks from site.
2. "Development Limitations" map identifies environmental features of site
3. "Proposed Development Plan" identifies the pattern of development on the site with high (apts.) and medium (townhouses) density development around the new lake that will be built and single family housing on the eastern side of the site. A new neighborhood center and commercial office park will be also provided.

City Obligation

The city will be expected to provide financing for new sanitary and storm sewers, to maintain the streets and parks, and operate the neighborhood center.

Assignment

Conduct an Urban Impact Analysis of this proposal by:
1. Meeting small brainstorming groups to identify the *positive and negative impacts that can be expected in each of the following areas:*
   a. Physical environment
   b. Economic Impacts on the private economy
   c. Social Impacts on adjacent residents
   d. Government Impacts
2. As a group, analyzing each impact for each of the areas:
   a. Rating each impact on a scale from A (very positive) to E (very negative)
   b. Explaining the reason for each rating (refer to the physical characteristics of the site, the number of people who will be living there, etc.).

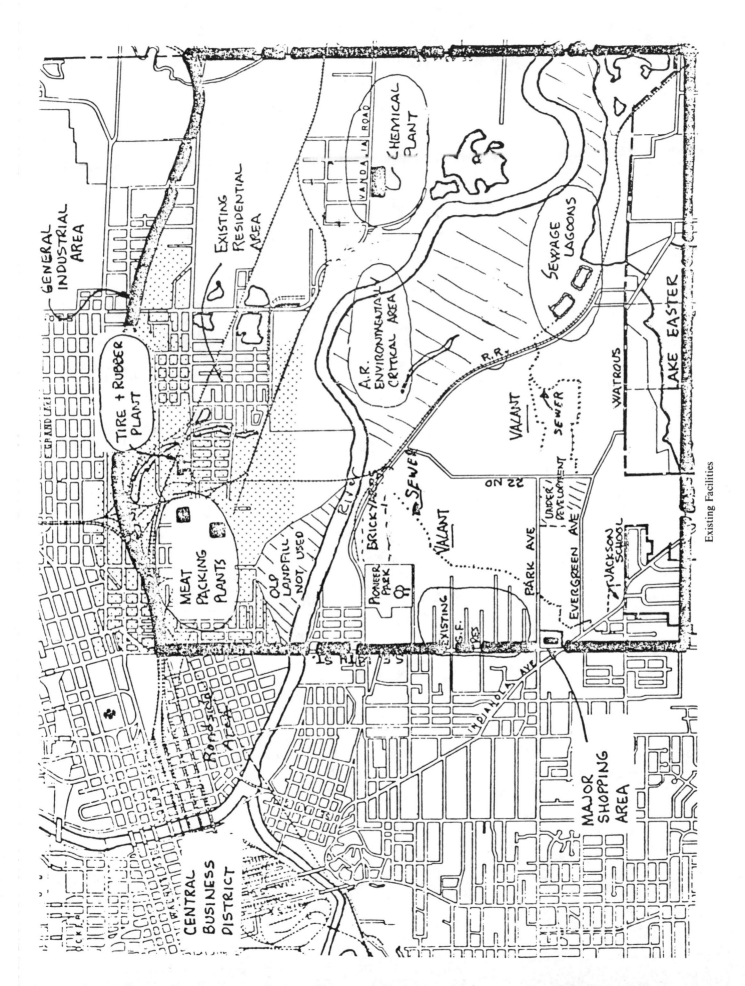

Existing Facilities

GENERAL INDUSTRIAL AREA

EXISTING RESIDENTIAL AREA

CHEMICAL PLANT

VANDALIA ROAD

SEWAGE LAGOONS

LAKE EASTER

A.R. ENVIRONMENTAL CRITICAL AREA

R.R.

WATROUS

SEWER

VALANT

UNDER DEVELOPMENT

VALANT

TIRE + RUBBER PLANT

GRAND AVE

MEAT PACKING PLANTS

OLD LANDFILL NOT USED

BRICKYARDS

River

PIONEER PARK

EXISTING S.F.

PARK AVE

EVERGREEN AVE

JACKSON SCHOOL

CENTRAL BUSINESS DISTRICT

Raccoon

INDIANOLA AVE

MAJOR SHOPPING AREA

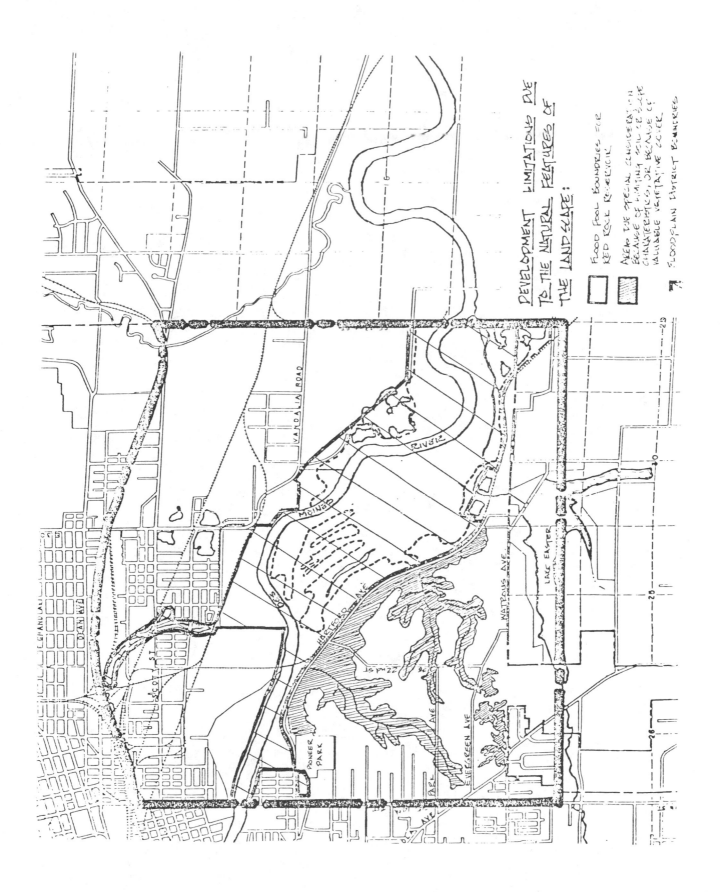

DEVELOPMENT LIMITATIONS DUE
TO THE NATURAL FEATURES OF
THE LANDSCAPE:

FLOOD POOL BOUNDARIES FOR
RED ROCK RESERVOIR

AREAS DUE SPECIAL CONSIDERATION
BECAUSE OF LIMITING SOIL OR SLOPE
CHARACTERISTICS, OR BECAUSE OF
VALUABLE VEGETATIVE COVER

FLOODPLAIN DISTRICT BOUNDARIES

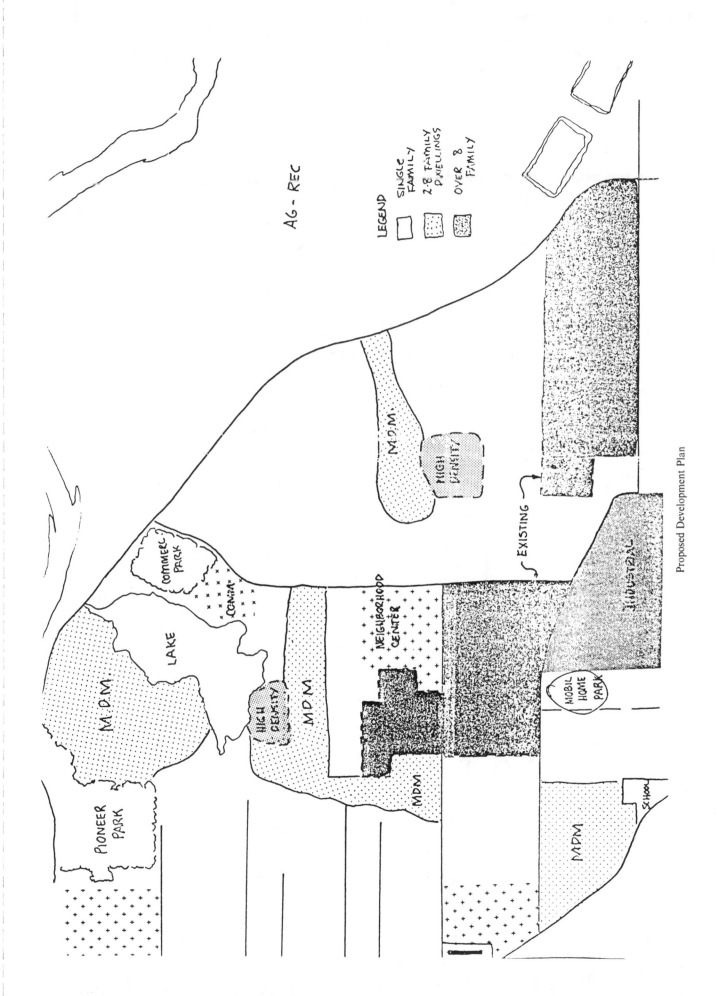

Proposed Development Plan

The Landowner's Game

You own rental property in the city. The neighborhood is an older one, and it is starting to show its age. The sidewalks are cracked, the streets are crumbling, and the garbage doesn't always get collected. The neighborhood is changing; it used to be a working-class area, but now more and more of the residents don't seem to have regular work. Many have given up looking. Your buildings are past their prime, too. They need new roofs, the windows are no longer airtight (many even have broken panes), the plumbing is starting to rot and the electrical service is antique. Needless to say, all your buildings need paint.

It will cost money to make the repairs, and you're not sure you'll get it back in rents. If you spruce up your place and no one else does, you'll hardly be able to raise your rents at all because the buildings will still be in a tough neighborhood. And the other landowners—who put nothing into repairs—will be able to raise their rents just as much as you do! On the other hand, if a bandwagon gets started and most of the buildings are rehabilitated, then the neighborhood could get a reputation as a "hot" place to live and you could get more back in rent than you paid for repairs. If enough of the landowners are involved, you might even convince the city to initiate a special "code enforcement" program to push the holdouts into line.

What do you do?

The Play: Each person in your group (it is easiest in groups of 10) represent a landowner in the district. You must decide whether to improve your property this month or not. *You must make your decision in private* without colluding with your fellow landowners.

As each of you announces your vote (written in advance so you are not tempted to cheat), it is recorded on a large sheet of newsprint taped to the wall, so all can see. Once the voting is done, each player's "earnings" (or losses) are recorded, using the schedule below. Play continues for 10 rounds or until everyone in the group votes the same way 3 times in a row.

Goal: Maximize Rents

Cost of Improvements: $20/unit
Return from Improvements:

10%	upgraded	+	$ 5
20– 40%	upgraded		10
50–60%	upgraded		15
70%	upgraded		20
80–90%	upgraded		25 (holdouts fined $5)
100%	upgraded		30

When the game is completed, tally the scores and calculate the net gain for the neighborhood, the top rent-earner in your neighborhood, and the percent upgrading in the last round played. If your neighborhood stopped playing before ten rounds elapsed, count the unplayed rounds as earning the same as the previous three rounds.

The Analysis: Compare your neighborhood's performance to that of the other neighborhoods in the class.

What seems to be the best strategy for maximizing rents for *all* the landowners in a neighborhood?

What seems to be the best strategy for maximizing the rents to a *single* landowner?

What is the relation between these two strategies (i.e., how does pursuit of one affect pursuit of the other)?

How did the dynamics of the players in your group affect the outcome in your neighborhood?

What does this game tell you about the dynamics of neighborhood decline and removal? Why are there slumlords? Why isn't everyone a slumlord?

Build Your Own Neighborhood

Materials

1 sheet, assorted structures
    8 bungalows
    8 duplexes
    8 4-plexes
    3 8-plexes
    2 Commercial/Office/Light Industrial
1 sheet, base map
scissors, tape, glue-stick
extra paper/graph paper (as needed)

The Rules

1. The base map and the structures are to the same scale, 1"=50'. Unless otherwise instructed, assume:
   - 1 Acre=43,000 sq. ft.
   - 1 block = 280 x 560 ft.
   - 1 lot = 7,000 sq. ft.
   - front setback=35 ft.
   - side setback = 5 ft.
   - rear setback = 10 ft.
   - Street R.O.W.=60 ft.

   Household sizes are:
   - 1 bungalow = 4–5 persons
   - 1 duplex = 3–4 persons ea.
   - 1 4-plex = 2–3 persons ea.
   - 1 8-plex = 1–2 persons ea.

   Employment ratios are:
   - 1 commercial=1 employee/1,000 sq. ft.
   - 1 office=1 employee/250 sq. ft.
   - 1 lt. industry=1 employee/400 sq. ft.

   Parking needs are:
   - bungalow = 1 space
   - multifamily = 2 spaces/unit
   - commercial = 1 space/500 sq. ft
   - office = 1 space/400 sq. ft.
   - industry = 1 space/600 sq. ft.

2. The Task:
   a. Assemble a neighborhood block, using the dwelling units provided (you may need to make extras).
   b. Working in groups of 10, assemble a district of blocks. The district must average 120 persons per block, and must provide enough employment for 100 people.
   c. Assemble 13 of your districts into a neighborhood. The neighborhood must average 175 persons per block, and must provide enough employment to hire one person from each household. It must have a commercial center, at least 4 neighborhood parks (1.5 acres each, minimum) and 1 school for each 1,000 bungalows or 1,500 duplexes (each school is 3.67 acres).

3. Try to lay out each block in as *interesting, cheap, and convenient* a fashion as possible.

4. When you, and later your group, are satisfied with the layout, glue the buildings onto the base map and draw the sidewalks, roads, parking, and open space on the site plan.

5. Evaluation: Each block, district, and neighborhood should be evaluated using the following assessment form:

Assessment Form

	++	+	0	+	++	
Attract.						Unattract.
Conven.						Inconven.
Cheap						Expensive

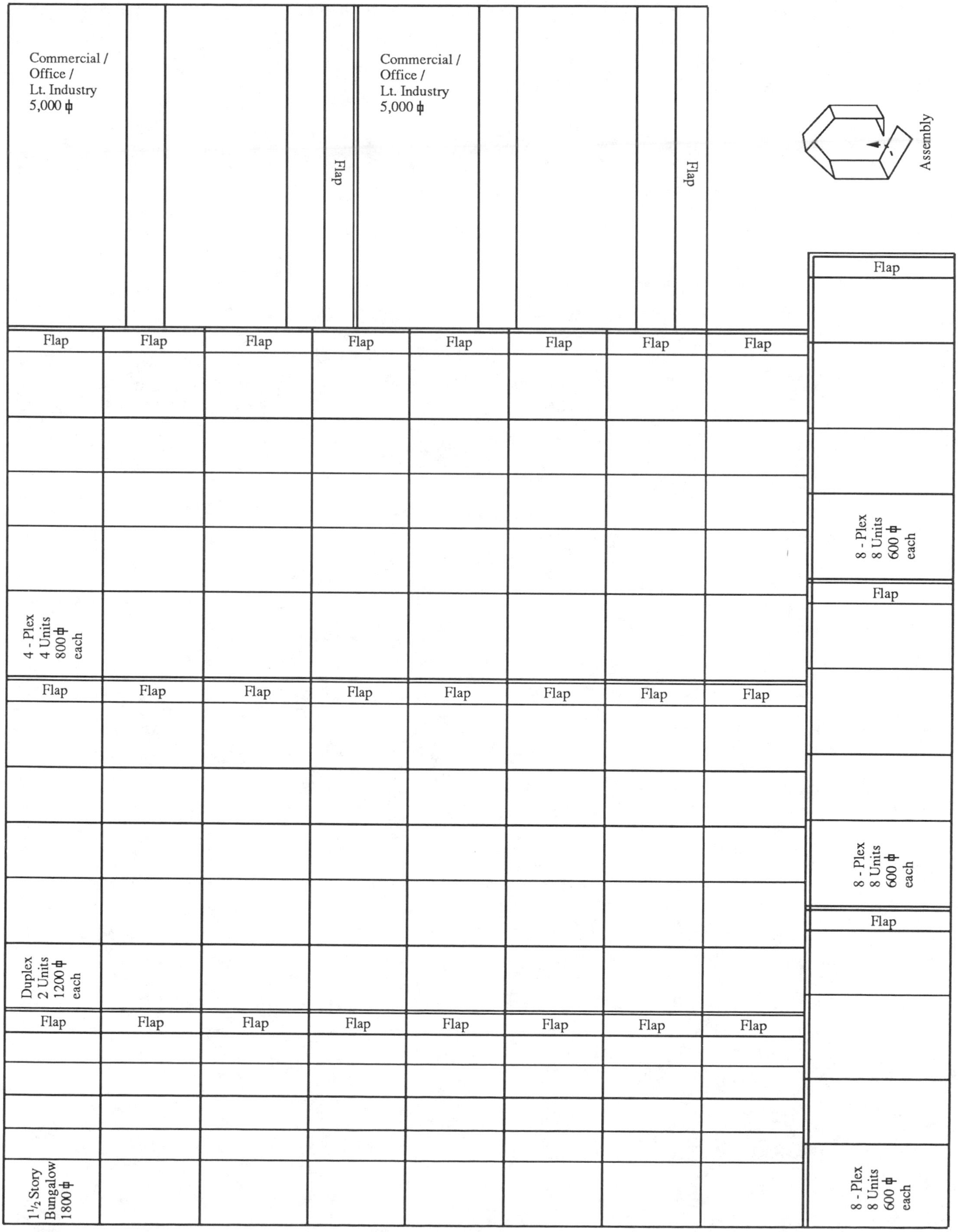

Assembly

Commercial / Office / Lt. Industry 5,000 ₵				Commercial / Office / Lt. Industry 5,000 ₵			

Flap

Flap

Flap

Flap	Flap	Flap	Flap	Flap	Flap	Flap	Flap

4 - Plex
4 Units
800 ₵
each

Flap	Flap	Flap	Flap	Flap	Flap	Flap	Flap

Duplex
2 Units
1200 ₵
each

Flap	Flap	Flap	Flap	Flap	Flap	Flap	Flap

1½ Story
Bungalow
1800 ₵

Flap

8 - Plex
8 Units
600 ₵
each

Flap

8 - Plex
8 Units
600 ₵
each

Flap

8 - Plex
8 Units
600 ₵
each

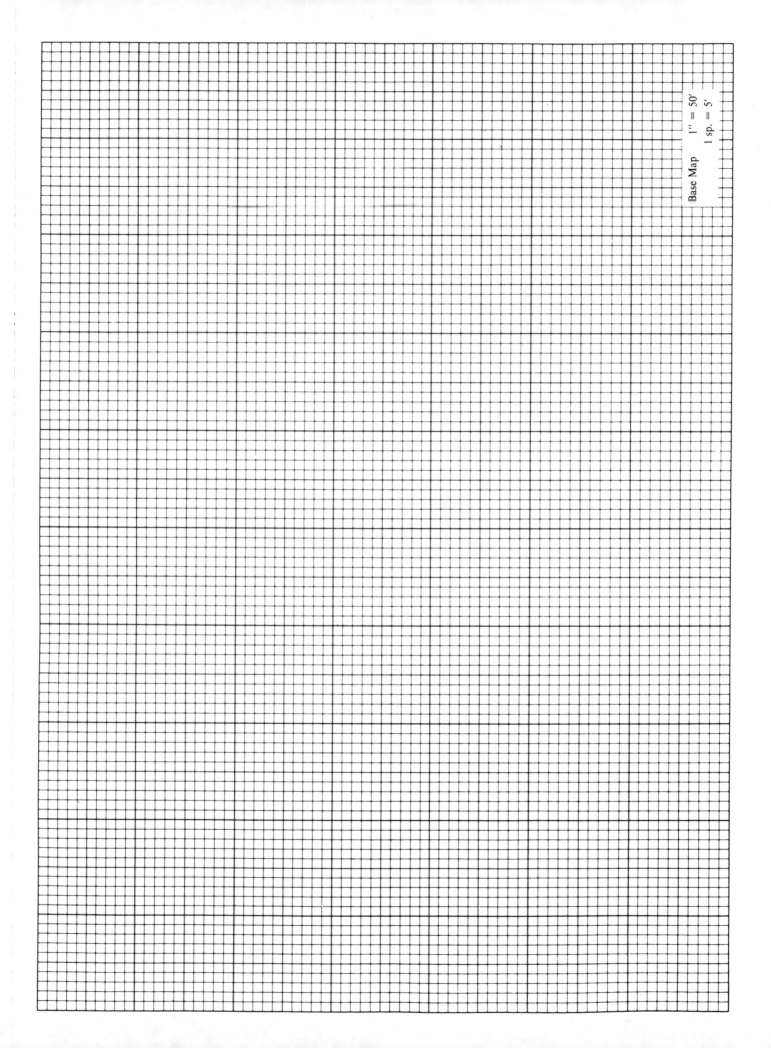

Base Map 1″ = 50′
1 sp. = 5′

Urban Opinion Survey Project

Purpose

In order to gauge the attitudes of your fellow students about living and working in the city, you will administer the attached questionnaire, analyze the results, and write a summary report of your findings.

Assignment

Implement the project by following five steps:

1. Make twelve photocopies of the questionnaire on the next page.
2. Locate ten students who have not taken this course in the past and are not currently enrolled in the course. These students can be friends or strangers in the student union.
3. Ask the students to complete the attached questionnaire and complete one *yourself*.
4. Tabulate survey findings by using a blank questionnaire to fill in the number of total responses to each question.
5. *Analyze* the results by writing a report which discusses:
   a. Has the experience of students been more positive than negative? Are they aware of urban amenities (e.g., landmarks, plazas, etc.) in town? What services do they support?
   b. What does your survey reveal about students' interest in living and working in cities? Where do they want to live (size of city? city vs. suburb?)
   c. Did the findings of your survey support or deny information presented in class? Explain and be specific.
   d. What do you feel was the most significant finding of your survey?

Submission

You should submit your report, your *completed survey questionnaires,* and your tabulation sheet.

Urban Opinion Survey Project

1. Have you taken or are your currently enrolled in an introductory course about cities?

    _____ Yes (do not proceed)   _____ No (proceed with survey)

2. When you think of cities over 50,000 population, has your experience visiting or living in such cities been basically positive or negative?

    _____ Positive   _____ Negative

    COMMENTS:_____

3. If you could live anywhere you wished, which one of these places would you prefer:

    _____ Large city (1 million population)   _____ Small town (2,500–9,999)

    _____ Medium city (100,000–999,999)   _____ Rural area, on a farm

    _____ Small city (50,000–99,999)   _____ Rural area, non on a farm

    _____ Large town (10,000–49,999)

4. If you needed to live in a metro area (region which contains a city of at least 50,000 people), would you prefer to live in the city or in the suburbs outside the city?

    _____ City   _____ Suburbs   WHY?_____

5. If you could live anywhere you wished, which region of the country would you prefer?

    _____ Northeast   _____ Midwest   WHY?_____

    _____ South   _____ West   _____

6. Would you be willing to move into an older house in the central city, and spend your time fixing it up, if you could purchase the house at a very low, affordable price?

    _____ Yes   _____ No   COMMENT:_____

7. If it would improve the quality of service, for which of the following services would you be willing to pay higher taxes?
    (check all that apply)

    _____ Elem. & secondary education   _____ Welfare

    _____ Police   _____ Low-income housing

    _____ Fire   _____ Street Maintenance

    _____ None of above COMMENT: _____

8. Do you use public transit in town?

    _____ Yes   _____ No

9. Identify an historic landmark in town:

10. Identify a space in town which is oriented toward pedestrians:

12. Name of respondent _____

13. Age _____   14. Major _____

15. Class: ____ Fresh.____ Soph.____ Jr.____ Sr.____ Other

Comparison of Urban Documents

Background

In order to appreciate the various approaches that cities are taking to address issues in the areas of housing, economic development, transportation, etc., it is best to examine actual reports and plans that have been produced in specific cities. Urban documents describe the nature of urban problems, the alternatives strategies for addressing the problems, and the preferred approach.

Assignment

You are to read two local government documents and compare them. Using either the school library, the public library, or the city's planning library (if it is open to the public):

a. Choose a city which interests you (e.g., your home town, a nearby city, etc.) and pick two documents you would like to review.
b. As an alternative, you could pick one document from one city and a second, similar document from another city.

Read the two documents thoroughly. After reading them, write a report describing them. In your report, be sure to cover the following points:

1. *Purpose of Reports:* What are the major issues or problems that the reports are addressing? Why do you think these reports were needed?
2. *Content of Reports:* What information is presented in the documents? What type of data was gathered? Who was consulted? What are the recommendations:
3. *Graphic Critique:* How well is the material presented in the reports? Is the narrative easy to read? Are the tables, maps, etc. interesting to look at (visually attractive)? Were pictures included?
4. *Evaluation of Reports:* Do you think the reports are understandable by the average citizen or was it written just for professionals? Do you think the information presented in the reports is still accurate/valid? How do you think the information was used?

Suggested length of Your Paper—2–3 pages, typed. Photocopy the table of contents of your two reports and attach them to the back of your paper.

Index